DATE DUE

AUG 17 1994			

Demco, Inc. 38-293

Automating School
Library Catalogs

AUTOMATING SCHOOL LIBRARY CATALOGS

A Reader

Edited by
Catherine Murphy

1992
LIBRARIES UNLIMITED, INC.
Englewood, Colorado

LIBRARIES UNLIMITED, INC.
P.O. Box 6633
Englewood, CO 80155-6633

Library of Congress Cataloging-in-Publication Data

Automating school library catalogs : a reader / edited by Catherine
  Murphy.
    xvi, 211 p. 17x25 cm.
    Includes bibliographical references and index.
    ISBN 0-87287-771-X
    1. School libraries--Automation. 2. On-line bibliographic
searching. 3. Cataloging--Data processing. 4. Catalogs, On-line.
I. Murphy, Catherine (Catherine Ann)
Z675.S3A92 1992
027.8'0285--dc20   91-39329
                                                                 CIP

Contents

Part 1
Overview of OPAC Development

Part 2
Evaluating OPAC Systems

Part 3
Implementing OPAC Systems

Part 4
Issues in OPAC Development

**Part 5
OPAC Research**

Preface

The idea for developing a collection of articles about automating the school library catalog stemmed from the awareness that there is still little written about the subject specifically for this audience. In a broad sense, the automation process is the same for school library media centers as it is for other libraries—planning, selecting the system, converting catalog records, going online, and continuing to develop access. In reality, however, the school library often has less funds and fewer support staff than other libraries, and these factors impact the type of automated system and retrospective conversion process selected. The issues of access also tend to be different because of the younger age of catalog users and the need for information related to K-12 schooling.

With these perspectives in mind, the articles selected for *Automating School Library Catalogs* were culled almost entirely from the school library literature of the past three years. The one exception is the second section, "Evaluating OPAC Systems," which contains two excerpts from mainstream library literature to supplement Lynne Lighthall's comprehensive checklists. Each author has reviewed the information so that it is current as of publication date. In total, I believe that the collection is a comprehensive and unique compilation of the practical and theoretical literature on the topic of online public access catalogs (OPACs) in school libraries.

I have followed the online catalog market since 1982 when I began my doctoral investigation of standards and practices in cataloging in microcomputer OPACs. By 1988 it was apparent that sales of systems to school libraries were escalating because by then the technology and vendor services were becoming more compatible with school library budgets and needs. That impression spurred me to write the lead article in part 1, "Overview of OPAC Development," which outlines major issues and presents a sample of school library automation development. This article was selected for *The Best of Library Literature 1988*. Robert Skapura's article is characteristic of the style of this leader in the field; the decision-making process, for simplicity, is broken down into a choice between three hardware configurations—minicomputer, hard disk, and compact disk. However, more significant variables influence final selection, and this will be evident in the case studies in part 3, "Implementing OPAC Systems." The last two pieces in this first section are authored by two other well-known observers of school library automation. Mary Holloway places the emphasis on the online catalog as an instructional tool as she describes several pilot projects on which she served as a consultant. Lynne Lighthall, a professor at the University of British Columbia, profiles the school library OPAC market in Canada. Many of the systems are also selling in the United States. The data confirms that sales are increasing and that integrated systems continue to be desirable.

Another article by Lighthall leads part 2, "Evaluating OPAC Systems." It continues the theme established in part 1 about careful planning preceding the selection of a system and offers basic checklists to evaluate separate modules. Skapura's cost comparison of eleven OPACs is also a companion piece to his decision-making article in the first section. This article and the one in part 3 listing retrospective conversion vendors are meant to be representative rather than inclusive of the market. Henry Barnard's checklist for vendors is comprehensive without becoming overwhelming and might be adapted. The summary of observations and matrix of comparative data from *Library Technology Report* prepared by Joseph Matthews, Joan Williams, and Allan Wilson for twenty-four systems is unique and may serve as a series of benchmarks for any system.

Part 3 is concerned with implementing the OPAC system. Skapura's primer of retrospective conversion compares the amount of work or time spent by library staff on each method versus the cost of the service or product. Questions for the library staff and for vendors, as well as an updated comparison chart of vendor services, were originally prepared by me for the first of two preconferences on automation that Skapura and I cochaired for AASL in 1989 and 1990. I wrote the final article about the MARC record mainly to address the issue of content versus format of the record. In the push for school libraries to adhere to standards, the quality of the catalog record has sometimes been overlooked. Now that we are further along the path to automation, minimal content is recognized as unacceptable.

Several case studies in this section demonstrate that there are a number of ways to automate. The current recommendation in the literature is to develop an integrated catalog existing within a local or distributed network. Many smaller libraries may still be choosing the path described by Holloway in her article about a stand-alone circulation station (although a system at this level is very limited). If an interface with a bibliographic database on a compact disk is added to the system, this will minimize some data entry tasks and ensure the development of an integrated catalog with full MARC records. Ann Daniels's case study demonstrates that an existing cooperation between school and public library can facilitate the development of a minicomputer-based union catalog and interlibrary system. Doris Epler and Richard Cassel describe a statewide CD-ROM database project, completing three distinct and historical profiles of online catalog development in this section.

Part 4, "Issues in OPAC Development," is about general issues in access. My paper about the impact of automation on access was written for a research retreat preceding the AASL conference in 1989 and offers general background on the two levels of catalog development, implementing standards, and improving access for young users. Additionally, there are recommendations for practitioners and researchers in the field. Two issues that have received little treatment in the school library automation literature—collection development and screen design—are also included here. Skapura looks at catalog screens and search terms while Patricia Hooten also offers suggestions for designing screens understandable to children as well as making a plea for school and public libraries to coordinate catalog instruction. Linda Bertland reports on circulation analysis while I review the OPAC as a tool for collection development.

Part 5, the last section, "OPAC Research," pulls together the little research that has been done in the field of OPAC development in schools. My findings point to the need for the market to support *Anglo-American Cataloging Rules*, second edition (*AACR2*) standards as well as for enrichment of catalog records. The issue of OPAC systems and software conforming to MARC has been realized to a greater degree; it is in the 1990s that there will be more attention paid to particular needs of students and staff for information about literature and curriculum-related material in the catalog record. In another doctoral investigation, Kathleen Craver looked at the effect of access to an online catalog in neighboring academic institutions by college-bound high school seniors and found a positive impact in their increased use of materials and, overall, found implications for change in bibliographic instruction in high schools. Leslie Edmonds and her colleagues report on the results of the first Baber grant in which students' use of the catalog was determined by developmental level, experience, and training; they make recommendations for simplifying the catalog and improving training in its use. Roberta Lewis, an elementary school librarian, describes the results of an informal survey of fourth graders which bears out the pleas made elsewhere for more detail in the catalog record.

It is my hope that this collection will serve as a useful resource for all those who are developing online catalogs in school libraries. The recommended readings list contains other materials that provide more information about the broad topic of OPAC development. Because the readings come from a variety of previously published sources, no attempt has been made by the publisher to conform in these readings to a particular standard. For example, MARC is referred to in its extended form as both "machine-readable cataloging" and "Machine Readable Cataloging."

Catherine Murphy

List of Contributors

Kathleen Mehaffey Balcom
Director
Arlington Heights Memorial Library
Arlington Heights, Illinois

Henry Barnard
Systems Analyst
Library of the Port of Authority
    of New York and New Jersey
New York, New York

Linda Bertland
Library Media Specialist
Stetson Middle School
Philadelphia, Pennsylvania

Richard E. Cassel
Coordinator (retired) of ACCESS
    PENNSYLVANIA
Bureau of State Library
Pennsylvania Dept. of Education
Harrisburg, Pennsylvania

Kathleen W. Craver
Head Librarian
National Cathedral School
Washington, D.C.

Ann Daniels
Media Department Chair
Carmel High School
Carmel, Indiana

Leslie Edmonds
Youth Services Coordinator
St. Louis Public Library
St. Louis, Missouri

Doris M. Epler
Director of the School Library
    Media Services Division
Bureau of State Library
Pennsylvania Dept. of Education
Harrisburg, Pennsylvania

Mary Holloway
Training Services Coordinator
Follett Software Company
McHenry, Illinois

Patricia A. Hooten
Ph.D. Student, Adjunct Faculty
    Member
School of Library & Information
    Services
Indiana University
Bloomington, Indiana

Roberta Welsh Lewis
Librarian
Kittery School District
Kittery Point, Maine

Lynne Lighthall
Assistant Professor
School of Library, Archival, and
    Information Studies
University of British Columbia
Vancouver, British Columbia
Canada

Joseph R. Matthews
International Business Manager
Data Research Associates, Inc.
Folsom, California

Paula Moore
Head of Youth Services
Arlington Heights Memorial Library
Arlington Heights, Illinois

Catherine Murphy
Director of Library Media Services
Three Village Central School District
Stony Brook, New York

Robert Skapura
Librarian
Clayton Valley High School
Concord, California

Joan Frye Williams
Regional Representative Mid-Atlantic
Inlex, Inc.
Havertown, Pennsylvania

Allan Wilson
University Library
University of Calgary
Calgary, Alberta
Canada

Catherine Murphy

The Time Is Right to Automate

1

In 1988, automation of the card catalog has become a reality for many school library media centers. In 1985, when I was conducting research on the standardization of cataloging in microcomputer online public access catalogs (OPACs) in school library media centers, I found that only about 160 school sites with stand-alone circulation and catalog systems could be identified by vendors selling to this market in the United States and Canada.[1] The reasons for today's increased interest in automation can be attributed to technological developments that permit easier use of systems, expanded capabilities in searching and reporting, and interfaces between stand-alone microcomputers and distributed networks or compact disks. In addition to these improvements in the technology, vendors are providing services for retrospective conversion options that are geared to different budgets in the school market.

It is barely 10 years since the Apple was introduced in 1978, presenting an alternative to automation that was affordable for small libraries. The big online circulation systems had been introduced into university and other large libraries in the early 1970s and several years later some of these systems had grown into online catalogs for the public, influenced by the growth of online Machine Readable Cataloging (MARC) databases available from bibliographic networks and utilities, e.g., the Online Computer Library Center, Inc. (OCLC).[2] But, almost exclusively, the OPACs were turnkey systems developed by vendors into complete packages of hardware, software, training, and support. The minicomputer systems were too powerful and expensive for most school library media centers or any small library to consider. By 1981, *Computer Cat* was developed by the Costas for an elementary media center in Mountain View, Colorado;[3] and soon after that, there were a number of scaled-down OPACs designed for the microcomputer.

Source: Reprinted by permission from *School Library Journal*, November 1988, pp. 42-47. Copyright © by Reed Publishing, USA.

The early software for microcomputer catalogs promised new directions for school library media centers via improved library management and enhanced services to clientele. Most of the systems were essentially replicas of the card catalog, with searching options limited to first word or letters of the author, title, and subject, perhaps with other fields available in the nonpublic mode. Few of these stand-alone microcomputer OPACs offered key word or Boolean searching, processing was slow, and conversion of card records to electronic format was limited to manual data entry. In the last seven years, the technology has advanced, and the market has been tested enough by both vendors and school library media specialists to have caused an increase in sales of both microcomputer stand-alone systems and distributed network systems.

Although it is difficult to get exact figures for these sales, a few microcomputer systems vendors estimate their numbers of users in the thousands, while a number of others report hundreds of sales. It is probable that at this time there are 10,000 automated circulation and/or catalog sites in schools.

School library media specialists must plan carefully for automation, considering global issues as well as specialized needs, not only to participate in the automation revolution but to take a leading role. As sales increase, the market is correspondingly anxious to meet those special needs.

Preparing for Automation

The items that follow are a broad checklist of the considerations in planning for any automated system. Knowledge of these issues should be expanded by reading the literature, examining different systems at conferences or perhaps through purchasing demo disks, and finally, when the selection process has narrowed the choice, those systems should be reviewed in greater detail at a school site using the program.

1. *Standards.* There is only one standard for bibliographic records, the *Anglo-American Cataloging Rules,* second edition (*AACR2*), which includes the format for MARC records. School library media centers were not early subscribers to cataloging standards, evidenced in the research of Rogers and Truett and attributed to school library media specialists' lack of training in cataloging, lack of support staff in the building, and/or lack of endorsement by state supervisors.[4] The development of online catalogs in school library media centers that might be interfaced in multilibrary networks focused new attention on the school library media specialists' lack of awareness of mainstream standards. The fact that record conversion to electronic format in the pioneer days of microcomputer OPAC development was largely accomplished by keying in all data from shelf-list cards at the local site did not contribute favorably to adherence to standards. My doctoral research, mentioned earlier, confirmed that the lack of awareness of cataloging standards that existed in the card catalog era had been continued into the microcomputer online age; by contrast, those schools belonging to bibliographic utilities and networks were influenced to conform to cataloging standards.

All of this has changed in 1988. The microcomputer stand-alone systems, as well as the minicomputer systems, provide for storage of the full MARC record although vendors' claims for data storage should be verified. Automated system vendors as well as specialized data conversion vendors offer varied retrospective conversion options. There are still a few microcomputer software systems on the market that do not conform to the mainstream standard for bibliographic records and these programs should not even be considered for purchase.

2. *Networking.* Multilibrary networking offers to members various cataloging and interlibrary loan services as well as union catalog products that are online, on microfiche, or in CD-ROM format. School library media centers participate in many state and regional networks but only those that are automated provide direction, and sometimes financial support, in the development of local cataloging and OPACs. Examples of these automated database networks are ACCESS PENNSYLVANIA's LEPAC, Wisconsin's WISCAT, Minnesota's TIES, and the Western Library Network's LASER CAT. Just as critical is local area networking, the cabling of terminals in an on-site multiuser system, which has just come of age. (Recent technology allows several different stations to access the database simultaneously.) This development permits processing in one location and public access from several terminals in another area. It is also possible (though still in the experimental stage) to customize network software to access from the same menu both a MARC record online catalog database and a non-MARC record database of perhaps a film collection.

3. *Hardware—micro or mini.* The debate is between a system with terminals linked to a remote bibliographic database or a microcomputer stand-alone system (IBM, or more recently, Macintosh). There is a correlation between large school districts and extensive computer systems because of the greater cost of a distributed bibliographic network, but sometimes there are joint school and public library automation projects that favor the selection of an online system by a smaller school. The smaller library usually chooses a microcomputer system because both the start-up and maintenance programs are less expensive. The greatest advantage of the online system is that it has the most current database, but the distinctions between the two types of systems are blurring as the technology provides for off-line, more frequently updated databases on compact disks that can be interfaced with different computer systems.

4. *Cost.* Cost includes software and peripherals such as a bar wand or scanner, as well as hardware, but even more significantly, the retrospective conversion of the library's shelf list to machine readable cataloging. Once the decision is made between minicomputer and microcomputer systems, there are further variations in the price of single and multiuser networks, software programs, and retrospective conversion options. There are also vendor charges for yearly maintenance and support. The budget for automation should be based on planned obsolescence of hardware (perhaps 20 percent replacement cost per year over a period of five years) and software updates (change is constant as the vendor receives input from users and also tries to be competitive). An important aspect of the budget should be a one-time retrospective conversion of records, which may be transferred to a different system as needs change (this incurs far less expense than reentry of data). It should be remembered, however, that automation does not usually save money. The result of automation is an improvement in services. This improvement justifies any increase in costs.

5. *Order of conversion.* Many more circulation systems than public access catalogs have been sold, but this is changing. It was considered less costly and easier to begin automating by typing in a brief bibliographic record for a circulation system than to develop full bibliographic records for a public access catalog. Because the program vendors, as well as companies dealing strictly with retrospective conversion, are providing more options, school library media

centers are now just as likely to begin automating by developing a database of records that can be accessed for different functions in an integrated system. Automating circulation facilitates the handling and inventory of materials but also encourages use analysis for collection development. The automation of the catalog provides greater access to materials because of improved searching options and indexing. Circulation and catalog modules are the two major components of an integrated system, but acquisitions, serials, and inventory modules may be added. Data is shared between modules where needed.

6. *Retrospective conversion*. The vendors can provide brief records for a circulation system or full MARC records for a catalog. Vendors can convert all of the data entry from the library's shelf list or they can supply a software program which the school library media specialist uses to identify a title. The data entry disks are then forwarded to the vendor to be expanded into full MARC records. Alternatively, the school library media specialist can pull partial or full records into a circulation system or catalog by using a CD-ROM database of Library of Congress MARC records or a shared union catalog of MARC records, or they may use an online bibliographic utility. The cost of retrospective conversion will vary according to the method and how much data the vendor provides. Current records for new acquisitions may also be downloaded to the local database from a network terminal or compact disk, or they may be secured in the MicroLIF format provided on floppy disks by book suppliers (along with bar coded books). The MicroLIF format was cooperatively developed by the microcomputer circulation system vendors and a number of major book suppliers including Baker & Taylor, Brodart, and Follett.

When considering options for retrospective conversions, it is wise to plan for archival copies of the library's full MARC records to be stored on magnetic tapes or disks. The companies that specialize in retrospective conversion will hold those archival copies in-house; the vendors of circulation and catalog software may deliver the converted records but once these are loaded into the system, it is possible that they will be altered and will no longer be complete MARC records. The rule is to keep a separate set of archival tapes or disks somewhere outside of the system.

7. *Nonprint bibliographic records*. Because school library media center collections have more audiovisual materials than most other kinds of libraries, the lack of MARC records for these materials has been a particular problem. This will change as more schools participate in statewide library systems that develop union catalogs. Records for audiovisual materials in vendor conversions are beginning to appear on special databases. Several school districts in Maryland are sharing their audiovisual cataloging by sending floppy disks to their vendor, Library Corporation, Inc., who returns the combined cataloging to each site for downloading into the Intelligent Catalog system.[5]

8. *Reputation of the vendor*. There are continuous changes in the automation market, and it is wise to select a system that has been on the market for a while. This ensures that there are a number of users and that the bugs in the program have been worked out. Some vendors have a nationwide, as well as international, network of users who may be contacted by beginning users. Most vendors distribute newsletters that also connect users. There should also be telephone support available from the vendor during the workday via a toll-free number.

9. *Integration of school library software with school management software*. One of the newer developments in this area is the marketing of library management programs by some of the companies that offer school management software.

This increases the likelihood that some school library media centers will be automated because school records are computerized (perhaps it will also work the other way). The two programs can be integrated to facilitate the exchange of student data or the collection of overdue fines, for example. It is also technically possible to interface two different hardware and software systems — a school management program from one company with a library management program from another company — if a link is programmed to enable the exchange of necessary data.

10. *Subject access.* The real revolution in online catalogs must be in improved subject access for users; otherwise, the investment of resources in automation does little more than replicate the card catalog. Improved subject access means, to begin with, access to fields not conventionally indexed, such as call number, notes, and copyright as well as the author, title, and subject. Key word and Boolean searching options increase the retrieval of subject information. Online help menus, location maps, and audio tutors can guide the user from one step of the search to the next step.

Some vendors are providing on-line indexes that link to the MARC record to create even greater access. Authority files for authors' names and subject headings are important and have been standard in the big on-line systems for some time. Tables of contents and first pages of documents might also be linked to the main record. Enhancements to the record itself include local additions in the notes field such as curriculum units and grade and reading levels. Some vendors are providing or are planning to implement a number of these enhancements in microcomputer OPACs.

Survey

Media specialists and directors were contacted by telephone or at the American Library Association Conference in New Orleans, Louisiana, in July 1988 and asked what their school district automation status was at the time. They were also requested to define their task for the next several years. The respondents were in school districts of varying sizes and represent different approaches to automation, from development of a microcomputer stand-alone system to a minicomputer shared network. (See the table on pp. 6-7.)

Some Final Suggestions

It is apparent that there are some universal suggestions that all school library media specialists wishing to automate circulation and/or the catalog may wish to consider: become informed about the market by reading and attending conferences; learn what is going on with automation at the state and regional level that may affect local decision making; analyze the resources of the school district in terms of the budget, staff, expertise, and motivation necessary to implement an automated system; follow standards for retrospective conversion and new acquisitions of bibliographic records; and finally, form a committee in

(Text continues on page 8.)

Schools Automating Circulation/Catalog 1988

District/School		Respondent	Circulation	Catalog	Future Task
Brookline (MA) Public Schools	(9)	C. Markuson	Winnebago Circ. in high school (HS)	Winnebago Cat. in HS	Complete auto. other schools/union catalog
Broward County (FL) Public Schools	(170)	J. Klasing	Book Trak in 48 schools	(Book Trak has category searching)	Complete auto. other schools/union catalog
Carmel Clay (IN) Public Schools	(9)	K. Niemeyer	CLSI in HS	CLSI in HS/Public Library; OCLC for cataloging	Complete auto. other schools/INTELNET for interlibrary loan
Concord (CA) Public Schools	(37)	R. Skapura	Circ Plus in two HS (one is the original test site for Circ Plus)	Card catalog	Complete development of Circ Plus
Glen Ellyn (IL) Public Schools	(5)	D. Adcock	Circ Plus in junior high school (JHS)	Card catalog	Circ Plus in 4 elem. schools
Greensboro (NC) Public Schools	(38)	J. Davie	Circ Plus in 10 secondary, 1 elementary	OCLC for cataloging and interlibrary loan	Consider Circ Plus for other schools; plan for Cat Plus
Henrico County (VA) Public Schools	(52)	E. Browning	Pueblo Library System in 7 HS (designed for Henrico)	Pueblo in HS/Public Library	Complete auto. other schools

Site	(No.)	Contact			
Madison (WI) Public Schools	(32+)	C. Cain	Circ Plus in HS	Cat Plus in HS (was test site	Circ Plus and Cat Plus in all HS/MS, then elem. schools
Provo (UT) Public Schools	(16)	K. Berner	Dynix 2 in HS, 2 in MS	Dynix 2 HS, 2 MS with Public Library; OCLC for cataloging	Extend Dynix to other schools, plan collection development
Robbinsdale (MN) Public Schools	(17)	B. Nemer	Winnebago Circ in 11 elementary schools	Bibliofile to get ready for conversion of catalogs in 6 HS	Complete auto. other schools/union catalog
Sante Fe (NM) Indian School	(1)	A. McGrattan	Card circulation	Intelligent Catalog for Indian collection	Complete conversion of collection; auto. circ.
Shoreham/Wading River (NY) Public Schools	(5)	J. Bennett	Mandarin in HS; Utlas MSeries 10 in MS; Book Trak in MS; Utlas MSeries 10 in elem. schools	Same as circulation (database developed on Utlas)	Develop multi-user network, interface HS catalog and non-MARC CD-ROM ERIC, Info Trac, etc.
Stamford (CT) Public Schools	(17)	E. Kogan	Circ Plus in elem. schools	CLSI terminal access to public lib. from HS, pilot site for Project Amoeba (CT interlibrary loan database on CD-ROM)	Complete plan for automating schools
Tower Hill School, Wilmington (DE)	(1)	N. Minnich	Circ Plus in Upper and Lower Schools	Intelligent Catalog in Upper School, Bibliofile for conversion	Auto. based collection development for curriculum
Wichita (KS) Public Schools	(105)	J. Meyers	Card circulation	Notis at 51 schools, links in HS to Wichita State Univ. Notis catalog	Put other elementary schools online, auto. circ.

the school that involves all of the participants in planning for site automation. It is necessary to add that the technology is constantly changing and everyone must be aware of the inevitability that systems will become obsolete. On the other hand, this is an exciting time to automate because the technology, while costly, at last promises to deliver real improvements in the managing, indexing, and retrieval of library materials.

Notes

[1]Murphy, Catherine. *Microcomputer Stand-Alone Online Public Access Catalogs: Practices and Attitudes of School Library Media Specialists Toward Standardization.* Doctoral dissertation, Columbia University, 1987.

[2]Seal, Alan, ed. *Introducing the On-line Catalogue: Papers Based on Seminars Held in 1983.* Bath: University of Bath, 1984.

[3]Costa, Betty and Marie Costa. "Microcomputer in Colorado—It's Elementary." *Wilson Library Bulletin* 58 (May 1981): 676-678+.

[4]Rogers, JoAnn V. "Mainstreaming Media Center Materials: Adopting AACR2." *School Library Journal* 27 (April 1981): 31. Truett, Carol. "Is Cataloging a Passé Skill in Today's Technological Society?" *Library Resources & Technical Services* 28 (July/September 1984): 268-275.

[5]"Networking a CD-ROM System: Bibliofile in Maryland." *Library Journal* (February 15, 1987): 96.

The Decision(s) to Automate
the Card Catalog

2

The decision to automate the card catalog is really made up of a whole series of smaller decisions. It begins with choosing the method of doing retrospective conversion and ends with the installation of hardware and software. And in between are many other little decisions.

In the fall of 1989, the *CMLEA Journal* focused on the options for retrospective conversion with four case studies and a cost-comparison chart. Perhaps a quick summary is in order. The process of converting your paper shelf list into a format that a computer can read is called retrospective conversion. There are basically three ways of doing it. You can do all the work on-site, part of the work, or none of the work. If you do all the work on-site, you will end up with forty to fifty floppy disks that contain the MARC records of your shelf list. Those libraries that are already using a circulation system have already done part of the work; the circulation backup disks can be matched against a large MARC database. You do part of the work (entering brief circulation records), and an outside company does part of the work (building your MARC database). But the easiest method is, of course, one in which you do none of the work. You box and send your shelf list to a company that will do the conversion off site. When an outside firm does the conversion, the MARC records can be stored on either floppy disks or a nine-track tape. How you load your collection later into an automated catalog will determine which format you will choose.

When considering computerizing the card catalog, it's best in a sense to start at the end, that is, the hardware configuration of the finished product. Like choosing a car, there is no one product that best fits all situations. The car analogy is apt; there are many good cars to choose from. At one time in my life a

Source: Reprinted by permission from *California Media and Library Educators Association Journal* 14, no. 1, (Fall 1990): 9-12.

four-door sedan was best, especially for getting the kids in and out. Then there was the station wagon. And now there's my two-seater sports car.

Mainframe/Minicomputer Configuration

Automated catalogs divide themselves along hardware lines. Each configuration has advantages and disadvantages, and any decision will be a trade-off. First, there is a mainframe/minicomputer configuration. In the last few years, the lines between a mainframe and minicomputer have blurred. Mini-computers have become progressively more powerful so that now they frequently outperform mainframes of a decade ago. A minicomputer is capable of storing a very large database (frequently a half-million unique titles) with multiple sites, each with a number of terminals accessing the same database. The minicomputer "watches" each keyboard terminal and responds so quickly that the user thinks that he is the only person using the system.

Advantages of a Mainframe/ Mini Configuration

A major advantage of a mainframe system is that all the users have access to the entire database. Large school districts or cooperative ventures between public and school libraries would find this very inviting. Dumb terminals, rather than microcomputers, can be used at each station and these can be purchased for about $400. The maintenance of the database is done off site, usually at some district processing center. If book ordering and processing are currently done centrally, the maintenance of a computer database would simply be an extension of something already done. As books and materials are received and processed, instead of typing catalog cards, data is added to the computer. Frequently this bibliographic information is provided on disk by the book vendor, automating even this process. This means that as books are added to the collection the new additions are instantly reflected in the catalog.

Most mainframe systems include not only the catalog but also circulation. When a student finds a book during a search, the shelf status (whether the book is in or checked out) of that book is displayed on the screen as well as the bibliographic information. Neither the librarian nor the student would go to the shelf looking for a book that is already checked out.

Mainframe programs are usually designed to accommodate off-site access via a phone modem. A student with a computer and a modem at home could easily dial in when the school library is closed and begin his research without even being in the library.

Disadvantages of a Mainframe/ Mini Configuration

Because the database contains more than the single library where the student is searching, the bibliographic citation usually contains a location line that tells the student what library has a particu- lar book. If the student does not look at the location code, he could go off looking for a book that is not even in that building. Some systems are so sophisticated that they filter out all other collections and initially present only materials in the single library. Only on command will the search be expanded to other libraries. But this is one more thing to teach that the infre- quent user might not remember.

Because a single mainframe or minicomputer runs the whole system, if the computer goes down, all the sta- tions (terminals) go down. Everything depends on the reliability of a single computer.

The various sites communicate with the mainframe via telephone lines. This requires a dedicated phone line, and the monthly line charge must be factored into the cost of maintaining

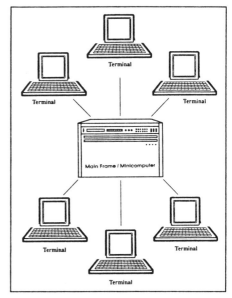

Mainframe/mini configuration.

the system. An additional concern is the speed with which the data is sent to and from the mainframe. The speed of transmission is called the *baud rate*. While the technical aspects are unimportant, generally faster is better. A 2400 baud rate is common now, but many people believe that 9600 baud will replace that in the next few years. Mainframe computers can search and retrieve data at lightning speeds, but the speed with which the terminal responds and displays information is not determined by the computer but by the rate of transmission down the phone lines.

The off-site maintenance of the database was mentioned as an advantage, but this is true only if the off-site staff is both good and cooperative. If, however, it is part of the general data processing staff for the district, library processing could take a back seat to personnel, payroll, and the student management system.

There are a number of library companies that have already developed mainframe programs for public and academic libraries. Many are now turning their attention to school systems where the technological problems of maintaining multiple sites via phone lines are very similar. A librarian looking for a mainframe configuration will find a number of established companies from which to choose.

Hard Disk Configuration

A hard disk configuration or local area network (LAN) is appealing to a single library that wishes to automate. Although people refer to an IBM or IBM clone generically, there is a real range in the speed and performance of the various models. Although IBM stopped making some models years ago, the clone makers have continued to manufacture a full range of what were once IBM models. The IBM models (and clones) that you find in advertisements today can be listed, in terms of power and speed, as follows: IBM PC, 286s, and 386s. In addition to the clone makers, IBM now produces its own newer PS/2 model 30 through model 80. It is unimportant that you know the technical aspects of all these models. It is important only that you know that a local area network requires one high-end computer (usually PC 386 or PS/2 model 50 through model 80) to run the system, while the individual stations can be low-end computers. For the Macintosh user, the high-end computer can be an SE 30 or Mac II.

The high-end computer holds the database on a hard disk (40 to 120 megabytes) and is referred to as a file server. The individual stations generally do not have hard disks and are attached to the file server by a cable. Physically, the file server could be in a back room with the individual stations out in the library. The data is generally backed up on floppy disks, another hard disk, or tape drive specifically for this purpose.

Advantages of a Hard Disk Configuration

The advantages to using a LAN are similar to those of a mainframe configuration. Updates are instantaneous and shelf status is continually updated by the circulation system. Response time on the stations is generally very fast since microcomputers are attached by cable directly to the file server. The data is therefore not slowed down by transmission over a phone line. With a direct connection the rate of data exchange is usually 19,600 baud.

Book vendors now deliver books with the bibliographic data on floppy disks. These can be loaded into most systems by simply putting the disks into the floppy disk drive and choosing some kind of an import function. Gone forever is the task of filing catalog cards. Books can appear in the catalog faster than they can be put on the shelf.

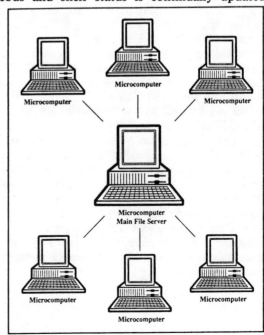

Hard disk configuration.

Disadvantages of a Hard
Disk Configuration

Maintaining a local area network becomes a *local* responsibility and this usually means the librarian. Not only must you update the database, but you will also have to make sure that the hardware is working correctly. I do not want to give the impression that local area networks are troublesome. They simply require a different level of sophistication. It's much like graduating from using only a floppy disk drive to a hard disk. I had to learn a number of new things to use a hard disk, but the benefits made the learning worth it. Some of the library companies require that you have a modem attached to your file server so that if you're having a problem, they can dial in and see on their screen exactly what you are seeing. This makes troubleshooting a problem much easier for them and for you.

In a LAN, each computer is attached to the file server through a networking card that fits into one of the slots in each computer. Networking cards currently cost hundreds of dollars each. The system itself is managed by networking software. Some companies develop their own networking software; most use commercially available systems, the most common being Novell™ cards and software.

There is a physical limit to how many stations can be added to a local network. This is determined by the power of your file server, the quality of the networking software, and the physical distance between the server and the stations. It's unlikely any single library would outgrow a local area network.

Most book vendors now deliver bibliographic data on floppy disks ready to be loaded into your system, that is, if everything goes right. Because updating the collection is a local responsibility, problems with reading in data, hard disk crashes, and entering uncataloged materials now become the local librarian's responsibility.

Many small businesses use local networks, so this configuration has a track record and many computer companies have wide experience in setting up and troubleshooting problems with them. It is a relatively safe technology to go with.

CD-ROM Configuration

Until a few years ago, there were only two possible configurations. The advances in CD-ROM technology have created a third alternative. A CD-ROM (Compact Disk — Read Only Memory) can hold an incredible amount of information, for example, *Grolier's Academic American Encyclopedia*. Read by a computer through a CD-ROM player, this technology enables a microcomputer user to search large amounts of data very quickly.

Although the technology is slightly different, advances in audio compact disk players will continue to have a trickle-down effect on reducing hardware prices. Currently CD-ROM players for information systems are between $400 and $800. Large school districts can usually receive a substantial discount on volume purchases.

Advantages of a CD-ROM Configuration

A CD-ROM station is basically a stand-alone system. A low-end (inexpensive) microcomputer can be used at each station since it is the access time of the CD-ROM player and not the speed of the computer processor that accounts for its speed. CD-ROM disks themselves are rugged, and after the master disk is produced, disks for additional stations are usually less than $20 each. The fact that many magazines and reference databases are being put on CD-ROMs promises that this is a technology that will endure. Because of the pioneering audio technology, we can expect to see prices continue to decrease.

Because each station is essentially a stand-alone station, if one malfunctions, the others are unaffected. Some libraries have an extra CD-ROM player in reserve, so a quick substitution can be made if one must go out for repair.

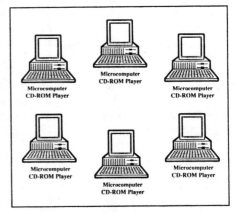

CD-ROM configuration.

Disadvantages of a CD-ROM Configuration

A CD-ROM disk can hold a great deal of information, certainly far more than the typical twenty thousand volumes of an average high school library. Creating the master disk, however, is prohibitively high for most school libraries to absorb out of their operating budgets each year. Cutting a master CD-ROM costs between $1,500 and $2,000. There is plenty of space, however, to put a number of library collections on the same disk, say, twenty or thirty school library collections. Sharing the cost among many libraries brings the cost to an individual library down to less than $100 each. The software provided by most of these companies is capable of *masking all the other collections* on a particular CD-ROM and displaying to the student *only* the materials in that library. On command the search can be expanded to include all the collections on the disk. The cooperating libraries could be in the same district or area or just have come together to share the cost of cutting the CD-ROM. All of this, however, involves coordinating a number of libraries and goes beyond a single library's decision to automate.

Because new titles can be added only when a new CD-ROM is mastered, updating the catalog happens only periodically, not simply when new books are purchased. Most libraries try to do this twice a year, but even then it means having books on the shelf for months before they are reflected in the catalog.

On the hardware side, each individual station requires not only a microcomputer but also a CD-ROM player and search software for each machine.

Some companies grant a site license for the software; others charge a per station fee and frequently limit the license to one year.

Since the CD-ROM database is independent of the circulation system, the shelf status of a book does not appear as part of the book record. CD-ROM companies tell me that they are working on this feature, however.

Common to All Configurations

There is a last consideration no matter which configuration you choose for your library: Do you attach a printer to the catalog stations? Most students want to walk away from a search with titles and call numbers on a piece of paper. If the student writes down the information, it increases the time he's at the station; if you attach a printer to every one or two stations, there is another machine to maintain and supplies to keep it printing. Most libraries that have installed printers have opted for "ink-jet" printers because they are virtually silent.

How Much Does It Cost?

The "bottom line" is always the bottom line. The cost of automating the card catalog can be broken down into eight parts, and systems should be compared on the basis of all of them, not just one feature.

Hardware. This includes all the computers, the wiring if necessary, and the printers. Some configurations call for networking cards or CD-ROM players. Others require a modem.

Software. Features must be kept in mind. Some search software is more expensive because, very simply, it does more. On the other hand, paying for features that you'll never use is a waste of money. But the many different features in search software muddies the water when trying to make side-by-side comparisons.

Loading the Collection. After retrospective conversion has been done, someone must put the collection on either a hard disk or a CD-ROM. Some companies expect you to load the collection yourself. Others load it for free or for a small per-record charge.

Training. Some companies provide no training beyond the manuals that accompany the software. Others require that training be part of the package. Some train the entire staff, while others train a single person who then trains the rest.

Hardware Maintenance. Some companies require that you buy or lease hardware from them. Others set the specifications, but allow you to buy the hardware anywhere. The crucial issue is who will be responsible for the hardware when something doesn't function properly. Splitting the hardware and software purchases between different vendors frequently puts the librarian in the middle. When something goes wrong, the software company says it's the hardware; the hardware supplier says it's the software.

Software Updates. Search software constantly gets better. Generally, there is a yearly charge for updates.

Support. Possibly this is the most important aspect to consider when purchasing a system. Probably the best way to evaluate the quality of the support *before* you buy a system is to insist on talking to a number of customers who are already using the system. Good support is never free. Either the cost will be included in the purchase price or be listed separately, but common sense tells you support is not free. Some companies have a toll-free number, some don't, and still others require communication through a modem.

Updating the Collection. Whenever new books or materials are added to the collection, they must be added to the catalog. Some systems are updated with floppy disks provided by the book vendors. In that case the update is essentially free. CD-ROM vendors require that you send them MARC records (book vendor disks will usually suffice), and there is a small charge for merging these records with the large database, indexing the entire collection again, and then creating a new CD-ROM master.

There is no one best system for all situations. Large school districts might want union catalogs as well as catalogs in individual schools. An isolated rural school library simply does not have the same requirements as a school that's part of a large district. There are, in fact, many good systems to choose from and they just keep getting better.

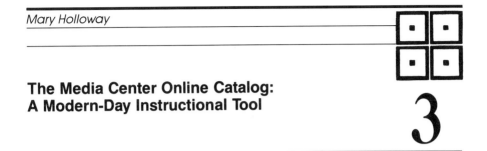

The Media Center Online Catalog:
A Modern-Day Instructional Tool

3

In the past the tools of the library trade included printed indexes, circulation desks, card pockets, date due stamps, and the card catalog with drawers and drawers of cards to provide access to the library collection. The increased emphasis in education on accountability and test scores and the need for a better-educated work force, coupled with the increased availability of educational technology that includes microcomputers, electronic databases, CD-ROM products, and distance learning via satellite, have changed the media center and its tools of the trade forever.

Micros in the Media Center

Today's media center may feature four areas where technology tools enhance and extend the learning possibilities and provide better management of resources: a utility station, a desktop publishing station, a telecommunication and information retrieval station, and an automated circulation and catalog station. At the utility station one might find such software as *Bibliography Writer*, *Grade Manager*, *AppleWorks,* or *Slide Shop*. The desktop publishing center might include a Macintosh or other microcomputer with *MacWrite, MacDraw, MacPaint*, the *Children's Writing and Publishing Workshop*, or *MECC Writer*. At the information retrieval station could be online access to DIALOG or Dow Jones News/Retrieval, or to CD-ROM products such as *Grolier's Academic American*

Source: Reprinted by permission from *Wilson Library Bulletin*, September 1990, pp. 27-30, and by Training Services, Follett Software Company.

Encyclopedia or *Compton's Multimedia Encyclopedia.* The circulation/catalog stations could have automation software that utilizes bar code technology and complete bibliographic records cataloged using MARC standards.

In North Carolina, the Computer Services section of Media and Technology Services in the Department of Public Instruction has developed and coordinated several projects in these areas. The pilots were designed to set up a working library site to learn the costs involved, the hardware and software needed, the training and staff development required, and the impact on the instructional program of the school. The most recent project involved the development of an online catalog at two secondary school sites in the state to serve as a model for other schools. The project was to include both audiovisual and printed resource materials.

Pilot Sites

Two secondary school sites, already using Follett's automated circulation system, Circulation Plus, were chosen. West Davidson Senior High in Lexington, North Carolina, is a small secondary school, grades 9-12, with 30 to 35 faculty members and 650 students. The collection contains 9,000 books, plus audiovisual materials. Plans at this site were to utilize existing equipment along with new equipment purchased for the project. The retrospective conversion was contracted from a vendor. West Davidson is also a test site for the new Alliance Plus CD-ROM product from Follett Software. This tool will be used in-house to build additional database records.

The second site, Central Davidson High School, also in Lexington, North Carolina, has 62 faculty members and 980 students in grades 9-12. The collection includes approximately 13,000 items, housed in a two-level facility. At Central, the staff is using BiblioFile to retrieve data for the catalog database. Central will also be a pilot site for the Alliance Plus CD-ROM product, a database for retrospective conversion for school libraries. Any new materials orders from vendors at both sites will include a disk for uploading MARC records of the new materials into the catalog using MicroLIF, a data interchange format used by vendors who market to small- and medium-sized libraries.

The project began during the early fall of 1988 with planning, ordering, and installation of equipment. In January through May 1989, there was loading of some data and trial of the system before final setup and use. The 1989-90 school year featured continued building of the database, further introduction to students and staff, and greater use of the complete system.

Online Catalog Setup

The process of establishing the online catalog is best described in three stages: the setup of the software, hardware, and network; the database; and the use of the system.

Software

The online catalog software chosen for the demonstration site was Follett Software's Catalog Plus. This product was chosen because the schools selected were currently using Circulation Plus, the program utilized the MARC record standard for the database, the software company had a representative in our state, and the company supported the product via consultants and a toll-free telephone service.

Hardware

The hardware configuration for the sites included a Tandy 4000 with 3MB of extended RAM in addition to the 1MB originally in the machine and a hard disk as the file server/host computer; a Tandy 3000 with 640K and a hard disk, originally used for circulation at the circulation desk; and a Tandy 1000 with 640K as the access or search station, in the media center. The Tandy 4000, located in the media center office, has one 3½-inch disk drive, one tape backup installed in the second disk drive slot, a monochrome monitor, and a Okidata printer. The circulation station has one disk drive, a monochrome monitor, and the light pen attached. At the access station, the Tandy 1000 has one 3½-inch disk drive, a color monitor, and a printer. For student searching, the West Davidson site has two Tandy 1000 machines with color monitors that share a printer. Plans are to add another microcomputer so there will be access to the catalog on the second level of the Central Davidson media center. The color monitor is recommended for student use for its motivational factor and for the better visibility of the software selection display in inverse video.

Although one machine can be used for both the file server/host and circulation, the configuration of a file server/host in the media center office and a separate microcomputer for circulation benefits the library opration and provides greater data security. One media center staff member can update the catalog database, do original cataloging of items, or print overdues while another is circulating items or searching the catalog database. With a single machine at the desk for host and circulation, on the other hand, one must purchase an intelligent scanner card to operate the light pen and also forgo the ability to update and maintain the database during circulation/catalog activities.

MS-DOS microcomputers other than the Tandy equipment will operate the software and network. For example, an IBM PS/2 Model 60, 65, 70, or 80 with extended memory and a hard disk could be the file server/host. A Personal System 2 Model 30 could be the circulation station, and Model 25s could function as access or search stations for students. There are schools in our state using this combination successfully.

Network

All of the hardware is linked with Follett's Plus Link Network. Each microcomputer has a networking card connected by a drop cable through a junction box to the main networking line. The networking line uses base-band, twisted-pair, telephone-like cable with modular jack connectors. The network, purchased from and supported by the software vendor, is easily installed by the library staff and the computer coordinator of the school district. The cable was run up the wall from the file server and above the dropped-in ceiling tiles to the circulation desk and then out into the media center and down a column to the search station(s).

The overall cost for the online catalog setup including hardware, software, supplies, networking, off-site data conversion, and in-house data conversion via the BiblioFile CD-ROM was $10,000 per site.

The planning, purchasing, and installation of the hardware were just the beginning steps; it is the catalog database that is the key to a successful automated catalog system.

Online Catalog Database

From the initial planning stages, the goals for the database were to use MARC standards for the records to permit the electronic sharing of records later, to have the most complete records possible to provide the greatest access to the searcher, and to eliminate the upkeep of a paper catalog and shelf-list database.

With these goals in mind, several different approaches to building the database were explored to test the costs, effectiveness, and resources needed. At West Davidson, the Circulation Plus titles disks that the media center had already created, with as many LC card numbers as available, were forwarded to Follett for retrospective conversion at a cost in 1989 of $800. The hit rate was less than 25 percent, due to the age of the collection, the lack of extensive weeding prior to automating, and the inclusion of paperbacks, audiovisual materials, and equipment in the Circulation Plus records. One must remember that the vendor matches Library of Congress card numbers (LCCNs) and a few characters of the title against the MARC record tapes of the Library of Congress for hits. Early materials (prior to 1969) and most audiovisual materials are less likely to be found. Another site in our state with a fully weeded collection of more recent vintage achieved a 69 percent hit rate. In any case, more than one method of building the collection database is required.

The West Davidson site will now use the Alliance Plus retrospective conversion product, since it permits searching of the LC database via author, title, subject, series, and standard book numbers. An advantage of this approach is the ability to edit records retrieved that are close to present holdings but need a few changes. This should garner additional complete records.

At the Central Davidson site, the Library Corporation's BiblioFile setup was used for retrospective conversion. This process involves creating a printed list from the Catalog Plus software of items with brief records and LCCNs, searching the CD-ROM Library of Congress database of MARC records to retrieve full cataloging data, saving that data to floppy disks, converting the data into MicroLIF format via Follett's BibLIF software, and batching the full records into the catalog database.

The pilot study indicates that one could successfully retrieve, edit, save, convert, and batch between seventy-five and one hundred records per hour. Edited records can have added local call numbers or local holdings. Currently, bar codes are transferred from Circulation Plus data. There is an increase in the hit rate with the in-house process because of the ability to both edit records that are close to current holdings and visually judge if the records are identical to current holdings. By March 1990, approximately a year following the catalog hardware installation, the Central Davidson site had searched BiblioFile for all its print materials. The BiblioFile searching occurred at a separate Tandy 1000 machine to be used later as the second search station. The hit rate for the second school was approximately 82 percent for nonfiction and 50 percent for fiction.

For the remaining items without extended records, there are three choices: use the brief Circulation Plus record with limited access points for the life of the item, contract with a REMARC vendor to search for hits on pre-1969 records, or do original cataloging of the materials via the Catalog Plus software.Many changes are happening in the marketplace currently that will affect retrospective conversion. Companies are developing specialized databases on CD-ROM with emphasis on school materials and Sears subject headings and are also combining with REMARC services to retrieve early (pre-1969) records. The following factors should be considered when choosing a method or methods for retrospective conversion:

- Accuracy and completeness of MARC records

- Costs

- Ease of batching into the catalog system

- Quality of MicroLIF records generated

- The process for batching those records into the catalog program database

- Staff and collection size and needs

Since the catalog data is not static, plans are needed for keeping the collection information up-to-date. The project sites will acquire MicroLIF disks from library vendors and do original cataloging to keep the records current once the retrospective conversion is complete. The media specialists at the sites are aware that MicroLIF records vary from vendor to vendor and will need to be checked before or after entering into the database to maintain data quality. Baker & Taylor, Brodart, Bound to Stay Bound, Demco, Econoclad, Follett, and Perma-Bound are a few of the companies that can supply MicroLIF data disks for materials purchased from them.

Tremendous energy has been spent to bring the catalog project to this stage, but the true test was to be in the use of the system and its value to the instructional program. In addition, the staff wanted to explore the changes and improvements in the technical and support area of media center management.

Use of the Catalog System

One of the media specialists described the automated catalog well when she said, "One can hardly keep students from using the system!" They do indeed gravitate to the new technology, but some advertising and training still was planned to introduce the technology and increased capabilities and benefits of the new system.

Helpful hints for student and faculty training include:

- Provide an introduction for faculty and staff first.

- Introduce the systems to students during orientation rather than at research or term paper time.

- Work with fellow teachers to support instruction for keyboarding and Boolean search strategy skills.

- Train a cadre of student assistants to become the first level of support. Students often came to the search station in pairs or groups, and peer teaching is a useful tool.

- Introduce the concept in classes or groups, preferably with some visuals.

- Prepare some audiovisual aids for learning: videos of steps and results with student and faculty actors, guide sheets and posted step-by-step charts near the terminal, slide/tape productions, charts, and transparencies.

- Post simple procedures nearby. Be sure to display items graphically or visually for all levels of learners.

- Use the school handbook or media center newsletter to announce the system and to follow up on progress.

- Be prepared for active, enthusiastic users.

In addition, four items need highlighting. First, take the time to weed, weed, weed. Since tremendous amounts of time and energy are needed to convert and load data, make sure the books you have are worth the effort. Second, the easiest way to match MARC records is by number, usually the Library of Congress card number. To speed this process, make sure LCCNs or other standard book numbers are on the shelf-list card or in the circulation data. Third, a color monitor at the search station is a great advantage and worth the cost. Finally, plan to allow at least a year to build the database for existing schools.

A Powerful New Tool for Learning

The project is successful! The school media centers truly have a powerful new tool. The online catalog is an excellent management tool, a motivational tool, and an impressive instructional tool.

As a management tool, the online catalog provides better inventory control with access to current data about the media center collection. This increased knowledge of the collection, of its use and its strengths and weaknesses, becomes a positive, objective collection development and planning tool for both the media staff and the school faculty. The increased access points to the collection ensure better information about the collection and better use of the resources. One vivid example is the ability to create and print current bibliographies with annotations for students and teachers. The management gains far exceed the limited manual system that is so expensive to set up and maintain.

In addition to the management of resources, the online catalog proved to be a tremendous motivational tool. Students and teachers flock to the terminal to search for information. Very young students, students who experience difficulty with the paper catalog, and reluctant teachers have all successfully used the online catalog. Students are eager to demonstrate the catalog and the process and share their skills with others. Since the online system is more forgiving and less intimidating, users are thrilled to be able to locate materials with a few keystrokes and then to check if those materials are available to circulate. This success rate reinforces continued use of the automated system. Even teachers who may be uncomfortable with the technology are attracted to the system's ready reference abilities, quick retrieval features, and the bibliographies. The media center has high visibility as it harnesses the power of the information age for its users with this new tool. Students and teachers *wanting* to use the catalog—what a powerful public relations tool to draw patrons to the media center and to help with instruction.

Getting patrons to use the catalog is, however, only the first step; the online catalog should be developed for its instructional impact. In this area the catalog can be a tremendous tool for the development of higher-level thinking skills. The faster, better, easier access to resources removes the drudgery of searching and provides practice in search strategy and analysis of findings. Less time searching and checking for availability of resources means time for a greater emphasis on use of the information located. The synthesis, organization, and presentation of data can be stressed. Since almost every business wants employees who can access information, think clearly and logically about it, and use that information to its greatest advantage, the school's instructional program needs every tool at hand to achieve that goal. The new library tool of the online catalog permits greater development of student skills so necessary for survival in their new world.

The microcomputer and media management software give media specialists a tool to affect the instructional program. As the Central Davidson principal said:

> Automating our media center helps students to better understand how computers can be used to access information quickly and easily. It has encouraged the use of technology in the curriculum areas through our school. We find our students are enthusiastic about using the online catalog terminal to access books and materials for classroom assignments. As a high school principal, I believe this is a good

step for any school since it stresses to students and to faculty the importance of the use of technology.

Project Summary

Goal

Develop and implement an online catalog as a model for users

Hardware

File server: a Tandy 4000 with 3MB in RAM, a monochrome monitor

Circulation: Tandy 3000 with 640K, a monochrome monitor

Access stations: Tandy 1000 with 640K, a color monitor

Tape backup: Network cards for each, plus connecting cables

Printers: Okidata

Retrospective conversion: Tandy 1000 with 640K, a monochrome monitor, a Hitachi 1503S CD-ROM player

Software

- Circulation Plus
- Catalog Plus
- PlusLink
- *BiblioFile*
- CD-ROM LC records

Costs

The average cost was $10,000 per site for two sites. Total expenditures were $19,649.83 with some existing hardware.

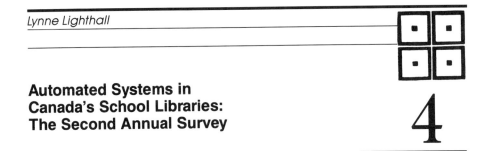

Lynne Lighthall

Automated Systems in
Canada's School Libraries:
The Second Annual Survey

4

The primary purpose of this report is to present a capsulated picture of the Canadian automated school library system marketplace to the end of 1990. A secondary purpose is to inform the marketplace about what systems suitable for the school library setting are available.

The emphasis on personal computers in this survey is deliberate and based on the fact that the cost of implementing and maintaining a large system is beyond the fiscal capacity of individual schools and even many school districts. As well, there is not usually the expertise in a school to run and maintain the necessary hardware.

Large Systems

This does not mean that large systems ought to be excluded from the consideration of those responsible for school library automation. There are certainly vendors, including Canadians, who make such products and offer services appropriate to the school library market. In fact, in the early 1980s, the Vancouver School Board automated its large centralized cataloging function, using a minicomputer-based system, the former Easy Data System. And the Calgary Board of Education recently negotiated a contract with the Sobeco Corporation (505 Rene Levesque Blvd., Montreal, QB H2Z 1Y7) to automate their school libraries using MultiLIS. A telephone conversation with Daniel Boivin of Sobeco confirmed the arrangement with Calgary, mentioned a possible arrangement with another school board, and included the news that MultiLIS is available in a PC-based version as of the fall of 1991.

Source: Reprinted by permission from *Canadian Library Journal* 48, no. 4 (August 1991): 244-53. Copyright © Canadian Library Association.

PC-Based Systems

All of the systems reported in this survey are meant to run on personal computers, the vast majority on the IBM/MS-DOS (or compatible) family (Card Datalog and Winnebago also run on IBM's PS/2). Card Datalog also runs on the Macintosh family of microcomputers, as does Follett's Circulation Plus (but not Catalog Plus). Library 4, the Mac Library System and Mac School Library operate on Macintosh. MicroCAT stands alone among the systems surveyed as operating both in the Xenix environment and the IBM.

The Macintosh family of computers appears to be becoming very popular with teachers, teacher-librarians, and others in school settings. There has been an increase in the number of Macintosh-based installations in 1990 over those in 1989 as well as in the number of vendors reporting on Mac-based systems. Will future surveys show a continuation of this trend? Can we expect to see increasing numbers of schools looking to Macintosh-based products to automate library functions?

Card Datalog stands alone as a *turnkey* system, with the vendor supplying all the hardware, software, and technical support needed to install, implement, and maintain the system. But as Laura Chakravarty, account manager with Avec Technical Services Inc. says, "We supply turnkey systems, but as well take any orders including software only." All other respondents reported that their systems are of the software and support variety. This is very much the industry norm and what teacher-librarians and others working in school library settings expect.

MARC Standard

Just as all the systems included in this survey run on personal computers, so too should they be integrated, modular systems utilizing the full MARC record via one or more MARC interfaces. As Joe Matthews in his article for *Library Technology Reports* says, "Full MARC records constitute the *lingua franca* of library automation."

Teacher-librarians, and others involved in school library automation, should be as concerned as their colleagues in other types of libraries with adhering to internationally-accepted standards and guidelines. Participating in a union catalog project, resource sharing with other schools within (and even without) a district, and possible transference of a complete database to another vendor's system at some point in the future are all good reasons for choosing to use the full MARC record. The more immediate and practical reason is that a quality database can be created more effectively this way.

All the systems included in the present study are capable of accepting or downloading a full MARC record. What usually happens next is that the full MARC record is "massaged" or converted into the format specified by the particular software package and stored in the system in this modified format.

To date, few micro-based systems surveyed offer the capability to store records in full MARC format and to export them. Many argue that only these capabilities allow for the true flexibility of the MARC record, freeing the user from being tied forever to a particular software package. It remains to be seen whether teacher-librarians and others working in school libraries will consider this capability a "must have" when deciding upon a software package or whether brand loyalty (or other factors) will prevail.

Integrated, "Modular" Systems

All of the systems surveyed, except Utlas' M/Series 10 (see below), are "integrated" in that they combine, using a single database, *at least three* of the usual six library functions. Mac Library's OPAC function is available as a separate product, MacLAP. The functions that are of the most concern to an individual school library and included in this survey are cataloging, online catalog (OPAC), and circulation. The figures show that all sites have installed the cataloging/online enquiry function; 72 percent have also installed the circulation function.

Eight of the systems reporting allow for the installation of one or more additional functions—acquisitions, serials control, or media management. Of these, Card Datalog, Eloquent and Library 4 allow for all six functions. However, installations of these other functions lag far behind the cataloging/OPAC circulation installations. Table 1 shows the various functions modules available for the systems surveyed.

Table 1.

Available Functions.

	CAT	OPAC	CIRC	ACQ	SER	AV	OTHER
The Assistant	✓	✓	✓	✓	✓	X	
Card Datalog	✓	✓	✓	✓	✓	✓	1
Circ/Cat Plus	✓	✓	✓	X	X	✓	2
Columbia	✓	✓	✓	✓	✓	X	
Dynix	✓	✓	✓	✓	✓	✓	3
Eloquent	✓	✓	✓	✓	✓	✓	4
Impact/SLiMS	✓	✓	✓	X	X	X	
Lexifile	✓	✓	✓	X	X	*	
Library 4	✓	✓	✓	✓	✓	✓	5
M/Series 10	X	✓	✓	X	X	X	
Mac Library	✓	**	✓	✓	X	X	
Mac School	✓	✓	✓	✓	X	***	6
Mandarin	✓	✓	✓	X	X	X	
Mediafile	✓	✓	✓	X	✓	✓	
Microcat	✓	✓	✓	X	X	X	
Molli	✓	✓	✓	****	X	X	7
Winnebago	✓	✓	✓	X	X	X	4

*   Can transfer files to and from CAE software.
**   Available as separate product "MacLAP."
***   Available as separate product "Mac School Advance Booking."
****   Link possible.

OTHER functions include:
1. CIRSELF module for self-service circulation.
2. "Alliance Plus"—CD-ROM product for reconversion.
3. Homebound circulation module; patron dial-up; community resource module.
4. Union catalog.
5. Graphics; word processing.
6. Link to student information system (SIS).
7. Link to borrower's records from any automated source.

Utlas M/Series 10

As noted earlier, the Utlas M/Series 10 is not an integrated system as defined here; it does not allow cataloging per se. Users cannot enter catalog records into their local systems and only "capture" for their own use records that are already in the Utlas database. Records that are unique to a particular location and not already in the Utlas database may be entered by the school or by Utlas staff into the school's portion of the Utlas database for use by the school and by anyone else, but they are not part of the local database. This is both a strength (it provides the potential for an excellent union catalog capability) and a limitation (it means the school doesn't have its own holdings on a database in-house). Rumors always seem to be circulating that Utlas will allow its members to have their own databases, but no firm plans have been announced yet. Utlas corporate uncertainties have, for the time being, been set aside with the recent announcement that OCLC's offer to buy Utlas had fallen through. Utlas is now seeking other alternatives in order to continue to provide products and services to its many customers. Other corporate news in 1990 included the merging of Columbia Computing Services into CTB Macmillan/McGraw-Hill.

Four of the respondents describe their systems as completely modular, meaning that the various modules for the different functions can be purchased and installed one at a time and in any order. Card Datalog, Columbia, MicroCAT and Winnebago CIRC/CAT fall into this category, although MicroCAT's respondent recommends installing the cataloging module first, then the OPAC, and then the circulation module.

One advantage to installing and implementing a system, module by module, means the school can spread out payments, training, etc. over several budget periods and get only what is wanted or needed at the time. A disadvantage to this approach is that it can cost more in the long run as the school may not be able to take advantage of package deals or quantity discounts. Also, it may mean the wrong decision about what to automate and in what order.

Building a quality database first, using MARC records, and adding other functions afterwards is the best approach. Even though circulation is a function which readily lends itself to computerization, it is not recommended that circulation be automated first. Circulation is too busy and visible an activity to be experimenting with. Also, circulation can be carried out successfully with a very abbreviated bibliographic record in the database, and these abbreviated records are not very good for searching. This means those six vendors who offer a modular system for which a base module (allowing for the cataloging/data entry function) must be purchased and installed first are reinforcing the idea that the creation of a quality database ought to be the first step. The vendors of Circulation/Catalog Plus, Eloquent, Lexifile, M/Series 10, Mac School Library and Mediafile all describe their systems as "partially modular" in the sense just noted.

The remaining four systems, Library 4, the Mac Library System, Mandarin and Molli are not modular in that all modules must be purchased and installed as a package. Molli's Liz Erdmer makes a very good case for this approach citing the one "look and feel" for the system throughout—one manual, one installation procedure, and one technical support agreement and price, as well as a better price overall than if the modules are purchased separately. But with such packages the clients may get more than they want or need; too much all at once can lead to confusion and frustration. As ever, it is *caveat emptor.*

The 1990 Survey

In the spring and summer of 1990, *Library Technology Reports* published a two-part study evaluating 29 microcomputer-based library automation systems. The study provided the field from which systems were chosen for this 1990 survey of automation in Canadian school libraries.

Eleven software packages were excluded because they either did not meet the broad definition of an integrated system, or they did not have the capability to utilize records in the MARC format. (Such systems may be adequate for small school library resource centers; they are generally easy to use and maintain and their lower price tags make them very attractive. However, they are hardly state of the art and their limitations soon become obvious.)

Twelve of the 18 qualifying systems from the *LTR* study had been included in the 1989 survey (*CLJ*, August 1990). Three other vendors from the 1989 survey were included, as were three vendors new to the survey. This brought the total to 24 (13 Canadian, 11 American) who received the survey questionnaire in March 1991. All were known to produce and/or market and support in Canada automated systems suitable for school libraries.

Completed questionnaires came back from seventeen vendors (ten Canadian, seven American). One additional vendor reported by telephone, Bibliofiche, the vendor of Mandarin, a Canadian PC-based system, did not reply for 1990, although this company took part (and had installations to report) in the 1989 survey. *Therefore, the figures for and comments about Mandarin are based on the 1989 responses.* Names and addresses of the vendors who responded to the 1990 survey and reported Canadian installations appear at the end of the report.

Four American vendors did not reply most likely because they did not have any Canadian school library installations. The same assumption is made about Quebec's Best-Seller, and was confirmed for Sydney International Library Systems.

Questionnaire

Respondents were asked to report on the numbers of installations for their systems in three different school library "settings" or locations – individual schools, school districts or boards, and district resource centers. Respondents were asked also to break down their installations by geographic region (including those outside Canada for Canadian vendors), and to comment on their systems' makeup, capabilities, and special features.

Unfortunately, inconsistencies in the vendors' reporting methods continue to be a problem. The most common was for the vendor to list installations at individual schools when the client was the *school district*, which included installations at a number of sites within the district.

Adding to the problem was the refusal of some vendors to include client lists so that verifying numbers was virtually impossible. Whenever a vendor did supply a client list, it was checked very carefully to ensure that data there corresponded to what had been filled in on the questionnaire. In some cases data were modified to match both the definitions and what was on the client list.

In an attempt to offset the inconsistent reporting methods, it was decided to base this year's report on *separate installed sites*, regardless of whether they were independent schools or schools that were part of a school district or board, centralized school district sites, or district resource centers. Many vendors were recontacted by telephone to clarify or verify figures for total sites installed. Whether this is the best or fairest way to make comparisons is debatable, but it seemed the most straightforward approach for this year's report.

Using this approach the survey showed that automated school library systems were installed at 469 individual sites in 1990. Total installations to the end of 1990 were 1,324. Even taking into account the different reporting practices in 1990 compared to 1989, there is a substantial gain (21 percent) in the marketplace for 1990 over 1989.

Leading the Way

Utlas continued to maintain a very healthy market share both in 1990 (41 percent) and overall (48 percent). To the end of 1990, M/Series 10 had been installed at a total of 630 individual sites (schools and district resource centers) representing 27 school districts and one independent school. This total includes 191 "new" installations (189 at schools and two at DRCs), spread among 10 school boards in 1990, Utlas' M/Series 10 best year. Just how many of these new installations were in districts that were already Utlas clients and how many were in new districts is impossible to report as a current copy of the complete client list was not available. (The 27 board-level clients were verified from a recent list, however.) Readers are reminded that the purpose of the survey report is to show general trends and patterns and any conclusions must be those of the reader and equally general. Figure 1 shows relative market shares, based on numbers of installed sites, 1990 and overall.

Other Market Leaders

A newcomer to the Canadian school library market for 1990, Follett's Circulation/Catalog Plus is installed at 71 individual sites (including three school districts) in Canada. In addition, Follett has made two sales to schools in Ontario, but these systems were not installed at the end of 1990 (and are not included in the graphics). This gives Follett second place in 1990, edging out CTB/Columbia by one installed site. Both vendors have approximately 15 percent of the 1990 market.

Circulation Plus was developed in 1983 by Follett Software Company's development group specifically to meet the needs of the school library market. It is in place in more than 12,000 school libraries in the United States. Catalog Plus (essentially Follett's OPAC module) was released in January 1990 and there are now over 1,600 users of the integrated system. Alliance Plus, a CD-ROM product containing over 350,000 LC MARC/MicroLIF records for retrospective conversion, was also released early in 1990.

CTB/Columbia reported installations at 70 new sites for 1990 with many existing clients upgrading their systems by adding modules. With installations at 244 sites, this company has an overall market share of 19 percent, placing it solidly in second place after Utlas for total sites installed. Columbia moved into the district and DRC market in 1990 with one and sixteen installations respectively.

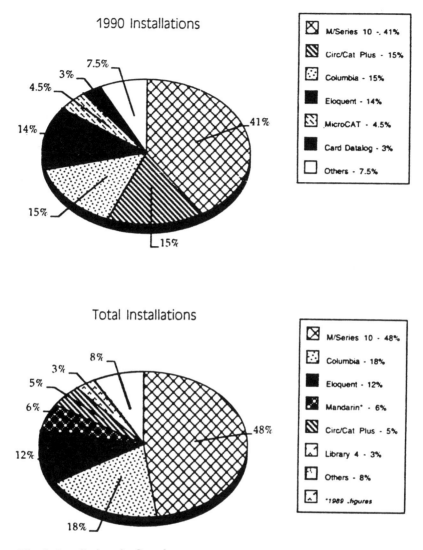

Fig. 1. Installations in Canada.

Eloquent continued among the front runners, reporting that 1990 was its best year to date with a total of 66 installations, and 9 new districts, and 5 new DRCs added to the client list. Eloquent continues to lead (with 19 total) in installations at district resource centers, most likely because the media management module was developed specifically for this setting with lots of input from DRC personnel.

Because a number of the districts using Eloquent are taking advantage of the union catalog capability to implement a districtwide automation for which schools may come online at different stages, it is difficult to give a definitive figure for individual Eloquent users. Jacki Hooker, product manager of library systems, clarified the total number of sites installed (including independent schools, schools part of school districts, central sites for school districts, and district resource centers) as 160 at the end of 1990, giving Eloquent 12 percent of total market share.

It is assumed the Mandarin Document Management System is still installed at the 76 sites reported for 1989 and perhaps at the additional sites which were reported as "sold but not yet installed" in 1989. However, with no 1990 data for Mandarin, it is impossible to give a true picture of its market share. Using the 1989 figure, it appears that Mandarin has approximately 6 percent of total market share, down from its neck-and-neck position with Eloquent last year.

Lexifile also slipped from last year's position due primarily to a strong showing for MicroCAT. 1990 was a very good year for MicroCAT, with 12 sites installing the DOS version of the software and 9 sites installing the XENIX version. Eight school boards are represented in these totals. This puts MicroCAT in fifth place for 1990, with 4.5 percent of the market, and in tenth place overall.

Card Datalog was installed at 14 individual sites in 1990, for a 3 percent share of, and sixth place in the 1990 market. The majority of these installations were for two school boards in southern Ontario, with four installations for one board and seven for the other. Overall, Card Datalog is installed at 24 individual sites including those which are part of six school districts. Card Datalog has no DRC installations even though an AV booking module is part of the system.

Following Card Datalog for 1990 is Molli, a truly Canadian product developed, marketed and supported by Nichols Advanced Technologies of Edmonton, and erroneously identified in last year's report as an American product. The company's client list shows installations at nine schools, one school district and one district resource center for 1990, slightly down from 1989, the company's best year with 16 installations. These were at six individual schools and two school boards one of which included nine schools. With five installations prior to 1989, Molli's total comes to 32.

Completing the Picture

The remaining 1990 market share (approximately 5 percent) is spread among five systems, including Lexifile. Library 4 is installed in 35 school libraries which are part of seven school districts, all in British Columbia (B.C.). Ten of these installations (in four school districts) were reported for 1990. Library 4 was mentioned in last year's survey as "Librarian 4" a name Kelowna Software could not continue to use for copyright reasons. The original package was developed in 1986, with the school library market in mind, in the West Kootenays of B.C. at the Trail and Rossland High Schools and the Trail Public Library. It is an integrated package system offering the usual six major library functions and including authority files, reserves, report and label generation, and inventory control. Graphic and word processing (with data merging) capabilities are available as options.

The Mac Library System was installed at four new schools and two new districts in Ontario in 1990, bringing the total number of installations in Canadian school libraries and districts to 11. The district installations are a new market for Mac Library System whose previous sales were all to individual schools.

Mediafile was developed in 1989, primarily for the school library market, by Hector J. LeBlanc of Silverdale Computers Incorporated. Mr. LeBlanc explains, "We want teachers and students together, to use Mediafile within the curriculum. Mediafile has a feature that can tie library holdings directly to a specific curriculum guide in the 'Canadian' context." The system is concluding a period of testing, updating, and polishing at sites in central and southern Ontario. It is not installed at two elementary schools representing pilot projects for two school boards, and at three district resource centers.

The Mac School Library's reference site list names a school district in B.C. and a private school in Montreal among the company's clients, but Rondi Rebak, director of marketing, reports that figures for sales and installations are now available. Developed by Chancery Software Ltd. of Vancouver specifically for school libraries, the Mac School Library software has been on the market since 1986. One of its strengths is that it is integrated with the Mac School Student Information System so that borrowers' records for circulation do not have to be keyed into the system.

Winnebago Software Company reported no installations of their products to school libraries in Canada for 1990. However, Eric H. Bjerke, marketing/bid coordinator, reported a good start for 1991 with some installations already in Ontario; these will be included in next year's survey.

Geographic Distribution

The western provinces and Ontario remain the most automated of the geographic regions, both in terms of numbers of installations and vendors represented. This was expected and makes good sense, as all the Canadian systems surveyed (except Mandarin which was developed in Quebec) were developed either in Ontario or the west. Interestingly, the American products included in this survey are also western (or midwestern) products.

Also as expected, the vendors had the largest share of the market in the regions in which their systems were developed, although incursions into other markets definitely increased over 1989. Columbia, for example, moved away somewhat from its traditional market base in the prairie provinces to approximately double the company's share in the Ontario market. Eloquent also made inroads into the Ontario market, and into Atlantic Canada, which, relatively speaking, was the major growth sector for school library automated systems in Canada in 1990; installed sites more than doubled over 1989. Follett's Circulation/Catalog Plus, Eloquent, and Molli all made significant gains there. Follett leads the way with 22 installed sites out of 69, and Eloquent is a very close second with 21.

Ten vendors are represented in Ontario, nine in the Prairies, seven in B.C., five in Atlantic Canada, and only two in Quebec. With 78 percent of the Ontario market, Utlas has left little room for the other nine vendors represented there. Columbia is coming on though with a total of 63 installations (9 percent) in Ontario. The situation is somewhat reversed in the Prairies where Columbia is the clear front-runner with 159 installed sites (51 percent) and Utlas is in second place with 59 installed sites (19 percent).

Lexifile's strength remains in the Prairies, but it was challenged for its position there in 1990 from another western product (MicroCAT) and a newcomer

(Circulation/Catalog Plus). Circulation/Catalog Plus also made a nice showing in B.C. but nothing near enough to challenge Eloquent's supremacy (58 percent). Columbia lost its second place in B.C. to Library 4 which now has 35 installed sites there to Columbia's 17. Figure 2 shows the major vendors' shares of the market in the various geographic regions of Canada.

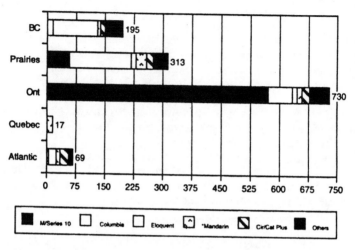

Fig. 2. Installations by region.

Configurations

Values from one to five were reported for the average number of terminals per installation in a school, with three the most common. Likewise, three was the most common number of terminals per installation for those vendors reporting on district resource centers.

When asked to describe the configuration for sites with more than one terminal, nearly all the vendors reported having multitask terminals within a local area network (LAN). Novell™ was the most frequently mentioned network software used to achieve the LAN with IBM-compatible equipment (seven vendors). Circulation/Catalog Plus currently must use Follett's Plus-Link Network System to achieve a LAN, but company programmers are reworking the system to operate under the Novell networked environment. Winnebago CIRC/CAT must use Netbios-compatible products. The Macintosh-based products, Library 4 and the Mac Library System, use Appleshare and Apple Talk respectively. No specific network software was mentioned for multitasking with the Mac School Library.

Ross Eastley, president and C.E.O. of TKM Software Limited, and the respondent for MicroCAT says, "The system also operates in a Xenix environment which we think is a preferred multiuser environment."

Unlike the other systems, Mediafile can be installed only at single terminals with a different function at each. Mediafile's developers designed the system to avoid networking because of the additional management burden they say LANs impose on teacher-librarians.

Union Catalog

As more and more teacher-librarians and school district staff recognize the advantages of a districtwide automation project and the union catalog approach, we should see more and more vendors directing their development time and talents to incorporating a union catalog capability into their systems. Although a few of the vendors responding to the 1990 survey could be said to have "true" union catalog capability, most of them, at least, are acknowledging the importance of this concept and are in the process of developing a union catalog function or perfecting what methods they already have to work towards this capability.

Four vendors reported that their systems did not have a union catalog capability at present. These are Library 4, the Mac Library System, Mac School Library, and MicroCAT. Follett's respondent stated that a union catalog was under development, and Mediafile's respondent claimed that the concept was feasible but that the vendor would have to merge files for a fee.

Using Card Datalog, it is possible to have separate schools, within a district, transfer their databases (via magnetic tape or floppy diskettes) to a central site which acts as the union catalog. School districts may mount a union database for the district on Utlas' CATSS database, but the M/Series 10 software does not allow for "scoping" of the union database down to a region or individual school. Winnebago has a separate product, Union Catalog, which acts as a centralized district level catalog and is capable of holding more than 300,000 records.

Lexifile can handle two databases simultaneously; one is usually a union catalog. The system can merge duplicate records, itemizing the location codes of the holding libraries. With Molli, multiple collections have always been possible. One may be designated the union catalog and it may reside on a hard disk alongside the local collection or at a central site. Portions of collections may be exported and numerous collections may be incorporated into one, using import and export functions.

One of the highlights of Eloquent's year was the release of their union catalog module. Using this module, the user can create a true union catalog that displays appropriate school locations for the whole district and from which titles can be exported to schools from the central site.

Alan Ball also reports a true union catalog capability for the Columbia Library System. It works from the cataloging module, where specified fields contain holdings information (and even variant call numbers) for a variety of locations which can then be displayed on the OPAC. Import/export and editing capabilities mean almost "automatic maintenance" at a central site.

Êtes-vous Bilingue?

Canada is an officially bilingual country and many schools and districts across the country offer French immersion or *Programme-cadre de français* classes. There also many dozens of schools in Quebec and elsewhere in Canada in which the entire instructional program is offered in French. Students in these schools must have access to French language materials in their school libraries. Not only the records for these materials should be in French but also the interface the students use to access the records.

There is also an increasing awareness in Canada's schools and school districts of the importance of preserving the language skills of immigrants. Many schools and districts have established first language or heritage language collections. If these collections are cataloged, classified, and used in the curriculum, shouldn't the records representing these materials be in the language of the materials and shouldn't students be able to access them in that language too? Library automation products that allow the user to query the system in languages other than English and that provide on-screen help messages, prompts, and documentation in languages other than English would seem to offer something desirable in the Canadian school library market. Consequently, vendors in this year's survey were asked, "Is yours a multilingual system?"

A few systems are currently bilingual or multilingual. Among these is Card Datalog which offers two-language versions of the system—English/French and English/Spanish. The Eloquent OPAC supports any number of additional languages that users can introduce on their own. Currently English and French versions of the system have been developed. Such is also the case with Utlas' M/Series 10 that supports separate English and French interfaces between which users can switch with a keystroke or two. Mandarin supports English and French records, interfaces, and documentation. Columbia's software will support up to four alternative languages. The system currently comes in English, French, and Dutch versions with a Spanish version under development.

A number of other systems are multilingual in the sense that the system will accept and store words and characters in other languages, but the screens, manuals, etc. are in English. Follett's Circulation/Catalog Plus, the Mac Library System, and Mac School Library are in this category.

Lexifile, Mediafile, MicroCAT, and Winnebago report that multilingual systems are in the planning and development stages. In the case of Lexifile, a user in France is working on translating the commands and online help messages. Mediafile's French version is 85 percent completed and will soon go out for testing. MicroCAT's next version will incorporate the French option into the searching screen, and Winnebago plans French and Spanish versions of the system. The remaining systems (Library 4 and Molli) are not multilingual.

Canadian Installations and Sales Abroad

Did Canadian vendors make any inroads into the American or overseas markets in 1990? With a total of 715 non-Canadian installations (214 in 1990), primarily in the United States, Molli is the leader for installations by Canadian vendors outside Canada. CTB/Columbia is in second place with a total of 552 installations outside Canada (223 in 1990). The majority of these are also in the United States as are the 165 systems Columbia has sold to schools but has not yet installed. Other sites are as far-flung as Europe and the United Kingdom, the Caribbean and Central America, the Far East and the South Pacific. Alan Ball reports, "1990 was the year in which CLS installations in the USA surpassed those in Canada.... Based on LTR counts for 1989 we believe that CLS is now #3 for installed sites in the USA."

Mandarin must also be counted among the front-runners for foreign installations, based on the vendor's 1989 report of 299 installations in the United States and United Kingdom and 67 systems sold but not installed. The Mac School Library's reference site list names a number of U.S. schools as clients, but since figures were not available, Mac School is not represented in Figure 3 that shows installations in and sales of automated systems to school libraries outside Canada by Canadian vendors.

Mediafile's Hector LeBlanc said he is looking for a U.S. distributor, but did not report any sales or installations outside Canada for 1990. Nor did any of the other vendors, except Utlas and TKM. Utlas' M/Series 10 is installed at ten sites (six in 1990) in the United States and MicroCAT at two (one in 1990).

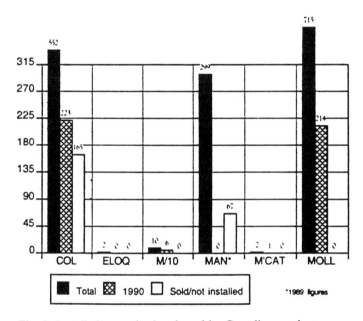

Fig. 3. Installations and sales abroad by Canadian vendors.

The Bottom Line

Prices for the systems remain quite competitive and a number of vendors indicated that site or multiuser LAN licenses were negotiable and that quantity discounts could apply. In fact, MicroCAT is available on a current promotion at $725 for a single-user and $1210 for a multiuser installation.

One of the reasons for Follett's new success in the Canadian school library market is undoubtedly the attractive price—an average $895 to install Circulation Plus in a school and $2295 for the complete package, including Catalog Plus. This latter figure is in the same range ($2,000/$3,000) reported by many of the other vendors to install a system in a school. District and DRC installations are understandably more expensive.

Outside the lower end of this range are Lexifile (an average of $1,000 per school) and MicroCAT. Card Datalog comes in at the high end of the scale with an average cost per installation of $3,600. However, this price includes a very complete package with all six modules. Once again, it is *caveat emptor*, and price alone should never be the determining factor in any automation decision. Teacher-librarians and others working in school libraries must know exactly what they want an automated system to do and base their decisions on those needs and expectations. It may not be cost-effective to purchase a system that does more than is required and certainly foolhardy to purchase one that does less on the mistaken assumption that money is saved.

Looking Ahead

Not all responses to the 1990 survey questionnaire have been included in this report for one reason or another. Allan J. McMillan, director of sales and marketing for International Library Systems Corp., reported no installations in Canadian school libraries. Further communication from ILS president Ron Aspe clarifies that the company is almost exclusively developing the Sydney Library Automation System for special libraries and is not targeting the school library market. This system has, therefore, been excluded from the present survey results and will not be included in future surveys.

On the other hand, IMPACT/SLiMS (Small Library Management System) from Auto-Graphics, Inc. (3201 Temple Ave., Pomona, CA 91768) and The Assistant from Library Automation Products, Inc. (352 7th Avenue, Suite 1001, New York, NY 10001) may well be included in future surveys if these systems break into the Canadian school library market.

In 1990, Auto-Graphics acquired the LIBerator Integrated Library system (developed in Parker, Colorado), renamed it, and proceeded with work on a major new release. To quote from Mark R. Parker, Auto-Graphic's library networking specialist,

> IMPACT/SLiMS is a microcomputer [and MARC-] based system for school, public, special, and academic libraries, with collections of up to approximately 50,000 titles. The system is sold as a total software package, with an optional LAN version for multiterminal operation. Included are a cataloging system, online catalog, circulation control module, reporting and statistical package, and an inventory system. The IMPACT/SLiMS software will run on IBM-compatible microcomputers.... We offer a complete line of systems and components, including LAN hardware, and barcode scanners, ... conversion services ... [and] CD-ROM catalogs, including multi-institutional data bases. Auto-Graphics was recently awarded the contract to create a provincial data base of public and college libraries for the Bureau of Library Services in Victoria.

Kerry B. Hanna, product manager for The Assistant, describes the product as a completely modular, fully integrated (acquisitions, cataloging, OPAC, circulation, and serials), IBM PC-AT or PS/2-compatible system capable of utilizing MARC records. It was developed in 1986 and revised to meet the needs of school libraries. The system has a location authority file to support union cataloging, but currently does not support the display or printing of diacritics. "However," Mr. Hanna reports, "we are working on it."

Last year's survey mentioned Dynix's announcement of a PC-based version of their popular integrated system. This is now available to Canadian school libraries as Dynix Scholar. A letter was mailed in the spring to 3,000 schools in Ontario as the first step in a marketing campaign. Ellen F. Crowne, automation specialist, says,

> Dynix is pleased to introduce to the Canadian market Dynix Scholar, a library automation system just for schools. The product will allow K-12 schools to implement and enjoy the functionality available to all of our clients around the world, at a fraction of the cost. Scholar includes software to automate cataloging, circulation, public access, a bibliographic utility interface, inventory control, acquisitions, media scheduling, and an ongoing student record load utility. Specific enhancements ... cater to the special needs of schools.... The Scholar runs on the X86 family of computers.... Dynix support ... is available at attractive rates.... Affordable training options ... are available as well.... Dynix Scholar boasts over 250 schools as clients in Australia and the United States. We are very excited to be able to offer our experience and expertise to Canadian schools.

Dynix did not report any sales to Canadian school libraries in 1990, but it remains a system worth watching, and no doubt will be included in the 1991 survey report if sales to other types of libraries, as reported in *Library Journal* earlier this year, can be taken as any indication. In the meantime, those interested in Dynix Scholar can contact Ellen Crowne or Craig Mann, sales and support representatives, at 1 Blue Springs Drive, Waterloo, ON N2J 2M1.

Conclusion

Growth and change will continue to characterize the Canadian school library automation marketplace as we move into the 1990s, although a less substantial increase for 1991 over 1990 is expected. Important decisions relating to the automation of a school's or school district's library functions take time. The decisions to install the systems which showed up in the figures for 1990 were most likely made in 1989 or even earlier, before the recession had made itself felt. Will future surveys show decreasing numbers of installations as a result of fewer decisions in 1990?

The market will continue to be competitive with existing vendors attempting to hold on to and expand their market shares by offering upgrades, enhancements, and special features more often and in greater numbers. Many of the vendors reported that new versions of some or all of their modules had been released in 1990. This trend should continue for 1991, as modules currently under development will be released. Additionally, the vendors will be looking to expand into new areas of products and services in order to tempt a larger share of the market. We should also expect to see the vendors attempting to move out of their traditional market bases into new geographic areas, perhaps with the help of a partner or distributor.

But gains and changes should be generally less dramatic than they have been as we cautiously move out of a recessionary economy. We are, as the Chinese proverb says, living in interesting times. What "interesting" things will next year's survey bring?

Vendors of Personal Computer-Based
Integrated School Library Systems

System Name	PC	Vendor/Representative
Card Datalog **(Data Trek, Inc.)**	IBM, Macintosh	*Marketed in Canada by:* Avec Technical Services Inc. 2261-A Royal Windsor Drive Mississauga, ON L5J 1K5 (416) 855-2924 (416) 855-2928 (Fax)
Circulation/ **Catalog Plus**	IBM, Macintosh (Circ only)	Follett Software Company 809 North Front Street McHenry, IL 60050-5589 (815) 323-3397 (815) 344-8774 (Fax)
Columbia Library **System**	IBM	CTB/Columbia Computing Services 1380 Burrard Street, Ste. 600 Vancouver, BC V6Z 2H3 (604) 739-5700 (604) 739-5727 (Fax)
The Eloquent **Librarian**	IBM	Eloquent Systems, Inc. 25-1501 Lonsdale Avenue North Vancouver, B.C. V7M 2J2 (604) 980-8358 (604) 980-9537
Lexifile	IBM	Lex Systems Inc. 513 Broadview Street P.O. Box 1438 Pincher Creek, AB T0K 1W0 (403) 627-2431 (403) 627-4957 (Fax) *Marketed in B.C. by:* CAE Custom Software Ltd. 2726 West 17th Avenue Vancouver, BC V6L 1A1 (604) 738-1062
Library 4	Macintosh	Kelowna Software Ltd. 2515 Winnipeg Road Kelowna, BC V1Z 2C6 (604) 769-3687 (604) 769-3587 (Fax)
M/Series 10	IBM	Utlas International Canada 80 Bloor Street West, 2nd Fl. Toronto, ON M5S 2V1 (416) 923-0890 (416) 923-0935

System Name	PC	Vendor/Representative
The Mac Library System	Macintosh	*Marketed in Canada by*: M.E. Phipps & Associates 143 Norfolk Street Guelph, ON N1H 4H9 (519) 836-9328 (519) 836-2623
Mac School Library	Macintosh	Chancery Software Ltd. 1122 Mainland Street, Ste. 450 Vancouver, BC V6B 5L1 (604) 685-2041 (604) 685-9669 (Fax)
Mandarin	IBM	Bibliofiche 9620 Trans Canada Highway Montreal, PQ H4S 1V9 (514) 336-4340 *Marketed in western Canada by*: United Library Services Inc. 7140 Fairmount Drive S.E. Calgary, AB T2H 0X4 (403) 252-4426
Mediafile	IBM	Silverdale Computers Incorporated 2304 Silverdale Road St. Anns, ON L0R 1Y0 (416) 957-7538
MicroCAT	IBM, XENIX	TKM Software Limited 839 18th Street, P.O. Box 1525 Brandon, MB R7A 6N3 (204) 727-3873 (204) 727-3338 (Fax)
Molli	IBM	Nichols Advanced Technologies, Inc. 1100 Royal LePage Building 10130-103 Street Edmonton, AB T5J 3N9 (403) 424-0091 (403) 424-7644 (Fax)
Winnebago CIRC/CAT	IBM	Winnebago Software Company 310 West Main Street P.O. Box 430 Caledonia, Minnesota 55921 (507) 724-5411 (507) 724-2301 (Fax)

References

Bridge, Frank R. "Automated System Marketplace 1991: Redefining System Frontiers." *Library Journal* (April 1, 1991): 50-62.

Lighthall, Lynne. "Automated Systems in Canada's School Libraries: The First Survey." *Canadian Library Journal* 47 (August 1990)): 247-54.

Matthews, Joseph R., Joan Frye Williams and Allan Wilson. "Microcomputer-Based Library Systems." *Library Technology Reports* 26 (March/April; May/June 1990): 131-289; 297-444.

Merilees, Bobbie. "Integrated Systems in Canadian Public, Academic and Special Libraries: Fifth Annual Survey." *Canadian Library Journal* 48 (June 1990): 171-79.

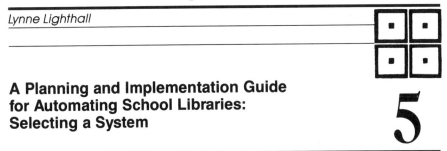

Part 2
Evaluating OPAC Systems

Lynne Lighthall

A Planning and Implementation Guide for Automating School Libraries: Selecting a System

5

Introduction and Overview

Today's educational programs actively involve students in the learning process through the meaningful use of a wide variety of print, nonprint, and human resources in order that students may develop the skills necessary for life-long learning and a commitment to informed decision making.

The school resource center is at the core of this process. A wide range of complex tasks must be performed by teacher-librarians and other staff to ensure effective programs.

Employing appropriate technologies to manage these tasks leads to enhanced resource center services and improved learning experiences for students. There are now many effective and reasonably priced microcomputer software programs available to automate resource center functions.

This guide:

- Outlines the issues facing teacher-librarians and school district staff in planning for resource center automation.

- Provides an overview of the options available.

- Explains the steps in the decision making process — moving from a "wish list" to a working system.

To meet these objectives three basic questions will be addressed:

- What do you want to do?

- What software is available to do it?

- What hardware will run the software?

Source: Reprinted by permission from *School Libraries in Canada* 8 (Winter 1989): 27-36. Copyright © Canadian Library Association.

This guide does not address the issue of the computer in the curriculum nor the issue of computer literacy even though the teacher-librarian may be responsible for these programs and/or the computers may be housed in the resource center. Many well-written and timely books and articles on these subjects are available. Consult them for guidelines on these issues.

School resource centers have lagged behind university and public libraries in introducing automated procedures. There are a variety of reasons, and at one time and/or considered in isolation they were all valid, but now are becoming less so.

Lack of funds is no longer a prime consideration as newer, faster and less expensive systems become available almost monthly. Hardware prices are decreasing more rapidly than at any time in the history of microcomputers. However, it is unwise to quote cost savings as an advantage of automation as this is rarely the case. Instead, stress cost-effectiveness and benefits to users through increased availability of staff and increased access to resources.

Lack of space and/or lack of appropriate staff are no longer valid reasons to put off automation. Most hardware configurations now take up very little space and do not require a special environment; most are "desk-top" systems. They are so user-friendly that very little training and experience are required to operate the systems efficiently and effectively.

No library is too small not to benefit from automation.

Other priorities vanish with the foresight to see how automating some procedures frees your time to enhance other aspects of your job.

Why Automate?

Computers are good at tasks that are repetitive, quantitative, routine, voluminous, logical, straightforward, and which require accuracy, precision, and speed in execution. Many library tasks are repetitive, quantitative, routine, and so on. Library operations are ideal candidates for automation.

Introducing computerized techniques into the resource center operation will:

- Eliminate some clerical, routine, or repetitive tasks or complete them more accurately and speedily.

- Increase productivity without wearing out the teacher-librarian and without having to hire new staff.

- Provide more time to work with students and plan with other teachers.

- Allow for improved and perhaps new services.

- Generate important "by-products" such as more and better information for decision making, more and better statistical reports, and more opportunities for cooperation and resource sharing with other libraries.

- Lead to increased computer literacy and fuller integration of the resource center into the curriculum.

How to Begin

Specific objectives are essential. What do you want the system to do in terms of volume, speed, accuracy, response time, specific functions? How will it be used and by whom? Clearly and concisely articulating these objectives makes a good point with administrators, officials, and purchasing agents. Garner support from your colleagues in the early stages of the project. Working from commonly held knowledge toward a commonly held goal increases your chances of success.

How do you acquire this knowledge? Start by learning all you can. Read all the articles in at least one computer periodical for the past several months plus the computer columns in the library journals. Talk to vendors and to users. Attend demonstrations, conferences, workshops, etc., and get some "hands-on" experience with different machines and software. Set broad goals and know why you want to automate. Do not assume that automating will automatically solve all your problems; avoid "computer bias."

Conduct a "needs analysis" in your resource center. Set the time range in which you will complete this analysis. It is time well-spent, but don't "overspend" — two to three weeks is sufficient for a smaller resource center. Begin by listing all the tasks now carried out in the resource center. Indicate who performs these tasks, when they are performed, and how long they take. Try to assign a dollar value to each task. Keep a logbook to aid your analysis.

Identify the strengths and weaknesses of each function as measured against the resource center's goals and objectives. Especially identify problem areas, e.g., functions that lead to inaccuracy or untimely information, tedium and inefficiency, lack of control. Examine the data you have gathered and ask the following questions:

- Can some tasks be eliminated?

- Is improving some manual tasks a valid alternative?

- What tasks are good prospects for automation now? ... in two years? ... in five years?

- Is appropriate software available?

- How much time and money are available for implementation?

- How visible will the system be?

- What benefits does it offer?

- Who will use the computer(s)?

- Where will it (they) be kept?

What to Automate?

Use the results of the needs analysis to prepare a detailed listing of your automation requirements.

Cataloging. The catalog or the resource center database is the core/key of any system; all library functions require some data provided by the catalog. By starting with the catalog database you enter data only once. Always begin with a full bibliographic record no matter what functions are to be carried out. It is much easier to ignore information that is not required than to try and access what is not there!

Cataloging programs are roughly divided into three groups depending on their output.

The online public access catalog (OPAC) is now the ideal. OPAC is more than just a replacement for the card catalog. It allows for the rapid location of appropriate resources, assists in the teaching of retrieval skills, and permits better access for disabled students. It easily generates bibliographies on special topics for particular lessons and heightens teachers' awareness of and positive response to the resource center. It enhances cooperative planning by readily identifying the collection's strengths and weaknesses. The online catalog is an excellent low maintenance, high quality access tool. It is also cost-effective. In a new school, installing an online catalog costs about the same as installing a card catalog, and the ongoing costs are lower.

Unfortunately some systems that feature online access do not have a label printing program. This is a very visible area in which to save time, effort, and money. In addition, the capability to print cards is also a useful feature as many teacher-librarians like the "comfort" and familiarity of maintaining a shelf list in card format. Make sure the system you select is able to print labels at least.

Ideal as OPAC may be it is not always practical or even possible in some situations. What are the alternatives?

Card production programs are reasonably priced, easy to use, and also allow for label printing. However, the card catalog has many limitations and failings in providing effective and timely access to the resource center's collection. Why perpetuate these limitations when automating? Even the more sophisticated and flexible programs result in a pile of cards that someone must file (or misfile).

Printed catalogs either in book or microformat are losing what popularity they once had due to lack of timeliness and flexibility and rising production costs. Many systems now offer print programs that allow you to put your print files on tapes or diskettes which can then be output on a laser printer or typeset commercially. This offsets some disadvantages of in-house production. Also, book and COM (computer output microform) catalogs serve a very important function in backing up the online system.

A checklist of features to look for in choosing cataloging software is on p. 55.

Circulation. Because of its high visibility and ease of conversion, circulation is the library function that is most frequently automated first. But because it requires daily input and updating, it is not "low pressure" enough to be a good first choice. Also, circulation requires only a brief record that will not serve other purposes. Therefore, it is best to add the circulation function after the database is built. On the other hand, it is foolish to ignore an existing database of circulation records and to dismiss all the effort that went into creating that database. It is also foolish and impractical to insist on beginning with the cataloging function. You can often convince administrators and others who are reluctant to undertake a full scale automation to proceed one step at a time and to start with a visible and "familiar" function.

Look for software packages that have programs to convert circulation records from other automated systems. Alternatively, look for packages that provide an abbreviated data entry screen to allow immediate creation of the brief records needed for circulation, but also provide the flexibility to later enter or download the full bibliographic records needed for searching and other functions.

A checklist of features to look for in choosing circulation software is on p. 58.

Acquisitions. In many school districts the ordering of resource center materials is handled on the district's mainframe computer and/or by another department. Introduction of automated acquisitions is an impossibility for some individual teacher-librarians or low priority in relation to other functions. An acquisitions module, therefore, is an option and you should not disqualify an otherwise effective software package because it lacks a purchasing module or has a poor one. However, you must still maintain records and files and these functions benefit from computerization. Using a general purpose program is a viable option here as is installing one of the nonintegrated acquisitions packages which generally cost less than $100 and require very little expertise to run successfully. But the better acquisitions programs now available are modules of larger integrated library packages.

A checklist of features to look for in choosing acquisitions software is on p. 60.

Serials Control. For most school resource centers sophisticated serials management is not a priority. Instead the teacher-librarian requires an easy-to-use and reliable method of keeping track of subscriptions. Integration with other modules like acquisitions and circulation is desirable, but not essential. Installing one of the many well-designed and dependable nonintegrated systems is a reasonable alternative. Do not disqualify a library package because it lacks a serials module.

In choosing serials control software ask, will the program:

- Order, renew, and/or cancel subscriptions

- Create records

- Receive issues

- Claim missing or late issues

- Route and circulate new arrivals

- Manage fund accounting

- Print periodicals lists

- Generate reports and statistics

- Provide other functions

Media Management. Cost-effective and careful management of expensive nonbook media is essential. Separate systems for media management including advance bookings programs and equipment inventory packages are currently available, but software developers will not be long in seeing the advantages of integrated packages. In schools or districts where media and resource center activities are integrated and/or where the teacher-librarian is responsible for both areas, planning to incorporate such a program into the resource center's overall system should be a priority. In these cases the media management program becomes the focal or starting point of the automation project. Those using the program to search for appropriate media to support activities at the school level get the benefit of training on the system and an advance look at what will be installed eventually in the schools.

A checklist of features to look for in choosing media management software is on p. 62.

Library Management. Library management included a variety of clerical and administrative tasks and record-keeping activities such as budget control, usage reports/statistics, etc. You want to be able to select, sort, and format data to produce reports tailored to your needs. Library programs frequently integrate these functions with the other modules or you may purchase software specifically designed for administrative functions. These all provide additional opportunities to enhance the resource center's services and profile.

In choosing library management software ask, will the program generate useful reports and statistics that will allow you to:

- Be aware of trends and changes?

- Make comparisons?

- Overview accounts and expenses?

- Analyse collection use?

- Prepare budgets?

Information Retrieval. A developing trend in school resource centers is the provision for students and teachers of access to major commercial databases, such as Globe and Mail Online, DIALOG, BRS, ERIC, etc. It is possible to trap data from these and a variety of other databases (even those at other schools) and make them part of your own database. The software needed for these functions need not integrate with the other library functions nor even run on the same machine. It may be preferable to have this function set up as a completely separate operation or running on a machine used for library management tasks.

Library Instruction. Commercial programs are available or they can be produced in-house. Either way you provide a meaningful learning experience for the students and a valid use of the microcomputer.

Considering Alternatives

Knowing why and what you want to automate is only partial preparation for choosing a system. You must also know what alternatives are available.

Retaining and Improving Manual Procedures

Manual systems have the advantages of being familiar and easy to understand; they have evolved over time and are easily modified. But manual procedures require large amounts of clerical time and effort; they are not cost-effective nor very efficient in the long run. Remember, however, that it is not necessary to automate all your library procedures, nor is it necessary to do it all at once!

General Purpose or "Horizontal" Packages

Word processing packages are good at dealing with text and can be used in the resource center for letters, memos and other correspondence and for reports of all kinds.

Spreadsheet packages are good at dealing with numbers and can be used in the resource center for budgeting, fund accounting, and statistical analyses.

Database management systems (DBMS) are good at sorting; they manage information very well. A DBMS allows you to define, create, edit, and delete records; search and sort records; and display and print records in a variety of sequences and formats. A DBMS can be used in the resource center for media management, equipment inventories, acquisitions files, teacher and student records, mailing lists, curriculum guides, and so on. A general purpose DBMS is not generally recommended for cataloging because of the large storage needs; however, some successful cataloging programs are available.

With a microcomputer and telecommunications package in place you can also subscribe to various bulletin board services, take advantage of electronic mail, and become involved in networking.

Specific or "Vertical" Packages

In-house or custom packages are completely developed by local staff and are unique to the local situation. If the system is particularly effective it can be marketed to others. A number of systems now on the market had such humble beginnings. However, with so many proven commercial packages currently available it is unwise to spend the time and effort needed to develop something new.

Purchased services are also impractical.

Purchased software is the most popular, affordable and practical approach, but which program? There is now an almost bewildering array of library application software programs from which to choose, but many alternatives can be eliminated immediately as not meeting your needs and expectations.

Stand-Alone Systems. Programs designed for stand-alone systems are "Model T" packages—very basic, inexpensive, and fairly reliable, but lacking in flexibility and expandability. They tend to satisfy only one function, usually circulation. Circulation is one of those routine, repetitive, voluminous tasks that lends itself so well to computerization. It is also carried out successfully with only a very brief entry in the database, but even very brief records require someone in-house to key in every record to build the local database. This process is slow and expensive in the long run and results in records that are nonstandard and too brief to be used for other functions.

Many stand-alone systems run with floppy disks and often require a lot of juggling of disks to successfully perform straightforward tasks. This wastes time and leads to frustration and errors. Stand-alone systems inevitably fail to keep pace with even the most basic demands and need replacement much sooner than more sophisticated systems.

Integrated Systems. The bibliographic record, no matter how it is presented (on a card in the card catalog, as an entry in a bibliography or book catalog, as an item on an overdue list, etc.), is the basis of all library work. It makes sense to create that record only once and use it in varying formats for different purposes. It also makes sense to ensure that the record is as standard as possible—one that is recognized and used by the largest number of locations—one that you can obtain from someone else. Integrated systems emphasize networking and depend on developing a database utilizing the full MARC record.

Cataloging information is complex and requires a multitude of access points for efficient and comprehensive retrieval. Until very recently microcomputers did not have sufficient memory and power to store and manipulate these data. But now more powerful micros with lots of hard disk storage are available at reasonable prices.

The questions now become: Do the apparent convenience and relatively low capital costs of a stand-alone system outweigh the staff costs, limitations of a short entry, and "isolation" that is imposed upon a library in terms of data and subsequent resource sharing? Do you want to be "outstanding in your field"?

To answer these questions consider the following:

- Does the program do what you want it to do in terms of specific tasks, speed, and number of records?

- What hardware does it require?

- Do the program and its developer(s) have a successful track record?

- How easy is it to learn and use and are training and support available? Is the system menu-based or command driven? Are the prompts meaningful? What about the "help" screens? What documentation comes with the system? How good is the documentation?

- What are the possibilities for expansion and/or data conversion? What about enhancements?

- Have you tried it?

The Selection Process

Software Evaluation

Deciding on the type of system is only one step in a fairly long-term project. Proceed carefully; don't be rushed. Use a formal RFP (request for proposal) or a more informal RFI (request for information) at this point or simply contact individual vendors. Use the checklists as guidelines and/or outlines for designing your own RFP or RFI. Decide which features of an automated system are "essential" to meet your needs and expectations, which are "desirable," which are simply "nice to have," and which are "not applicable." Weigh the features on an appropriate scale of 1 to 10 or 1 to 5, or A, B, C, D, etc.

Compare packages, hardware systems, and vendors. Determine which features are available already in the vendor's package, which are in development, and which are not available. For modules in development find out the expected release date or determine the vendor's priorities. Get written price quotations on the total system. Immediately eliminate systems that lack features you have heavily weighed as "essential." Don't waste time examining systems that are inappropriate to your needs.

What can you expect from the vendor at this point?

- *Demonstrations*: Go and see and use the system. Be aware that some systems operate from a very small demonstration database and may give false impressions.

- *References*: Get the names, addresses, and phone numbers of contact persons where the system is operational. Talk to these people; visit them if possible. Beware the overly enthusiastic or unduly negative response.

- *Equipment Requirements*: Find out exactly what is required to run the programs now and in the foreseeable future. There should be no surprises! Many software vendors offer a total package including hardware. But the obvious advantages of having to deal with only one vendor is lost if the vendor is out of town. A local vendor may offer a lower price and better support.

- *Training and Follow-up*: Make sure the vendor provides on-site training in basic use and maintenance. Make sure the manuals are clear and comprehensive. Make sure you have easy access to the vendor and his/her troubleshooting staff after installation. Local vendors are best in this regard, but don't abuse them. If the vendor is out-of-town ask about toll-free lines or collect calls. Are maintenance/service contracts available?

- *Contracts and Warranties*: Are they reasonable? Suggest changes, additions, and deletions of your own; and if there is anything you don't understand, ask! Have your board's legal advisor or computer consultant check the contract.

Hardware

The software vendor will provide the hardware specifications required to run the software. Visit and talk to hardware vendors. Sit in on demonstrations. Try the equipment yourself. Get the vendor to run your software or another program you know has the same hardware requirements and see what happens. Check with other users for their evaluations of the equipment.

Ask the following questions about the hardware:

- Will the software run on it? Be wary of claims that a "look-alike" is exactly compatible with the desired model.

- Is the dealer reliable, and is the price fair?

- Is the hardware standard or are a lot of special parts and pieces required to add a printer, for example? Are replacement parts readily available?

- What's included? Even monitors, keyboards, and disk drives may be separate—as may cables, interfaces, etc. How much memory is standard and is the operating system included? What are the warranties?

- Is the system expandable? Can memory and extra disk drives for storage be added? Is there an upper limit to the amount of data you can store? What about building a multiuser system?

- Is the system durable and reliable? Is it fast enough?

- Are the ergonomics right, i.e., is the system physically comfortable to use?

- How good is the documentation? Are the manuals comprehensive and comprehensible?

Cost-Benefit Analysis

Evaluation methods range from simple and subjective to complex and objective. The "least total cost" is one recommended method. Consider all the costs necessary to acquire, install, implement, and maintain the system over an approximate five-year period. Besides the basic costs of the software and the hardware include:

- Cables, interfaces, and special software needed to make the whole system work

- Special wiring or dedicated lines

- Structural alterations

- New furniture

- Telephones and lines

- Accessories, e.g., surge protectors

- Peripherals, e.g., printers, bar code readers/optical scanners and wands, color monitors, etc.

- Site visits and information gathering

- Database creation

- Bar coding and related activities

- Special insurance

- Lost productivity during training and implementation periods

Ongoing costs include paper, ribbons, disks, and other supplies; telephone and connect time charges; maintenance contracts; and software enhancements and equipment upgrades.

Measure the benefits of automation against these costs. Include the tangible benefits of increased staff productivity, time savings, elimination of multiple manual files and cost avoidance plus the more intangible benefits related to quality of service such as more and better access to and use of information.

Checklists

The checklists in this section provide a basis on which to judge library automation programs or modules. The features included are those that are useful in a school setting. Modify the lists as necessary to reflect your own priorities and use them to develop a personalized checklist for your resource center or district.

Decide which features are "essential" to meet your needs and expectations, which are "desirable," which are simply "nice to have" and which are "not applicable." Weigh the features on an appropriate scale of 1 to 10 or 1 to 5, or A, B, C, D, etc.

Determine which features are available already in the vendor's package, which are in development and which are not available. For modules or functions in development find out the expected release date or determine the vendor's priorities.

Immediately eliminate systems that lack features you have weighed as "essential."

Basic System Checklist

General. The vendor will:

- Provide on-site instruction in basic use and maintenance of the system and in system management and/or provide online tutorials for instruction and/or offer "hot line" support.

- Provide a full set of documentation upon installation.

- Provide software enhancements as outlined in the contract at minimal charge.

   The program will:

- Provide frequent and meaningful prompts.

- Provide comprehensive "help" screens for all steps.

- Provide an online tutorial for cataloging and searching.

- Accommodate current and future files in terms of numbers of titles.

- Be menu-driven.

- Have variable length fields.

Security. The program will:

- Prevent unauthorized use of all files.

- Prevent attempts to dump programs or damage database.

- Allow user to define operator codes and to modify them as necessary.

Statistics. The programs will:

- Display statistics online.

- Print statistical reports in a variety of sequences.

- Provide statistics for daily, weekly, monthly, yearly activities as appropriate.

- Provide statistics to monitor cataloging activities and OPAC use, e.g., items added, modified, deleted; types of searches and results.

- Provide statistics to monitor circulation activities, e.g., for items circulated, for reserves, for overdues and fines, for borrowers, for inventory.

- Provide statistics to monitor acquisitions activities, e.g., for items ordered, received, claimed, cancelled; expenditures per fund/school; vendor performance.

- Provide statistics to monitor media management, e.g., for items booked, confirmed, shipped, returned; for borrowers.

Cataloging Module Checklist

General. The cataloging program will:

- Interface with other modules especially circulation and acquisitions.

- Function independently from other modules.

- Function concurrently with other modules.

- Accept and store both full and partial records.

- Construct indexes automatically as records are entered/loaded.

- Automatically create item records for circulation.

- Print spine labels (and labels for borrower's cards and pockets).

- Print catalog cards.

- Print bar code labels.

- Print bibliographies and catalogs in a variety of sequences.

- Allow transfer of print files to diskette for subsequent laser printing or commercial typesetting.

Database Creation and Maintenance. The cataloging program will:

- Allow user to define record format, i.e., indicate which fields from the MARC record are needed plus provide the flexibility to add fields for local needs, e.g., "local" call numbers, reading level, subcollection, etc.

- Allow manual keying of records into database.

- Allow operator to learn data entry procedures easily.

- Alert operator if an error is made.

- Allow batch loading of records from other sources, e.g., MARC tapes, CD-ROM, etc.

- Overwrite records with those from another source as required.

- Allow online modification of all fields of catalog record.

- Allow online deletion of records.

- Alert operator when a record is about to be deleted.

- Automatically correct or delete index entries as records are modified.

- Print records to verify data entry.

- Provide programs to back up all files, preferably onto another medium.

- Provide procedures and programs to recover from hardware or software failure.

Authority Control: The cataloging program will:

- Include authority control to establish consistent forms for headings for persons, subjects, etc.

- Set no limit on the number of authorities that can be linked to a title.

- Allow online manual maintenance of all fields of individual authority records.

- Permit global changes to all authorities.

- Automatically relink modified authorities to appropriate titles.

- Include *see* and *see also* references.

- Disallow blind references.

- Print authorities by type, etc.

- Allow downloading of authorities from another source.

Searches. The cataloging program will:

- Provide access for a variety of predefined operators/users.

- Allow simple character-by-character author, title, subject and keyword searches.

- Allow truncation and enclosures on search items.

- Allow searches for any word "position," i.e., the words or character strings being sought do not have to be the first in the heading, title, etc., nor do they have to follow one another in order.

- Allow searches using Boolean logic.

- Ignore or forgive variations in punctuation, spacing, accents, upper- and lowercase.

- Qualify searches by date, language, material type, reading level, etc.

- Allow modification of search strategy throughout the search process.

- Permit "browsing" by displaying terms in alphabetic neighborhood of term entered.

- Provide a "sounds like" feature for searching names with variant spellings, e.g., Burton and Berton, etc.

- Disallow "no hits."

- Include user-defined stopwords.

- Provide an automatic flip to *see* references.

- Provide automatic display of *see also* references.

- Allow exits from long searches.

- Save search strategies.

Search Results. The cataloging program will:

- Inform searcher of number of items to be displayed.

- Provide "multilevel" displays, i.e., give each type of operator/user a different type of display.

- Provide both brief and detailed displays for all types of operators/users.

- Display search results in alphabetical order.

- Display search results with status, location, etc., shown.

- Allow searcher to select records to print (rather than printing whole list).

- Provide printouts of search results in sequence and format defined by user.

- Print catalog cards.

- Print bar code labels.

- Print bibliographies and catalogs in a variety of sequences.

- Allow transfer of print files to diskette for subsequent laser printing or commercial typesetting.

Circulation Module Checklist

General. The circulation program will:

- Interface with other modules especially cataloging and acquisitions.

- Function independently from other modules.

- Function concurrently with other modules.

- Accept and store both full and partial records. (Circulation records should contain at least author, title, call number, status, and bar code number if appropriate, plus provide the flexibility to include full bibliographic details.)

- Allow circulation status to display on OPAC.

- Allow user to define record format, loan codes and periods, borrower codes, materials codes.

- Provide access to files via a variety of points, e.g., title, call number, borrower, etc.

Loan Periods. The circulation program will:

- Allow variable loan periods and due dates.

- Automatically calculate loan periods and due dates or allow operator to enter them manually.

- Allow online modification of due dates.

- Display due date at time of checkout.

- Allow user to define resource center closing days and dates.

- Provide automatic holiday control.

Checkout and Check-In. The circulation program will:

- Check out materials using manual procedures or optical scanning.

- Check in materials using manual procedures or optical scanning.

- Verify that item is actually available to circulate.

- Verify that borrower is eligible to check out item.

- Provide various display options for operator to verify status of borrower or item.

- "Trap" borrower or materials, e.g., when borrower's card has expired, when borrower has materials overdue, when borrower has exceeded his/her limit, when materials have been reserved, etc.

- Allow operator to ignore/override traps.

- Allow operator to create borrower record online at time of checkout.

- Allow renewals by automatically recirculating and displaying new due date.

- Check for traps and block renewal if appropriate.

- Allow interlibrary loans.

Borrower File. The circulation program will:

- Allow user to create borrowers' records that contain at least an identification number, full name, and "location" plus provide the flexibility to add address, telephone number, parent's work number, borrower classification code, or whatever other details are required.

- Allow operator to modify borrowers' records online.

- Allow operator to delete borrowers' records online unless the borrower has overdue books, unpaid fines, etc.

- Retrieve and display borrowers' records by identification number, name, "location," etc.

- Print the borrower file in a variety of sequences.

- Allow downloading of borrowers' records from another electronic source, e.g., student records from school office.

Overdues. The circulation program will:

- Prepare and print overdue lists in a variety of sequences, e.g., borrower's identification number, borrower's name, etc.

- Prepare and print overdue notices.

- Allow user to compose overdue message and to modify message as required.

- Allow user to set timing of notices.

- Provide fines control, e.g., calculate and record fines, print fines notices, allow operator to forgive fines, etc.

Reserves. The circulation program will:

- Provide for reserves or holds.

- Set reserves on titles or on specific items as required.

- Produce a sequential reserve list, i.e., queue holds on an item in the order received.

- Prepare and print reserve notices.

- Automatically cancel reserve when item checked out.

- Automatically cancel reserve if item not claimed in a set period.

- Prepare and print recall notices.

Inventory. The circulation program will:

- Allow for inventory control by preparing copy file for inventory, printing inventory reports, etc.

Acquisitions Module Checklist

General. The acquisitions program will:

- Interface with other modules, especially cataloging and circulation.

- Function independently from other modules.

- Function concurrently with other modules.

- Accept and store both full and partial records. (Acquisitions records should contain at least author, title, publisher[s], date, binding, price, number of copies required, and ISBN, plus provide the flexibility to include full bibliographic details.)

- Allow acquisitions status to display on OPAC.

- Allow holds/reserves on items on order and in process.

- Allow user to define format for acquisitions records, purchase orders, claims, notices, cancellation notices, fund school files, vendor files.

- Provide access to files via a variety of points, e.g., author, title, keyword, etc., plus purchase order number, invoice number, vendor, requestor, fund school, order date.

- Allow interface with mail merge to produce personalized letters and notices.

Ordering. The acquisitions program will:

- Allow for verification against existing catalog.

- Allow for verification against existing on-order file.

- Allow duplicate orders for items in catalog, in process or on order using record already in database.

- Allow multiple copies to be ordered from multiple locations and charged to multiple accounts.

- Automatically check fund school accounts and alert operator if insufficient funds left.

- Allow overcommitments.

- Automatically change status of orders as each stage in the ordering process is completed.

- Allow online review of all titles entered for ordering before preparing purchase orders.

- Allow for individual or batch production of purchase orders.

Receiving. The acquisitions program will:

- Handle receipt of full or partial shipments.

- Automatically change status from "on order" to "received" and add date received.

- Automatically update all fund/school accounts.

- Automatically update vendor performance statistics.

- Prepare and print payment voucher for accounting.

- Track order closing dates and list materials not received.

Financial Records. The acquisitions program will:

- Allow user to create records to include fund/school identification number or code, fund/school name, amount budgeted, commitments, amount spent to date, balance.

- Automatically update all files for any items ordered, received, cancelled.

- Allow manual modification of records with automatic adjustments to balances.

- Prepare and print fund accounting reports.

- Track budgets by indicating total funds available, amounts committed, amounts spent.

Vendor File. The acquisitions program will:

- Allow user to create records that include vendor name, address, telephone number; local representative's name, address, telephone number; account number; timing of claims; cancellation period.

- Allow operator to modify and delete vendor records online.

Claims and Cancellations. The acquisitions program will:

- Search for, locate, and retrieve all items that are still on order after a set time period.

- Allow user to set timing of claims.

- Allow manual override of claims dates.

- Prepare and print claims lists or letters to vendors.

- Automatically change status from "on order" to "claimed."

- Allow user to set timing of cancellations.

- Prepare and print cancellations lists or letters to vendors.

- Prepare and print cancellation notices for requestors.

- Automatically change status from "on order" to "cancelled."

- Automatically remove commitments from fund/school accounts and adjust balances.

- Allow reuse of record for another vendor.

Media Management Module Checklist

General. The media management program will:

- Interface with other modules if desired.

- Function independently from other modules.

- Function concurrently with other modules.

- Accept and store both full and partial records. (Media inventory records should contain at least author, title, producer or issuing agency, call or identification number, media type, and vendor, plus allow the flexibility to include full bibliographic details including a content summary.)

- Allow user to define format for media inventory records, shipping lists, routing lists, packing slips, borrower file, and vendor file.

- Provide access to files via a variety of points, e.g., title, producer or issuing agency, call or identification number, borrower, reserve dates, etc.

- Allow operator to create, modify and delete records online.

- Print media catalogs in sequence and format defined by user.

- Allow transfer of print files to diskette for subsequent laser printing or commercial typesetting.

- Print shipping lists and labels, packing slips, and routing lists.

Loan Periods. The media management program will:

- Allow variable loan periods and due dates.

- Automatically calculate loan periods and due dates or allow operator to enter them manually.

- Allow online modification of due dates.

- Allow user to define resource center closing days and dates – provide automatic holiday control.

Bookings. The media management program will:

- Allow checkout of materials using manual procedures or optical scanning.

- Allow bookings up to one year in advance.

- Verify that item is available.

- Display alternative dates if first choice is not available.

- Display alternative media if first choice is not available.

- Display alternative title(s) on same topic if first choice is not available.

- Verify that borrower is eligible to book item.

- Print confirmation notices for borrowers.

- Automatically update all files on confirmation of booking.

- "Trap" borrowers or materials as required.

- Allow operator to ignore/override traps.

- Allow renewals by automatically calculating and displaying new due date.

- Check for traps and block renewal if appropriate.

Check-In/Returns. The media management program will:

- Allow rapid check-in of returned materials using manual procedures or optical scanning.

- Automatically update all files on check-in.

Borrower and Vendor Files. The media management program will:

- Allow user to create borrowers' records that contain at least full name, school location, delivery/pickup day(s), route number or code, borrower code or status, and equipment available at school, plus provide the flexibility to add whatever other details are required.

- Allow user to create vendor records that include vendor name, address, telephone number; local representative's name, address, telephone number; and account number.

- Retrieve and display borrower or vendor records via a variety of access points.

- Print borrower or vendor files in a variety of sequences.

Comparison Chart
for Public Access Catalogs

6

The Technology Committee of the American Association of School Librarians conducted a preconference in Chicago in June 1990. Eleven companies were invited to participate. The 11 were chosen because they had an established reputation in the library community and because they represented a *kind* of catalog configuration: mainframe/mini, hard disk, and CD-ROM.

There are certainly more than 11 companies that provide excellent automated catalogs. Time restricted the invitations to only eleven. Conspicuously absent was any Macintosh product. Three companies (Caspr, Richmond Software, and Library Management Systems) provide public access catalogs on the Macintosh, but the committee felt that none of the three currently had a large enough market share. Perhaps the lack of inexpensive Macintosh hardware has hurt that market, and if that's the case, the introduction of low-priced Macintoshes in October might change things dramatically.

The companies at the preconference were asked to list the price of their products. The old adage about apples and oranges is true here. It's unfair and impossible to compare packages when one includes hardware, software, and training, and another lists only the software.

An accurate comparison can only be made on a per-station basis. First, determine how many stations the library will have. Next, add up *all* the costs: hardware, software, installation, maintenance, training, and updates. Divide the total cost by the number of stations to get a per-station cost. The purpose of the cost comparison chart is to give you a feel for what each *configuration* costs. It is not a product comparison, since it does not even mention the features of each system.

Source: Reprinted by permission from *California Media and Library Educators Association Journal* 14, no. 1 (Fall 1990): 39-41.

Mainframe/Mini Configuration. Designed primarily for many users and/or multiple sites, this configuration offers real-time access to a number of collections by many users. Larger school districts, public library/school library cooperatives, and those districts wishing to maintain a central union catalog find this attractive. Terminals are less expensive than stand-alone IBM/PC compatibles.

Hard Disk Configuration. A high-end PC with a hard disk works as a file server while low-end PCs are connected through a local area network. Networking cards and networking software are required in addition to the search software for the catalog itself. This is the most common configuration for single school library sites.

CD-ROM Configuration. The cost of creating and updating the master CD-ROM almost requires a cooperative venture among many libraries to keep this within the typical school library budget. The ruggedness of the CD-ROM and the absence of wiring make this configuration attractive. Using two or three CD-ROM players in tandem makes it possible to search very large databases.

Directory of Automation Companies

Auto-Graphics, Inc.
3201 Temple Avenue
Pomona, CA 91768
(800) 776-6939

Brodart Automation
500 Arch Street
Williamsport, PA 17705
(717) 326-2461

CLSI
320 Nevada Street
Newtonville, MA 02160
(800) 365-0085

CTB Macmillan/McGraw-Hill
8101 East Prentice Avenue, Suite 700
Englewood, CO 80111-2936
(303) 773-6440

Dynix, Inc.
151 East 1700 South
Provo, UT 84601
(801) 375-2770

Follett Software
809 North Front Street
McHenry, IL 60050
(815) 244-8700

Library Corporation
14 Crow Canyon Road, Suite 105
San Ramon, CA 94583
(304) 229-0100

Media Flex
P.O. Box 1107
Champlain, NY 12919
(518) 298-2970

Nichols Advanced Technologies, Inc.
3452 Losey Blvd. South
LaCrosse, WI 54601
(800) 658-9453
(608) 787-8333

Winnebago Software Company
121 South Marshall
Caledonia, MN 55921
(507) 724-5411

WLN
4224 Sixth Ave., SE
Building 3
Lacey, WA 98503-1024

Company	Product	Hardware	Costs
Auto-Graphics	IMPACT/ SLiMS	IBM/PC XT and up with CD-ROM drive per station.	$4,000 plus 2.5¢ per record to build database and to create a master. $25 for duplicates. $100-250 per year per station for software license.
Brodart Automation	LePac	IBM/PC 640K with CD-ROM drive per station.	3-7 cents per title to create the master CD-ROM; $25-40 for duplicates. $90 per station per year for software licensing.
CLSI	CL-CAT	Altos Computer, 8-24 terminals.	$36,000 includes all hardware and software, loading of database and training.
CTB Macmillan/ McGraw-Hill	Columbia Library System	IBM/PC AT and up. Novell network and cards.	$1,295 ACQ, $1,095 CIRC, $1,295 CAT, and $695 SERIALS. $595 for MARC interfaces.
Dynix	Dynix Scholar	Dynix 286, 386, & 486 PCs; also UNIX-based miniplatforms: IBM, HP, DEC.	Turnkey system prices, including all hardware, $14,960 for two terminals on 286; $25,254 for six terminals on 386. Software includes CIRC/ CAT/PAC/INVentory, modem, training, first-year maintenance.
Follett Software	CATALOG PLUS	IBM/PC 386. Terminals 640K, one drive. Networking cards.	$895 CIRC PLUS, $1,295 CAT PLUS. $1,000 for networking capability software.
Library Corp.	INTELLIGENT CATALOG	IBM PC/AT Compatible 80286 with CD-ROM drive, 40mg hard drive, printer per workstation.	$2,970 station, $500 software for IBM-comp. $495 per year station maintenance, monthly updates/ remastering.
Media Flex	MANDARIN	IBM/PC 286 and up. Terminals 640K, one drive. Networking cards. Voice to data modem.	$1,500 for single user; $2,000 for multiuser.

(List continues on page 68.)

Company	Product	Hardware	Costs
Nichols Advanced Technologies, Inc.	MOLLI	AT, 286+. Novell/Network.	$1,795 for single user; $2,695 for multi-user. Includes PAC, circ. inventory, import module.
Winnebago Software	Winnebago CAT	IBM/PC 286 and up. Terminls 640K, one drive. Networking cards.	$995 for PAC. $180 for MARC compatibility module. $1,995 for union catalog. $1,000 for networking license.
WLN	LaserCat	IBM/PC XT and up with CD-ROM drive per station.	$400 set up charge. 6 cents a title to build database and mastering charge. $15 a disk for duplicates. Search software included.

Online Catalog/
Authority File Checklist
Submitted to Vendors

7

The following numbered items are not in priority order. Please reply to each of the basics of the *current* capabilities of your system. An attachment may indicate whether the feature *could* be developed.

1. Menu driven versus command driven:
    a. It is preferred that the basic approach is menu driven.
    b. Command-driven systems require the user to learn the commands — a possible impediment.
    c. Should have the option, however, of overriding the menu approach to default to a command-driven system.

2. System should not require a log-on procedure for the user:
    a. Initial menu should be resident on the screen, ready for input.

3. System should log off automatically after each user:
    a. After set amount of time without activity, system should default to original menu.

4. Is the format for search terms/keys:
    a. Full name of author, complete words in title, complete words in subject heading?
    b. Is search key "derived," i.e., based on a certain number of letters? For instance, for the author, John H. Smith, a 4, 3, 1 derived search key would be smit, joh,h.
    c. Full name/complete word approach is preferred.

Source: Reprinted with permission from *Library Software Review* 6, no. 1 (January-February 1987): 31-33. Copyright © 1987 Meckler Publishing, 11 Ferry Lane West, Westport, CT 06880; (203) 226-6967.

5. Search term truncation is available to retrieve all terms with the same stem.

6. System employs a stop list:
   a. Can a library change the words on the stop list?

7. Search terms can be qualified by:
   a. Date of publication or range of dates.
   b. Publication type, i.e., monograph, serial, microform, etc.
   c. Language.

8. System allows selective dissemination of information profiles to be set up online for patrons:
   a. Such a profile might consist of subject headings and call numbers automatically matched against subject headings and call numbers in updates to the file.

9. System provides the user with an interface to an online authority file:
   a. Which displays adjacent terms.
   b. Provides scroll forward/scroll backward capability.
   c. Displays postings for each entry.
   d. Includes personal names, corporate names, series, and subject headings.

10. System provides for automatic cross-referencing in the online catalog, based on *see* cross-references in the authority file:
    a. System displays the actual cross-reference before taking the user to the bibliographic records in order to eliminate any possible confusion.

11. Retrieval displays:
    a. System indicates number of postings.
    b. Provides a brief display of records when there are more than one.
    c. Provides for a full display of a record upon request.
    d. Uses English tags to explain each bibliographic element.
    e. Separates and displays bibliographic elements in a logical manner.

12. User can save results of searches online.

13. System provides for a terminal/printer interface:
    a. Default option available to print all citations continuously, i.e., not one screen at a time, with user intervention required.

14. System allows for rearranging citations in various ways, principally for printing purposes, such as by subject, by author, by title, by date, etc.:
    a. Full or truncated records can be requested.
    b. Explain the default filing arrangement in the system by type of search, i.e., subject searches are automatically arranged or subarranged how?

15. System has a MARC interface that reads MARC records and converts *all* fields, *all* tags, *all* indicators, *all* subfield codes into their equivalents in the record used by the system:
    a. Full MARC supported so that 246 added entries and 780/785 print constants are generated from the indicators. Please reply to these two specific examples.

16. System provides for LC record structure for authority records—the revised LC authority record:
    a. If not, describe the record structure precisely.

17. System is capable of downloading records directly from OCLC via a dedicated terminal.

18. System accommodates a machine-readable patron I.D. number:
    a. System can use the above for statistical reports while providing for privacy.

19. System supplies online work forms for:
    a. Search key formulation.
    b. Locally input bibliographic records.

20. System supports changing or deleting records online:
    a. Records can be altered at the character level.
    b. System can display nonprinting MARC fields for such editing.
    c. Editing a record does not prevent patron access to it.
    d. Entire record can be edited before "sending" the record back into the file, i.e., the record does not have to be edited so that one field is sent at a time.

21. System distinguishes between staff and patrons:
    a. Only staff allowed to modify, add, delete records.

22. System supports online user assistance with easy access to help screens, instructional messages, and understandable error messages.

23. System provides statistical reports on:
    a. Types of searches.
    b. Number of bibliographic and authority records.
    c. Number of access points per record.
    d. Number of searches by call number range.
    e. Patron user statistics (see item 18 above).

24. System provides global search and replace edits through the authority file for headings on the bibliographic records:
    a. Is the text or "string" stored in the authority file record only?

25. System provides software that detects any discrepancies between headings in the bibliographic records and headings in the authority file:
    a. For every heading in the online catalog, there is an exact match in the authority file.
    b. An exceptions report is generated otherwise.

26. User documentation provided for:
    a. Library patron.
    b. Library staff.
    c. Data-processing department.
    d. Documentation has an index, illustrations, is readable.

27. Describe any diagnostic capabilities of the system.

28. Does the system provide for a copy utility for backing up the file?

29. *All* Boolean operators are available:
    a. And.
    b. Or.
    c. Not.

30. System can search the complete text of the bibliographic record.

31. System has what limits on:
    a. Record size?
    b. File size?

32. System can search the following access points:
    a. Titles.
    b. Personal authors.
    c. Corporate authors.
    d. Linking entries.
    e. Notes.
    f. Publishers in the 260 field.
    g. Call numbers.
    h. ISBN and ISSN.
    i. OCLC control number.
    j. Purchase order number on temporary on-order records.
    k. Subject headings.
    l. STRN (027 and 088 fields).
    m. Uniform titles.

33. Concerning item 32 above, searches can be restricted to particular fields so that an author search, for instance, would be limited to a search of the 100, 400, 600, 700, and 800 fields.

34. System can search different combinations of different types of access points, i.e., an author/title search, a title/subject search, etc.

35. System can search by keyword or key phrase.

36. Is there a limit on the number of terminals supported by the system?
    a. System provides for both dedicated and dial access for remote access terminals.

37. System provides for display of holdings information in the online catalog, i.e., there is a link between the serials control subsystem and the online catalog.

38. System indicates circulation status in the online catalog and permits the patron to put a hold on a title.

39. System displays an on-order record in the online catalog.
    a. On-order record provided by downloading OCLC bibliographic record.
    b. In the event there is no OCLC order or bibliographic record, system provides a work form for a locally entered on-order record.

40. Vendor sells each of the four major components of the system — online catalog/authority file, circulation, acquisitions, serials control — separately.

41. System flags blind cross-references.

42. System "normalizes" initialisms, abbreviations, acronyms, singular and plural forms so that it does not matter what form of the word the user enters.

Joseph R. Matthews, Joan Frye Williams,
and Allan Wilson

Observations and Comparative Data with References to Vendors and Equipment: A Summary from "Microcomputer-Based Library Systems: An Assessment"

8

Libraries in the market for a micro-based automated library system should consider the following issues.

1. You must begin by identifying the library's own needs. This is most important, given the great diversity in product strengths and features. (See table 1.) Only after a careful assessment of local priorities and service requirements can the library weigh its needs against the capabilities of available systems.

   Note that this may be an iterative process, especially if project funding is slow in the coming. Both needs and products will change over time. The fast pace at which this technology has evolved means that some products, impressive in their day, have failed to improve and are now essentially obsolete.

2. Be aware that resource sharing and telecommunications protocols (codes and procedures for linking one computer system to another) are based on the Machine Readable Cataloging (MARC) record format. Regardless of the amount of data stored in a library's database, that data is significantly reduced in value if it cannot be output or converted to MARC format. For example, a library that plans to add records to a union catalog will encounter considerable difficulty and increased conversion costs if it doesn't start with bibliographic records in the MARC format.

3. Very brief patron records can cause problems since patrons may not be uniquely identified. (See table 2.)

Source: Reprinted by permission of the ALA from *Library Technology Reports* 26, no. 3 (May-June 1990): 431-38.

Storing a few additional characters is not likely to drive up the cost of the system—opt for completeness whenever possible.

4. Generally, it is more economical for libraries to order preprinted labels than to print their own bar code labels. Printing bar code labels takes both time and energy that could be better spent elsewhere. Commercially printed bar code labels are of much higher quality and will last considerably longer, since they come with a Mylar™ protective covering.

5. Storing data in uppercase letters only does the library user a disservice. The library must go to considerable expense to create its records. Uppercase only data is significantly harder to read on the screen and will not, in most cases, be compatible with regional resource sharing-databases or other cooperative projects in which the library may one day wish to participate.

6. Combined title/item records are expensive to create and store. Instead of reentering the bibliographic data for every copy in the collection, it is preferable to link multiple item records to a single title.

7. The improved searching power associated with authority control makes this capability extremely desirable. "See" and "see also" cross-references greatly enhance retrieval. Only a few of the more expensive systems provide authority control as part of a circulation/catalog package. (See tables 2 and 3.)

8. The primary measure of a system's power is its searching capability. As seen in table 3, the number of indexes or access points varies considerably from one system to another.

9. Libraries should examine the size and financial strength of any prospective vendor. Of the 16 vendors' offerings reviewed in the 1986 *LT Report*, six products have either disappeared or are being marketed by different firms fours years later.

10. Actual hands-on operation of a system can be quite revealing. Don't hesitate to pay for a user's manual and demo diskette; they can pay for themselves many times over in valuable information. If possible, visit a nearby library that has a candidate system installed to see how it works in a live situation. Talk with colleagues at conferences about the strengths and weaknesses of the systems they have installed.

11. In general, micro-based systems should do a fair amount of error checking of user input. When an error is made, the system should be able to provide an informative error message telling the operator what the error is and how to correct it. At the request of the operator, the system should tell the operator what the valid choices are.

12. Multiple micros, linked together using a LAN, can be expensive. The price of installing a LAN typically includes the LAN cabling, the LAN

software, a LAN interface for each micro and physical installation costs. LAN management and fine-tuning on an ongoing basis can also require a significant investment of staff time. Be sure to budget accordingly.

Vendor Name Index

NAME OF VENDOR	PRODUCT
AccuWare Business Solutions	RCM
Barscan, Inc.	TLS
Caspr, Inc.	MLS
Chancery Software	Mac School
COMPEL	MELVIL
CTB Macmillan/McGraw Hill	Columbia Library System
Data Trek, Inc.	Card Datalog
Eloquent Systems, Inc.	Eloquent Librarian
Follett Software Company	Catalog Plus
Foundation for Library Research	ALS
Gaylord Information Systems	SuperCAT
International Library Systems Corp.	Sydney Library System
K-12 Micromedia Publishing	K-12
Lex Systems, Inc.	LexiFILE
LIBerator Information Systems & Services, Inc.	LIBerator
Library Automation Products	The Assistant
Library Corporation, The	BiblioFile
Library Interface Systems, Inc.	MacBook
Nichols Advanced Technologies, Inc.	MOLLI
Professional Software	Professional Software
Ringgold Management Systems, Inc.	Nonesuch
Scholar Chips Software, Inc.	PCemas
TKM Software, Limited	MicroCAT
Winnebago Software Company	Winnebago CIRC/CAT

Table 1.
Summary of the circulation functions provided in each of the systems tested.

	Check-out	Renewal	Check-in	Calculation of Fine	Reserve (Holds)	Reserve Book Room	Inventory Control
ALS	Y	-	Y	Y	Y	-	-
Assistant	Y	Y	Y	Y	Y	-	Y
BiblioFile	Y	Y	Y	Y	Y	-	Y
Card Datalog	Y	Y	Y	Y	Y	Y	Y
Catalog Plus	Y	Y	Y	Y	Y	-	Y
Columbia	Y	Y	Y	Y	Y		Y
Eloquent	Y	Y	Y	Y	Y		Y
K-12	Y	Y	Y	-	-		-
LexiFILE	-	-	-	-	-		-
LIBerator	Y	Y	Y	Y	Y		Y
MacBook	Y	Y	Y	Y	Y	-	Y
Mac School	Y	Y	Y	Y	Y		Y
MELVIL	Y	Y	Y	Y	Y		Y
MicroCAT	Y	Y	Y	Y	-		Y
MLS	Y	Y	Y	Y	Y		Y
MOLLI	Y	Y	Y	Y	Y	-	Y
Nonesuch	Y	Y	Y	Y	Y	Y	Y
PCemas	Y	Y	Y	Y	Y		Y
Professional SW	Y	Y	Y	Y	Y		Y
RCM	Y	Y	Y	Y	Y		Y
SuperCAT	-	-	-	-	-	-	-
Sydney	Y	Y	Y	Y	Y	-	Y
TLS	Y	Y	Y	Y	Y	-	-
Winnebago	Y	Y	Y	Y	Y	-	Y

Table 2.

Summary of the data elements in each of the systems tested.

Due to space limitations, tables 2 and 3 have been split up. Read these tables horizontally, or across the page, rather than vertically.

	Full MARC?	Bibliographic Record No. of fields/ Total No. of characters	Authority Record No. of fields/ Total No. of characters	Item Record No. of fields/ Total No. of characters	Patron Record No. of fields/ Total No. of characters
ALS	N	18/407	-	-	13/164
Assistant	N	17/2,770	4/1,580	5/64	18/321
BiblioFile	Y	varies/MARC	-	varies/	varies
Card Datalog	N	21/1,245	-	10/209	26/459
Catalog Plus	Y	varies/MARC	-	13/110	11/123
Columbia	N	18/8,364	2/2,000	14/2,183	30/441
Eloquent	Y	varies/MARC	7/MARC	7/varies	10/175
K-12	N	1/32	-	-	4/ 41
LexiFILE	Y	varies/MARC	-	-	-
LIBerator	N	19/581	-	-	12/198
MacBook	N	25/819	-	-	27/387
Mac School	N	23/1,236	-	-	11/246
MELVIL	N	17/1,896	-	-	-
MicroCAT	Y	varies/MARC	-	-	9/233
MLS	Y	20/varies	-	-	10/varies
MOLLI	Y	varies/MARC	-	6/48	8/169
Nonesuch	N	7/120	-	11/46	16/129
PCemas	N	28/588	4/82	-	14/161
Professional SW	Y	varies/MARC	-	9/140	13/153
RCM	N	17/925	-	3/69	9/186
SuperCAT	Y	varies/MARC	-	-	-
Sydney	N	17/62,687	5/124	6/29	12/526
TLS	N	5/224	-	8/30	13/156
Winnebago	N	14/228	-	-	10/140

Table 2 (*continued*)

Summary of the data elements in each of the systems tested.

| | Serials Data | | | | Acquisitions Data | | |
	Biblio. Record	Vendor Record	Bindery Record	Receipt Record	Order Record	Vendor Record	Accounts Record
ALS	-	-	-	-	-	-	-
Assistant	20-287	17-462	-	6-85	16-306	11-272	-
BiblioFile	-	-	-	-	-	-	-
Card Datalog	30-626	11-204	41-997	-	25-439	-	-
Catalog Plus	-	-	-	-	-	-	-
Columbia	-	-	-	-	-	-	-
Eloquent	-	-	-	-	-	-	-
K-12	-	-	-	-	-	-	-
LexiFILE	-	-	-	-	-	-	-
LIBerator	-	-	-	-	-	-	-
MacBook	-	-	-	-	-	-	-
Mac School	-	-	-	-	-	-	-
MELVIL	-	-	-	-	-	-	-
MicroCAT	-	-	-	-	-	-	-
MLS	-	-	-	-	10-88	8-varies	8-varies
MOLLI	-	-	-	-	-	-	-
Nonesuch	-	-	-	-	*	*	*
PCemas	21-343	11-180	-	-	5-63	11-180	5-79
Professional SW	-	-	-	-	-	-	-
RCM	-	-	-	-	-	-	-
SuperCAT	*	*	*	*	*	*	*
Sydney	-	-	*	-	-	-	-
TLS	-	-	-	-	-	-	-
Winnebago	-	-	-	-	-	-	-

* = Data stored unknown

Table 3.

Summary of the online access points in each of the systems tested.

Bibliographic Record

	Author	Title	Subject	Call No.	Publisher	Year	Series	Location
ALS	Y	Y	-	-	-	-	-	-
Assistant	Y	Y	Y	Y	Y	Y	Y	Y
BiblioFile	Y	Y	Y	Y	-	-	-	Y
Card Datalog	Y	Y	Y	Y	-	-	Y	-
Catalog Plus	Y	Y	Y	Y	-	-	Y	-
Columbia	Y	Y	Y	Y	-	-	-	-
Eloquent	Y	Y	Y	Y	-	-	-	-
K-12	-	-	-	-	-	-	-	-
LexiFILE	Y	Y	Y	Y	-	-	Y	-
LIBerator	Y	Y	Y	Y	-	-	Y	-
MacBook	Y	Y	Y	Y	-	-	-	-
Mac School	Y	Y	Y	Y	Y	Y	-	-
MELVIL	Y	Y	Y	Y	-	-	-	-
MicroCAT	Y	Y	Y	Y	-	-	-	-
MLS	Y	Y	Y	Y	-	-	Y	Y
MOLLI	Y	Y	Y	Y	-	-	-	Y
Nonesuch	Y	Y	-	-	-	-	-	-
PCemas	Y	Y	Y	Y	-	-	-	-
Professional SW	Y	Y	Y	Y	-	-	-	-
RCM	Y	Y	-	-	Y	-	-	Y
SuperCAT	Y	Y	-	Y	-	-	-	Y
Sydney	Y	Y	Y	Y	-	-	Y	Y
TLS	Y	Y	Y	Y	-	-	-	-
Winnebago	Y	Y	-	Y	-	-	-	-

Table 3 (*continued*)

Summary of the online access points in each of the systems tested.

Bibliographic Record

	Mater. Type	Doc. Type	LCCN	ISBN ISSN	Record Seq #	Note (Full Text)	Author Keyword	Title Keyword	Subject Keyword	Other Keyword
ALS	-	-	-	-	-	-	-	-	-	-
Assistant	Y	-	-	Y	-	-	Y	Y	Y	-
BiblioFile	-	-	Y	Y	-	-	Y	Y	Y	-
Card Datalog	-	-	-	Y	-	-	-	-	-	-
Catalog Plus	-	-	Y	Y	Y	Y	Y	Y	Y	Y
Columbia	-	-	Y	Y	-	Y	Y	Y	Y	Y
Eloquent	-	-	Y	Y	Y	Y	Y	Y	Y	Y
K-12	-	-	-	-	Y	-	-	Y	Y	-
LexiFILE	-	-	Y	Y	-	-	-	Y	Y	-
LIBerator	-	-	Y	Y	Y	-	Y	Y	Y	Y
MacBook	Y	Y	-	-	-	-	Y	Y	Y	-
Mac School	-	Y	-	-	-	-	-	Y	Y	Y
MELVIL	-	-	-	-	-	-	-	-	-	-
MicroCAT	-	-	Y	Y	Y	Y	Y	Y	Y	Y
MLS	Y	Y	Y	Y	Y	Y	Y	Y	Y	-
MOLLI	Y	-	-	-	Y	-	-	-	-	-
Nonesuch	-	-	-	Y	-	-	-	Y	Y	-
PCemas	-	-	-	-	-	-	Y	Y	Y	-
Professional SW	-	-	-	-	-	-	Y	Y	-	Y
RCM	-	-	-	Y	Y	Y	Y	Y	Y	-
SuperCAT	-	Y	Y	Y	Y	Y	Y	Y	Y	-
Sydney	Y	Y	Y	Y	Y	Y	Y	Y	Y	Y
TLS	-	-	-	-	-	-	-	-	-	-
Winnebago	-	-	-	-	-	-	-	-	-	-

(Table 3 continues on page 82.)

Table 3 (*continued*)

Summary of the online access points in each of the systems tested.

	Authority Record					Item Record	Patron Record				
	Author	Corp. Author	Con-ference	Series	Subject	ID #	Patron ID #	Patron Alt ID #	Patron Name	Patron Alt Name	Patron Type
ALS	Y	–	–	–	–	Y	Y	–	Y	–	–
Assistant	Y	Y	–	Y	Y	Y	Y	–	Y	–	Y
BiblioFile	–	–	–	–	–	Y	Y	–	Y	–	–
Card Datalog	–	–	–	–	–	Y	Y	–	Y	–	–
Catalog Plus	Y	–	–	–	–	Y	Y	–	Y	–	–
Columbia	Y	–	–	–	Y	Y	Y	–	Y	–	–
Eloquent	Y	Y	Y	Y	Y	Y	Y	–	Y	–	–
K-12	–	–	–	–	–	–	Y	–	–	–	–
LexiFILE	–	–	–	–	–	–	–	–	–	–	–
LIBerator	–	–	–	–	–	Y	Y	–	Y	–	–
MacBook	–	–	–	–	–	Y	Y	–	Y	–	–
Mac School	–	–	–	–	–	–	Y	–	Y	–	–
MELVIL	–	–	–	–	–	Y	Y	–	Y	–	–
MicroCAT	–	–	–	–	–	Y	Y	–	Y	–	–
MLS	–	–	–	–	–	Y	Y	–	Y	–	Y
MOLLI	–	–	–	–	–	Y	Y	–	Y	–	–
Nonesuch	–	–	–	–	–	Y	Y	–	Y	–	–
PCemas	Y	Y	–	Y	Y	Y	Y	–	Y	–	Y
Professional SW	–	–	–	–	–	Y	Y	–	Y	–	–
RCM	–	–	–	–	–	Y	–	–	Y	–	–
SuperCAT	Y	–	–	–	–	–	–	–	–	–	–
Sydney	Y	Y	Y	Y	Y	Y	Y	–	Y	–	–
TLS	–	–	–	–	–	Y	Y	–	Y	–	–
Winnebago	–	–	–	–	–	Y	Y	–	Y	–	–

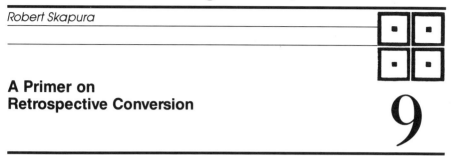

Robert Skapura

A Primer on
Retrospective Conversion

9

The task of converting a paper shelf list to a form that a computer can read is like putting bar codes on all your library books: it's so awful, you don't ever want to have to do it again for the same collection. To ensure that the first time you do it is also the last, it's important that the information on your shelf list is put into a standard format. Since the 1960s that standard format has been MARC records. The term "MARC" stands for the phrase "Machine-Readable Cataloging records." The Library of Congress originally devised this standard format in order to share its cataloging information with libraries using large mainframe computers. It's not necessary that you understand the technical aspects of MARC records (tags, subfield codes, headers). It's enough that you understand conceptually the importance of the MARC standard. A good analogy comes from the field of word processing. Every word processing program writes out a document on a floppy disk in a slightly different way. This means that the person using AppleWorks cannot just give a disk to a person using Word Perfect and expect that person to use it in his machine. In fact, the six authors for this issue used six different word processing programs. If everyone is using the same word processing program, however, everyone can share information with everyone else easily and directly.

It certainly is possible to develop a homegrown computerized card catalog and to type in the bibliographic information in the same way that you type words into a word processor or information into a database. This is not to say that a homegrown system will not work well. It will, however, be an *isolated system* if it cannot read in and write out MARC records.

Putting your records in MARC format opens the door for cooperative ventures with other school or public libraries. Many schools are currently looking at CD-ROM-based catalogs

Source: Reprinted with permission from *California Media and Library Educators Association Journal* 13, no. 1 (Fall 1989): 6-8.

because they're so rugged. A CD-ROM disk can hold hundreds of thousands of titles, but the cost of pressing a single master CD-ROM is between $1,000 and $2,000. After the master is pressed the copies are quite inexpensive, but few school libraries could afford to press a master each year. Twenty school libraries, however, could easily put their collections on a single CD-ROM and share the cost of the master. The software can be told to "mask" all the schools but yours, so students searching the system will see only the books from *your* library, even though there would be twenty collections on the same CD-ROM disk.

Shared ventures like this are only one reason to adhere to the MARC standard. Book vendors can also deliver MARC records on a disk with any new book order so that the information can be automatically added to your computerized card catalog. That means no more filing of catalog cards.

Adhering to a standard is also insurance for the future. If you ever outgrow your system or your vendor goes out of business, you will be able to easily load your MARC records into any other system.

Even though there is only one standard (MARC) for retrospective conversion, there are a number of ways of getting there. It's like traveling from point A to point B. You can walk, you can ride, or you can fly. Or you can travel one way for part of the journey and another for the rest. There are basically three methods of converting your paper shelf list to MARC records:

1. You do *all* the work.

2. You do *some* of the work.

3. You do *none* of the work.

MARC records can be put on either floppy disks or nine-track tapes. The nine-track tapes are used by large mainframe computers to read data very quickly. Only large companies can produce and read them. MARC records created on a microcomputer will be saved on floppy disks. It doesn't really matter on what media the records are stored. Most companies can transfer from one to the other, although there might be a small charge to go between the two.

Most libraries select the computerized card catalog before beginning the retro project. Many companies that sell computerized card catalogs also sell retrospective conversion services or products, but these two things can be viewed separately. It is quite safe to use one company or product for the conversion and another for the actual catalog.

Needless to say, it's least expensive if you do all the work on site, but that takes staff and time. It's most expensive if the vendor does the entire conversion off site. A conversion project like this, though, is a one-time expense, and frequently it's easier to find funds for a special project instead of hiring extra staff.

You Do All the Work

There are a number of products that make on-site retrospective conversion possible. One such product is Mitinet/MARC, a software package that runs on IBM, Apple, and Mac computers. It presents the user with screen prompts (Title, Author, Call Number, etc.) instead of arcane MARC tags. After you fill in the screen, the program writes out the data on floppy disks in MARC format. Many librarians may reject this method out-of-hand because of the amount of data that must be typed in. But no matter what *other* method you choose, there are always a number of titles that vendors can't find. So this product can be used in conjunction with others to complete a conversion.

A second way to accomplish in-house conversion is to *match* your shelf list against a large MARC database. Currently the most popular method is to use a CD-ROM-based product (Bibliofile or Laser Quest, for example) that uses an IBM PC (or clone) and a Hitachi CD-ROM player. The typical CD-ROM database contains between 3 and 6 million bibliographic records. Some contain only the original MARC records; others contain both original MARC and contributed records. The match is done by typing in a number (ISBN or LCCN) or a combination of author and title so that the computer can display the book that is on your shelf list. After you verify that the two match, you can then add your local information (call number, price, bar code number, etc.) and then write the record to a floppy disk. You can save about 200 MARC records on each floppy disk. With this method, if the CD-ROM database finds your shelf-list title, the amount of typing is relatively small.

You Do Some of the Work

With this method the MARC records are actually created by the vendor off site. You must, however, tell the vendor what books you have. This is usually done by typing in the LCCN or ISBN numbers on a special disk called a "batch disk." You must also type in your local information (call number, price, etc.). This is fairly fast, but since you just type in a string of numbers (ISBN or LCCN), there's no way to tell if you've made a typo until the mismatch comes back from the vendor. Finding the errors and correcting them can be time-consuming.

If you already have a circulation system installed, there's another way for you to do just "some of the work." It's possible to expand the brief circulation record into a full MARC record. For example, those libraries using Winnebago or Follett circulation systems can employ this method. The circulation record must, however, contain the LCCN or ISBN. Once that's done, the backup disks to the circulation system can be sent off to the circulation vendor, and MARC records will be returned on either floppy disks or nine-track tapes.

You Do None of the Work

If you can overcome the naked feeling of being without your shelf list for a while, the easiest method is full-vendor conversion off site. The vendor takes your shelf list and returns it to you in six to eight weeks along with MARC records on either floppy disks or nine-track tapes. Most vendors require a sample of your shelf list before they will quote you a price, because the amount of work they must do depends on how good (consistent) a shelf list your library has maintained. Some vendors have done whole states. Of course, the unit price goes down as the number of libraries in the contract goes up, so it's always best to be part of a large group in a conversion project.

There is no one method that is necessarily superior to another. Everything depends on the size of your collection and the size of your staff and budget. The end product of any of these methods will, however, ensure the possibility of shared resources, compatibility with future developments, and a guarantee that you'll never have to do it again.

Catherine Murphy

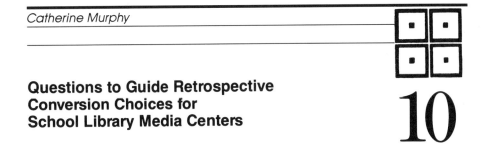

Questions to Guide Retrospective Conversion Choices for School Library Media Centers

10

As a library staff begins to plan for retrospective conversion, the number and complexity of decisions to be made may seem overwhelming. The questions in the first section are meant to help those beginning the process to evaluate their own catalog needs. The questions in the second section are to be asked of the vendors under consideration. The tables included with the article provide comparative data about various vendors and methods of retrospective conversion (see tables 1 through 3).

Questions to Ask Yourself about Your Library

1. *What is the size of your budget and staff?* The library with a large budget will most likely contract with a vendor for full service conversion. In that case, specifications are determined, and the shelf list is revised, edited, and mailed to the vendor.

   If the budget cannot accommodate full service, then partial in-house data entry is a good compromise. Search keys (usually the ISBN or LCCN) as well as local call number and copy information are entered on a data disk. Those records are then sent to the vendor who matches them against the vendor's database of records in MARC (machine readable cataloging) format.

   The third option of in-house full conversion, using compact disks to retrieve MARC records for the entire collection, is the least costly but the most labor-intensive method. If additional staff is not hired for the conversion, other library tasks may not get done.

Source: Reprinted by permission of the ALA from *School Library Media Quarterly* (Winter 1990): 79-81.

2. *What quality catalog records do you want to obtain?* The minimum quality that should be accepted is a full MARC record. Some databases include contributors' enhancements of those records such as additional notes and/or subject headings. One of the vendors provides grade and reading levels in some records. The vendor must be able to provide the school library with at least the standard MARC record.

3. *How large is your collection?* The vendor may base the price per catalog record on the number of records to be converted. The larger the collection, the better the price per item that can be negotiated. School libraries that are members of consortiums or are in very large districts have a price advantage when dealing with these vendors.

4. *What special features does your collection have?* School libraries want MARC records for audiovisual materials as well as for many curriculum-related books (even textbooks). They may also want Sears subject headings and/or Dewey classification numbers. A vendor that can provide these special records and features is desirable.

Questions to Ask Vendors about Their Conversion Process

1. *What is your fee structure?* Fees vary from a low price for a circulation record (MARC format but some fields are left blank) to a higher price for a full catalog record. Any special requirement in editing the records of a shelf list that is not in good condition will increase the cost.

2. *How many school retrospective conversions have you done?* The school library is looking for a vendor that has experience in school library conversions. These vendors understand that school library collections differ from those of other libraries and realize that the staff and budget may be small. In addition, vendors with school experience may have catalog records contributed by customers.

3. *How many catalog records are in your database or databases?* There will be a higher hit rate if the vendor has done school library conversions and runs your shelf list against this database as well as others.

4. *How many audiovisual records are in your database?* School collections have many audiovisual materials. Catalog records for these materials have not been readily available in the LC database. Other sources, such as contributors' records, may include them.

5. *What enhancements are available in the database records?* The databases of contributors' records offer more than the pure LC MARC record, although the enhancements may not always be acceptable. Sears subject headings, Dewey call numbers, grade and reading levels, analytics, and notes may all be considered enhancements.

6. *How are records matched?* Some vendors do only machine matching; some use operators to evaluate records and increase the number of hits. Matching by ISBN/LCCN is the most common process, but a vendor may also search by title, author, or a combination of approaches. Libraries sometimes accept "fuzzy" matches, a catalog record that is not identical but is close enough. Later, the entry may be edited.

7. *What is your school conversion hit rate?* The hit rate is the number of exact matches that a vendor is able to make between the school collection and the vendor database of catalog records. The hit rate should be available as an average from the conversions that the vendor has done.

8. *What do you do with nonhits?* You will want to know how the vendor handles nonhits. Some may create a record in MARC format. Possibly there will be an additional charge for this service, and these records may contain only the data on the shelf-list card. Other vendors do not provide for nonhits. You should also know what written reports of matching will be provided.

9. *What is the error rate of the conversion?* Errors may occur at the library or vendor site because of mistakes made in entering data. The vendor may have information about the error rates in different methods of conversion.

10. *Do you provide authority control?* If the retrospective vendor does not edit records for conformity in at least author and subject names, then authority control will have to be developed within the automated system.

Vendor Addresses

Brodart Automation, 500 Arch Street, Williamsport, PA 17705.

Catalog Card Corporation, 4401 N. 76th St., Edina, MN 55435.

Dynix, Inc. 151 E. 1700 South, Provo, UT 84601.

Follett Library Software, 809 N. Front St., McHenry, IL 60050-5589.

General Research Corporation, 5383 Hollister Avenue, Santa Barbara, CA 93111-9929.

Information Transform, 502 Leonard Street, Madison, WI 53711.

Library Corporation, One Research Park, Inwood, WV 25428.

Marcive, Inc., P.O. Box 47508, San Antonio, TX 78265.

RetroLink Associates, Inc., 175 N. Freedom Blvd., Provo, UT 84601.

UTLAS International, 80 Bloor St. West, Toronto, Ontario, Canada M5S 2V1.

Winnebago Software, P.O. Box 430, Caledonia, MN 55921.

WLN, 4224 6th Ave., SE, Bldg. 3, Lacey, WA 98503-0888.

Retrospective Conversion Options for School Library Media Centers

Table 1.
Full vendor contract. (You do none of the work.)

Vendor	Cost Estimate	Database Records Searched
Auto-Graphics	15 cents per record from existing non-MARC machine readable record, 50 cents from shelf list, up to $1.00+ for keying nonmatched records and additional copy	12 million LC, preMARC, and user files
Brodart Automation	50-90 cents per record depending on level of editing or condition of shelf list	9-10 million LC, GPO, CONSER, and selected customers' files
Catalog Card Company	46 cents per record; 3 cents per bar code	3 million LC, Dewey/Sears 450,000
Dynix, Inc.	50 cents per record for 100% of entries; includes keying in from shelf list of all no hits	11 million LC, LSSI, original entry in-house
Follett Library Software	44 cents for hits in match of shelf list; for misses, 30 cents for brief record, 75 cents for full record.	400,000+ LC selected for smaller libraries including 28,000 AV; 25% enhanced with *Sears SH*, reading levels, and review sources.
Library Corp.	10 cents per record for hits, 50 cents for creating a record	7+ million LC; Sears, Nat. Lib. of Canada, AV Access, GPO, and contributed records
Marcive, Inc.	45 cents per hit record, title, and numeric search	4.6 million LC, GPO, Nat. Lib. of Canada, NLM, nonauthoritative school contributed records
Retro Link Associates	50-90 cents per record	10 million LC, LSSI, in-house
Winnebago	39 cents per record includes preprinted bar code label and Mylar™ protector	2-3 million LC
WLN	50+ cents per record depending on level of editing, adding holdings to the databases	7 million, nonduplicate records, including LC, GPO, Nat. Lib. of Canada, NLM, and members' contributed records

Table 2.
In-house partial data entry. (You do some of the work).

Vendor	Software	Hardware	Cost Estimate	Database Records Searched
Brodart Automation	Micro-Check	IBM, Apple	10 cents per record plus $15 per month or $1,650 flat fee	2.5-3 million LC
Marcive	Cataloging Input System	IBM	45 cents per hit record, title, and numeric search; 90 cents to key nonhits	4.6 million LC, GPO, Nat. Lib. of Canada, and NLM
UTLAS International	M100	IBM	20 cents per LC record; 40 cents per contributor record; 21-50 cents per record	60 million LC, GPO, Nat. Lib. of Canada, NLM, and members' contributed records
UTLAS International	DISCON (Compact disk)	IBM, CD Player	$1,000 monthly rental; $850 if used more than a year and 25 cents per record	6 million LC, REMARC brief records
WLN	Micro Recon	IBM, Apple	$75 for software plus 15 cents per hit or 5 cents per miss	7 million nonduplicate records, including LC, GPO, NLM, Nat. Lib. of Canada, and members' contributed records

Table 3.
In-house full data entry. (You do all the work.)

Vendor	Software	Hardware	Cost Estimate	Database Records Searched
Brodart Automation	PRECISION ONE	IBM, CD Player	PRECISION ONE – retrospective disk, $300; PRECISION ONE – current, $450; subscriber monthly updates	1 + million records that comprise 95% of titles most frequently held by school and public libraries
Follett Software	ALLIANCE PLUS	IBM, CD Player	Initial cost $950, annual subscription renewal $450 includes quarterly CD updates	400,000 LC on CD disk; selected for smaller libraries; includes 28,000 AV; 25% enhanced records
General Research	LASER QUEST	IBM, CD Player	$2,200 license for first year; $500 subsequent years; $2,100 annual subscription fee	6 million LC and members' contributed records
Information Transform	MITINET/ MARC	IBM, Apple II Mac	IBM, Apple II: $399 Version 2. Mac: $399 Version 1. Both include 6 months free support and upgrades followed by $150 annual cost	Interfaces with more than 50 automated circulation and catalog systems. Creates MARC records from data in shelf list or material, requiring no previous user knowledge of MARC
Library Corp.	BIBLIOFILE	IBM, CD Player	LC $2,250 first year, $1,090 subsequent years for quarterly updates; Sears/Dewey $850 per year	3 million LC, LC foreign, Nat. Lib. of Canada, AV Access, GPO, and other contributed records

Table 3 (*continued*)

Vendor	Software	Hardware	Cost Estimate	Database Records Searched
WLN	LASER CAT	IBM, CD Player	$975 school subscription; no membership required	3.2 million LC plus contributors' records; includes Dewey, AV holdings

Comparison prepared by Catherine Murphy (Prices confirmed as of October 1991)

Key to abbreviations: CONSER = Conversion of Serials (an LC database); GPO = Government Printing Office; LC = Library of Congress (covering 1968 - present); Nat. Lib. of Canada = National Library of Canada; NLM = National Library of Medicine; REMARC = MARC record for pre-1968 (an LC database covering 1898-1968).

Catherine Murphy

The MARC Record in the
School Library Media Center

11

This essay explores the nature of the MARC record (that is, a record following the Library of Congress Machine Readable Cataloging standard) in microcomputer online circulation and catalog systems in school library media centers.

I developed one of the early microcomputer online public access catalogs (OPACs) in a junior high school in 1982 and implemented a second one in an elementary school the following year. I began to realize the potential of computer systems to enrich the catalog record, but at the same time they had limitations affecting bibliographic standards. Jane Hannigan encouraged me to investigate these developments as a doctoral research project; I followed her advice, and have been very glad that I did so, because I completed my doctoral dissertation on this subject, with Jane as my advisor, at Columbia University's School of Library Service in 1987.[1] This essay continues my role as observer in the field.

Getting Started: The Research

In 1985, I decided to study the bibliographic attitudes and practices of the school library media specialists who were in various stages of developing sixteen different microcomputer circulation and catalog systems. COMPUTER CAT was the first turnkey microcomputer OPAC, developed in 1981 by the Costas for an Apple II Plus in an elementary school in Mountain View, Colorado.[2] Some of the systems that followed were similar in their inability to employ the standard Machine Readable cataloging (MARC) format.

Source: Reprinted by permission from S. Intner and K. Vandergrift. *Library Education and Leadership Essays in Honor of Jane Anne Hannigan*, (Metuchen, NJ: Scarecrow Press, 1990).

The majority of the respondents to my survey did not seem to understand mainstream library standards and they were not conforming to them. This finding was not surprising and confirmed, with similar conclusions, earlier research by Rogers and Truett in card catalog practices.[3] The exceptions were a small number of school library media specialists using OPACs that were more MARC compatible than the majority of systems named in the study; these survey participants apparently were influenced by the system itself to adhere to the *Anglo-American Cataloguing Rules*, second edition (*AACR2*), which the MARC format was designed to incorporate.

Interestingly, I also found that a significant number of respondents to my survey were creating special subject headings for curriculum and reading materials, possibly in an effort to enhance the online catalog records to meet the needs of their school users. The Follett Library Software Company replicated my survey, with similar results for enhancements but finding more favorable attitudes toward the MARC standard. Their survey was distributed at a later date and the timing, as well as Follett's efforts to create awareness of bibliographic standards, may account for the difference in attitude toward the MARC standard.

The Follow-up: Contemporary Issues

In 1989, there were probably more than ten thousand microcomputer circulation and/or catalog systems in school library media centers in the United States and Canada. Some of the early experimental software programs have disappeared, and now the microcomputer OPACs conform almost universally to MARC (as much as larger minicomputer-based systems do). Awareness of school library media specialists about mainstream library standards is much greater than it was in the early days of automation. It is likely that everyone in school library media centers knows that there is a MARC record, and that conformity ensures the sharing of records between systems. There is a lack of widespread understanding, however, that the content of the MARC record may differ (in the sense that there is more or less information in the fields), depending on the retrospective conversion source and/or the system into which it is loaded. The following questions raise issues about the content of MARC records.

What is a full MARC record? MARC is defined by Walt Crawford in *MARC for Library Use* as "a set of standards for identifying, storing and communicating cataloging information ... a standard way to communicate bibliographic information between users and between computers."[4] If the school library media specialist fully understands that MARC is a structure as well as a communications format, but not a guarantee of cataloging content, then a more intelligent choice between retrospective conversion options can be made.

Crawford notes that a MARC record for a book may be as little as 250 characters or more than 2,000, although the average number of characters is less than 1,000.[5] The answer to the question as stated above, is that the record is guaranteed "full" only in the sense that the STRUCTURE is there (this issue will be further explored in the next question). Consider the possible differences in data in the fields of bibliographic records acquired in the following ways:

1. USMARC records are distributed by the Library of Congress, either on magnetic tape or from a Compact Disk-Read Only Memory (CD-ROM) database. These records will not include any local enhancements. Some records are released with only Cataloging-in-Publication (CIP) data, a skeletal record containing basic information gleaned from prepublication sources such as galleys or page proofs.

2. MARC records are available from bibliographic utilities, such as Online Computer Library Center (OCLC), Western Library Network (WLN), or Utlas, either online or on CD-ROM disks. The records will contain information contributed by members of the networks, which may include more data, such as additional headings or less data, depending on the contributors' policies and circumstances.

3. MARC records may be secured from a vendor who offers conversion services, e.g., BroDart, the Catalog Card Company, etc. The library may ship off its entire shelf list or may enter a key identifier for each record on a series of floppy disks sent to the vendor. In any case, the bibliographic records generally vary because in-house databases have different enhancements or omissions.

4. The MARC record may be created in house entirely from the information on the shelf-list card or in the material itself.

Is a MicroLIF Record the same as a MARC record? The microcomputer systems vendors and the book vendors developed Microcomputer Library Information Files (MicroLIF) cooperatively to ensure compatibility between their systems. In addition to the cataloging structure, the MicroLIF format provides for circulation data. This format has been advertised as a full MARC record, but not only can the individual record vary as described in the first question, but the directory, an essential part of a MARC record, is deleted in every MicroLIF record. The directory follows the leader in the MARC format, and identifies each field by tag, length, and starting position relative to the beginning.

The microcomputer systems vendors have argued that the directory is not read by the computer program in a microcomputer in the same way that it is read by a mainframe computer system, and it is, therefore, not necessary. The rebuttal from the mainframe automated systems representatives is that the directory is an essential component of the MARC communications format. Without it, the bibliographic record cannot be considered a full MARC record.

As a school representative, I was requested by OPAC vendors to participate in MicroLIF Committee meetings at the American Library Association conference in January 1989. At that time, both groups of vendors came together and it appeared that the MicroLIF format would undergo some changes to allow the directory to be recreated if records are exported to another system. School library media specialists interested in purchasing an automated system and, possibly, using it on different computers in the future would be wise to request that prospective vendors demonstrate the program to recreate the MARC communications format. For additional insurance, it is a recommended practice for all libraries to maintain an archival copy of their databases outside of the automated system. These backup databases protect their records from unauthorized editing or destruction due to system malfunctions, fires, etc.

Regarding the term MARC compatible, Crawford makes the point that precise compatibility, or what he calls strict identity as exemplified by USMARC records distributed by the Library of Congress, is too limiting for most libraries because it excludes local information. Crawford prefers a MARC compatible system (which, he says, describes most systems as one that "should be able to process USMARC records directly ... as needed, writing or restoring them, without loss of content, content designation, or structure."[6]

Is there anything wrong with developing brief MARC-compatible records for a circulation system, and later upgrading the records to full MARC for an OPAC? It depends. Although the current trend is to develop a database with full bibliographic records to support an integrated system, it is sometimes a question of economics or a desire to go slowly in implementing automation which suggests beginning with a circulation system. This is particularly true for school libraries, which frequently have smaller budgets and fewer staff members than other types of libraries. Many schools have begun automating by purchasing the hardware and software for a stand-alone circulation terminal. They have handled retrospective conversion by entering data at the keyboard as well as bar coding books as they circulate in a process described as "on the run." One software company reports that 60 percent of their users have implemented circulation in this way, as opposed to 20 percent who have converted all records before start-up and another 20 percent who have contracted with the vendor to handle the conversion.[7] The data entry is minimal at the circulation level; only an identifying title, author, and local call number will be keyed in. The record must be converted to full MARC by searching for a match in a bibliographic database, which may be done at an in-house CD station or a vendor's site. Implementing the system in stages has the added advantages of allowing the staff more time to become comfortable with automation, to clean up the shelf list and catalog records as they go, and to feel they are in control of the time it takes to develop records (although it may take longer in actual weeks or months for the conversion to be completed).

What are the negatives of this approach? Having in-house staff type in data "on the run" may result in more errors in bibliographic record conversion. If the library sends the shelf list to a company specializing in retrospective conversion they might expect the process to produce a more complete and accurate database. Some school library media specialists would contest this statement, however; records in vendors' bibliographic databases also contain cataloging errors, and some records may not be available. Retrospective conversion typically involves using records from more than one source. It is also more time consuming to have in-house staff do the conversion, along with other duties, and may cost more in the long run. If funds are available, either locally or otherwise, a vendor conversion to full MARC is preferable.

If a school is located in a state that has encouraged participation in a network or statewide system, there is more incentive to develop an integrated system as a first step. Usually there is financial support from the state education department for the conversion process and development support from the local educational agency.

Is there more than the MARC standard, or what enhancements to the catalog record are available (or might be made available), in microcomputer OPACs that meet the needs of school library users? Unless the online catalog revolutionizes subject access, it does little but replicate the card catalog. The amount of time, money, and energy that must be expended to convert the catalog demands not only adherence to standards, but movement beyond the standards to a state of enhancement.

Mandel noted that enrichment of the catalog record could take place either within the MARC format or by providing online thesauri or indexes that link to the record.[8] She favored the latter because it is more expensive to enhance the MARC record itself. Other observers in the field have noted that the number of subject headings in the MARC record may be inadequate, and the assignment of headings may be inappropriate. The implementation of improved design features within the automated system already is taking place. The following list describes some enhancements.

1. Keyword searching is now fairly universal in microcomputer systems. Not all of the systems, however, have keyword searching of every field in the record. If keyword access to every field were available, as well as right hand truncation, that is, the ability to search on word roots, these features would compensate for the difficulty users have in choosing appropriate subject heading terms.

2. The Intelligent Catalog microcomputer system developed by Library Corporation pioneered some innovative design features. Besides location maps and voice tutors, the prototype OPAC displays the first pages of fiction books. Displays of tables of contents and indexes also are mentioned as desirable enhancements to assist searchers in selecting the right book.

3. Some book vendors have additional information in the catalog records in their databases, such as grade levels and reading levels. Reading level was noted by respondents to my survey as the most desired information to be added to the notes field as well as in the Follett study mentioned earlier.[9] Both retrospective and current records (purchased with book orders) may be acquired from these vendors.

4. Quite a few years ago, Wehmeyer noted the need in card catalog records for more information about the material's relation to the curricula.[10] She suggested that library subject hedings were not adequate to indicate this relation, and that the terms already in use in educational computer systems could be linked to the catalog record. The current stage of development of microcomputer OPACs seems ripe to create such online thesauri, perhaps with linkages already established in a large district or state (such as California) where extensive and uniform curriculum development is in place; these thesauri might then be adapted by other users.

Conclusion

There is no doubt in my mind that all of these questions and issues offer the school library media specialist the opportunity to exercise leadership in the decision process of implementing automated systems. The management decisions that are made will affect our access to collections, our participation in networks, and above all, our service to the primary clientele, young people.

Notes

[1]Murphy, Catherine. (1987). *The Microcomputer Online Public Access Catalog: Practices and Attitudes of School Library Media Specialists Toward Standardization.* D.L.S. diss., Columbia University, New York.

[2]Costa, Betty, and Marie Costa. (May 1981). "Microcomputer in Colorado — It's Elementary," *Wilson Library Bulletin.* 58: 676-78 + .

[3]Rogers, JoAnn V. (January 1979). "NonPrint Cataloging: A Call for Standardization," *American Libraries.* 10: 46-48; Truett, Carol. (Fall 1983). "AACR Who? The Case for Using the New *Anglo-American Cataloguing Rules* in the School Library Media Center," *School Library Media Quarterly.* 11:38-43.

[4]Crawford, Walt. (1989). *MARC for Library Use.* 2nd ed. Boston, MA: G. K. Hall, 3.

[5]Ibid.

[6]Crawford, 264-65.

[7]Follett Library Software Co. (1989). Author's notes for a presentation at the School Library Media Section, New York Library Conference, 1 May, Lake George, New York.

[8]Mandel, Carol A. (January/March 1985). "Enriching the Library Catalog Record for Subject Access," *Library Resources & Technical Services.* 29: 5-15.

[9]Murphy, Catherine. (1987). *The Microcomputer Online Public Access Catalog.*

[10]Wehmeyer, Lillian. (Fall 1976). "Cataloging the School Media Center as a Specialized Collection," *Library Resources & Technical Services.* 20: 315-25.

Media Center Automation:
The Way to Go!

12

Today, library media specialists and coordinators must process greater amounts of data more quickly and more accurately than ever before. As a result, media center automation is being implemented in school districts across the country. When media coordinators in our state requested guidance in converting to automation, the North Carolina Media and Technology's Division of Computer Services developed a pilot program for online circulation.

After a number of media coordinators contacted us for information regarding online circulation systems, a specially created Advisory Task Force met to address the feasibility of automation. The consensus was to establish two pilot sites for demonstrating online circulation procedures, experimenting with various approaches, and keeping records and statistics for evaluation. Further, each site's administration agreed to purchase some hardware and/or software, or to be available for presentations and visitors, and to monitor these sites with an eye toward sharing our findings.

The project's theme: "The way to go." Our goal was twofold: to determine the hardware and software components for an automated circulation system that utilized student data from SIMS (Student Information Management System), our statewide automated attendance program, and to draw up a staff development model for implementing and evaluating an automated circulation system.

This article details the planning process and results of the two-year project, including the benefits of an automated circulation program: the reasonable start-up costs, the saving of administrative time, the limited data entry information required, and the capability of handling a large volume of circulation data. This program appears to be equally effective at both

Source: Reprinted from *School Library Journal*, August 1988, pp. 41-44. Copyright © by Reed Publishing, USA. Training Services, Follett Software, Co.

elementary and secondary levels. Suggestions based on our experience are also provided.

Equipment

The two schools that volunteered and continue to act as demonstration sites are the Frank Porter Graham Elementary School and the McDowell County Senior High School. The elementary school serves approximately 480 students in levels K-6 from an open media center with a collection of 12,000 books, plus audiovisual materials and equipment. Its weekly circulation is 600 to 700 items, borrowed by faculty and students. The high school has a two-story, open media center with multiple access points and an electric security system. It serves 1,460 students and 90 faculty members and contains approximately 12,000 resources.

To study the best hardware components, each site used different configurations. The elementary school used an Apple IIe with two floppy disk drives, a Profile hard disk of five megabytes, a monochrome monitor, and a light pen. At McDowell Senior High we used an IBM PC AT with 20 megabytes of hard disk storage, an Okidata 84 printer with a tractor-feed attachment, and a light pen. A battery-powered backup (a Tripp Lite emergency power supply costing $533.64) and an additional light pen were also purchased.

For software selection, we developed a comparison chart of the various circulation programs available at that time which vendors used for reviewing their programs. Program criteria included: (1) availability for both Apple and IBM machines; (2) a user-friendly program with good documentation; (3) support by an in-state vendor's representative; (4) a toll-free number for technical support and other vendor services; and (5) a cost of less than $1,000. Based on its response to the charts and our criteria, we selected Follett Library Software Company's Circulation Plus program.

Start-up costs (in 1985 dollars) ranged from $5,000 to $10,000. The maximum configuration was: hardware $5,541, software $695, and data entry services and item bar codes $2,250. Costs for supplies such as labels, cards, and Rolodex™ files were $984 for the high school: four Rolodex files $196; plastic Rolodex card covers $140; high-density diskettes $100; 2,000 continuous feed Rolodex cards $42; 1,600 patron bar code labels $56; and 13,500 label protectors $450. Supplies for the elementary school amounted to $1,260.

Implementation

As a preliminary step, the media coordinators verified their shelf lists against their collections. This allowed them to decide if the item should be weeded prior to the new system, check information accuracy, and add Library of Congress (LC) or ISBN numbers to the shelf list for data entry.

Once again, different approaches were tried at the two sites. The elementary location trained and used parent and student volunteers for the bulk of their data entry. Over a three-month period, fifth and sixth graders, working in teams in the computer lab adjacent to the media center, entered much of the book collection data from the shelf list. The media center staff and parent volunteers entered the remaining data. On the first 3000 entries, the margin of error was about 2 percent.

Other media coordinators in the district also helped with data entry as a way to learn about the new system.

While this was going on, the verified shelf list cards at the high school were boxed and sent to the vendor for data entry. At the end of the six-week time period, the batch disks for loading the circulation data and the shelf list cards were returned. In one and one-half days, the data was electronically transferred and the system was ready to run.

The bar coding of the book collection proved to be the more complex task. Attaching the coded label and its protector meant handling each item again. Both sites found that student help was not as effective in accomplishing this task and that once labels were on they should have been left as is, even if smudged or wrinkled. At first the media coordinators felt more secure with the bar codes attached inside the books—in the rear on the page facing the spine to provide a flat surface for scanning. Later, they felt that placing the labels outside was more advantageous, especially at inventory time.

Due to a shortened time frame to be up and running as a demonstration site, each media coordinator entered the student data and printed the Rolodex™ cards. The program, with the ability to move records from the student database in the principal's office, was tested at the pilot sites. This streamlined initial student data entry, the annual update of student locations, and the inclusion of new student records.

Repairs

The hardware setups at both sites have functioned well without extensive repairs. It isn't necessary to have the two-disk drive system at the elementary site; however, a printer is an absolute must. The IBM or MS-DOS equipment is more appropriate for future expansion. If one is purchasing new hardware and contemplates other automation such as an online catalog, then MS-DOS equipment is the best purchase due to its architecture and operating speed. Currently the new PS/2 IBM machines are all that are available directly from IBM. Once again for future growth and use of OS/2, the Model 60 with 44 or 70 megabytes seems the best purchase option. A heavier, mid-price range printer, similar to the Okidata, is recommended for producing numerous lists, reports, and notices.

The one repair was simple: the early replacement, by the vendor, of the elementary school's light pen. The other site purchased two pens, but has not needed the second one for regular circulation.

To date, the battery-powered backup to provide time to shut down the system whenever there is a power failure has not been utilized, although it frequently activates for power surges. Surge protectors are recommended for all configurations.

The high school setup includes a 3M book detection system that had implications for the circulation software data and equipment placement at the circulation desk. The program has worked well with the software and hardware, placed approximately 8 feet from the desensitizing device of the security system. Special care is taken when software disks and backup disks are anywhere near the desensitizing unit, which is located in one section of the circulation desk. Backups for the program are maintained on floppy disks as outlined in the manual. One archival copy is located someplace outside the media center as a further precaution.

Benefits

Inventory time was reduced drastically. One study conducted in our state showed that for a collection of approximately 7,500 books, the light pen could scan 833 per hour. What had previously taken one professional, one paraprofessional, and two student helpers five days to do could now be done in a day and a half.

Both of our schools documented similar savings. In the high school, the use of multiple machines and batching records to the hard disk accelerated the inventory (portable wands may offer greater savings of time, but our lack of success with this technology has made us cautious). At the next inventory we plan to test Follett Library Software Company's new PhD+ product. Its improved features of digital readout for code reading verification, plus the ability to become an auxiliary circulation station and to create purchase orders with it, makes this convenient, portable device worth testing.

Overdues also can be handled more efficiently. When students attempt to check out materials and have overdue items, the system signals the student assistant (we found that students often immediately retrieved missing books from their desk or locker). Because notices were sent on a regular basis, teachers and students began to collect and return items more promptly than ever before. End-of-the-year notices to teachers streamlined this previously hectic time.

As the systems have become fully functional the site staffs have worked to verify other anticipated automation benefits, including:

- Further time savings from automating circulation and overdues.

- The case of electronically transferring student data to the media center program.

- Increased inventory control and thus greater access to resources.

- New data generated to aid the media center planning process.

- The modeling of computer literacy in the library/media center in a "real world at work" environment.

- Increased time gained for the instructional program.

- The ability to reserve items with the system.

Among the unanticipated benefits:

- Student involvement and response to the system.

- Interface with SIMS for data entry and updates of students' records.

- Increased amount and accuracy of information for collection development—usage, areas to weed, areas needing new purchases, accumulated circulation statistics, status of items, and printed lists available.

AUTOMATING CIRCULATION

	Verifying	Entering Data	Labelling	Inventory
What is done	• Inventory • Weed • Check resources against shelf list • Record ISBN or LC number on shelf list • Assign each item a sequential number • Note the number on the resources and shelf list card	• For each item, enter author, title, ISBN, and price into the computer	• Locate item with number • Find and affix the corresponding label • Cover label with protector • Affix eye-readable label, if desired • Return item to shelf	• Follow program guidelines • Use the bar wand to scan all bar-coded items • Check database files for other locations of missing items • Print list of lost and missing items
Time needed per shelf of 50 books	One person: 60 min. Two people: 40 min.	30-45 min.	40-60 min.	Varies with label placement outside @ 833/hr.: 10/min. 7500 items 1 week/manual 1½ days auto
Location	Shelves	Microcomputer(s)	Shelves	Shelves
Benefits realized	• Organizes collection • Encourages weeding • Gives each item a distinct number • Familiarizes staff with collection • Prepares collection for data entry and labelling	• Prepares collection for automation • Increases awareness of collection • Gives success in computer usage • Prepares for printing of lists	• Assures accuracy of checkout records • Prepares collection for automated inventory • Completes automation project	• Assures accuracy • Saves time • Provides better inventory control

Recommendations

We offer the following suggestions for similar sites that vary in setups.

As an important first step, verify the shelf list. Be sure to include LC numbers preferably, since these numbers may be the best means for matching the book data later for electronically loading the complete book record on an on-line catalog. *Books in Print* was one source of numbers for books or cards that lacked this information. If you are thinking about converting to automation, begin now to ensure that your shelf list has these numbers.

Weed, weed, weed! This cannot be stressed enough. Old, out-of-date materials are not transformed by magic in the computer to useful, desirable resources.

Students can perform data entry efficiently without interference with their instructional day. A team of two students was assigned per station; one completed the data entry while the other verified the typing. By helping, these students felt more responsibility for the system. Remember that in-house data entry could be done by students, volunteers, a typing class, or the library club, but these groups will need training and guidance, especially with the shelf-list card arrangement and the data to be entered. It may be easier and faster to do the data entry in all caps without shifting from upper- to lowercase. The vendor data entry service accuracy rate was good and speeded the startup. Vendor entry is recommended if funds are available.

Assign each patron a unique bar code number for the system. We considered using the school management system identification number, but the length of the student numbers was a drawback (long series of numbers cause the system to sort more slowly when doing overdues, etc.). The student numbers were included, however, in the data entry for each student as a reference.

When doing inventory, consider assigning bar code numbers to the books and writing the numbers in the book and on the shelf-list card. Then when bar codes are purchased, books and codes can be matched without referring to the shelf list. The number on the shelf list can also be a backup should the book bar code be damaged. Neither site has had any difficulty with bar code removal by patrons. At orientation time, good citizenship with resources is stressed, and bar code removal or damage is discussed.

Place bar codes outside the books. We found this is important for speed and ease at inventory time. Suggested placement is in the top right hand corner on the back of each book. Then when taking inventory, simply tilt the book at a 45-degree angle to the shelf to scan the code. One site found that bar coding audiovisual equipment also worked well. Scanning pieces to be assigned to different teachers really speeded equipment disbursal at the beginning of the school year. A printed list of items assigned to each teacher was useful during and at the end of the school year for inventory and retrieval.

Keep patrons' cards at the desk. The elementary school organized its cards and labels on a Rolodex by class for ease of use. A looseleaf notebook with clear Mylar™ sheets is useful for putting all the individual teacher's cards together. The high school, with a larger enrollment, used several Rolodex files, one for each grade level. Then each file was covered with a different color plastic to indicate the grade level. (All plastic colors worked except blue, which prevented the scanner from reading the bar code.)

For student identification at circulation time, the high school distributes student cards that must be shown. This step also assists the process since it signals the student assistant which Rolodex file to check first and lessens the questioning of students during circulation. To avoid mistakes, the staff at the elementary school asks or says the child's name as they locate a card. They then scan the student's bar code in a box-type Rolodex file, arranged by individual teacher's classes and the bar codes on materials. Date due bookmarks are then inserted. In the high school, the assistants request identification cards before scanning a patron's card on Rolodex and the bar codes.

Presently, prestamped date due slips are used. We realize, however, that this date due process is time-consuming; new ideas are being considered, such as a circulation desk calendar with the due date highlighted or gummed stickers from a label gun affixed to the book.

Use student assistants as low as fourth grade; they can work the system well. One site developed a set of cards for students as a ready reference for using the system. Getting assistants isn't a problem—in fact, students can hardly wait for their turn at the circulation desk.

Arrange for maintenance. The payment of an annual maintenance contract fee means that you will get all updates during that year and get a higher priority for technical support via the toll-free telephone service. For these reasons, the pilot sites have continued the maintenance agreement. A word of caution about upgrades: each usually contains improvement and changes, but the changes may affect current practices and information. For example, version 7.0 of the Apple program made some changes to the category numbers. Then the elementary site found some of their data in the first categories were labeled differently. The media coordinator then had to relink the categories before printing accurate category reports. The data is not lost, but the user needs to be aware of the changes upgrades may mean.

Scheduling and Training

The media coordinators at both demonstration sites feel that a year is a reasonable time frame for planning and successfully implementing a project of this scope without additional help. A suggested schedule is:

1. At the end of the school year, complete the inventory and ready the shelf-list cards.

2. Complete data entry for materials and people and bar code resources during the next school year.

3. Introduce the new setup and procedures to all concerned and use the system for year-end inventory and for printed lists and records.

4. Begin using the full circulation system the next fall.

Training has two components: in house and outreach. Three areas needing attention immediately were the media center staff, the students, and the faculty and staff. Both site coordinators felt that the demonstration disk, complete documentation, and some support from the local school computer coordinator were sufficient to make the program operational. With the day-to-day operations, the staff is still learning the program's many features and uses.

A media center bulletin board graphically portrayed the new system along with a time line for start-up to keep everyone up-to-date. The school newspaper, the school handbook, and the media center newsletter also alerted faculty and students to the new procedures of the system prior to start-up. Special introductory classes were important before the elementary students started the system. The secondary library assistants were taught to man the system, except for maintenance and backup. Reference task cards at the desk provided assistants help with daily operations.

Ann Daniels

Online at Last!
An Odyssey of Automation

13

Our journey to an online catalog actually commenced in 1984. But first, let me set the stage. Carmel High School Library Media Center is part of the Carmel Clay School system—8,200 students in one high school (grades 10-12), two junior highs, and seven elementary schools. Carmel is an Indianapolis suburban community located in Clay Township, home to approximately 38,000 residents. (That's Carmel by the cornfields, not Carmel by the sea.)

Our card catalog is part of an integrated system that links the Carmel Clay School System (CCSS) with the Carmel Clay Public Library (CCPL). We share both a materials database and a patron database. Our system currently allows for the automation of circulation, statistics, overdues, intrasystem loans, and cataloging. All eleven school sites have been using CL-CAT, our online public access catalog, since December 1990. Full circulation is online at the secondary schools and two of the elementary schools. By now, the end of our odyssey of automation should be within reach!

The initiative to link all our libraries together came from the public library, as it wanted to network as a means of expanding services to the community. Discussions between the directors of the two library systems began as early as 1984.

Meanwhile, at Carmel High School (CHS), we had been investigating microcomputer-based circulation systems, looking for one that would not only give us an on-line card catalog and circulation control, but also allow us to network. We have three sites and four librarians to serve the 1,900 students on our two-building campus. So even though the term "network" wasn't in our 1984 vocabulary, that's what was needed at the high school. Our district supervisor had a grander voyage planned; she wanted to link *all* the schools together.

Source: Reprinted by permission from *California Media and Library Educators Association Journal* 14, no. 1 (Fall 1990): 15-18.

Other factors influenced our decision for a shared system. Indiana is one of twenty-three states that permits interlocal cooperation agreements between governmental units. That provided the legal basis for the shared system. The agreement was simplified by two factors: both the schools and the public library serve the same taxpayers and have identical geographic boundaries, and both have utilized the same legal firm for several years.

Also, a history of cooperation exists between the two units. For years we have shared both equipment and materials on an informal basis. The school courier includes the public library on his daily route. Two public librarians regularly attend the monthly school staff meetings. And last April, a successful American Library Association-sponsored "Night of 1,000 Stars," was a joint endeavor.

Finally, community attitudes were favorable. A pattern of cooperation already existed among other governmental units in Carmel. An exemplary school system prompts many moves to this area, so parents support ideas that enhance the schools. The school and library boards shared our vision of increasing access and improving services by sharing across the entire community.

Once the decision was made to link the school and public libraries, it was obvious that a mainframe computer was the solution. Four major items constituted our wish list in selecting a vendor:

1. The school libraries needed a system that would accommodate 134,000 volumes, 13,000 magazine issues, and 30,000 audiovisual items. The public library had 60,000 volumes in 1985. (As of June 1, 1991, our shared database contained a total of 323,400 items.)

2. Both partners wanted full MARC records. CCPL earlier had contacted nearby public libraries, but they were not committed to MARC at that time.

3. We all wanted an integrated system, more than circulation control. An automated card catalog was at the top of *my* list. CHS had begun online database searching of DIALOG, so we knew the capabilities of computers in retrieving information. (Incidentally, it is easier to sell the idea of automation to the superintendent and school board by stressing the advantages that *students* gain from an automated catalog, rather than the benefits that *staff* enjoy with automated circulation.)

4. The public library wanted a laser scanning system rather than bar code wands. The schools hoped to have the option of adding laser scanners as funds permitted.

Bids were let in May 1985. By July, CLSI had been selected as our vendor. We are still satisfied with that decision. Most of our problems were caused by the weakest link in our system—the telephone lines that physically tie us together.

Every voyage encounters rough seas. Retrospective conversion is the thunderstorm one endures to catch sight of the rainbow—and maybe find the pot of gold. Carmel Clay Public Library began its retrospective conversion using Microcon. Information from shelf-list cards was entered into a PC. The floppy disks were shipped to OCLC, and tapes of the matched records were returned. The resulting database needed to be "cleaned up," as there were false hits (i.e., a record for a different edition rather than an exact match), wrong call numbers, and inadequate cataloging.

Books from the first elementary school were matched against the CCPL database, then online with OCLC. They matched about 40 percent of their records. But in the spring of 1988 when we began converting the 24,000 volumes at the high school, we scored only about a 10 percent hit rate. This meant, unfortunately, that our conversion took longer and cost more than anticipated. On the other hand, it also meant that the high school books were *not* duplicates of those at the public library. Our goal of extending services and materials would be met sooner than anticipated.

The Carmel schools have a central processing center. A full-time cataloger matches each newly purchased book against the existing database. If it's a hit, then the book is added to the system. Each school has the option of using unique call numbers for any book. This allows for diversity among our collections and users. If the book is not a hit, then it's matched online with OCLC. Occasionally, the cataloger will input original records.

Even though we've been online for almost two years, our paper card catalog is still intact. No new cards have been added for more than four years, however; nor have we pulled cards for missing books. (Maybe we'll scrap it during National Library Week with a schoolwide contest or celebration.) The "backup" catalog proved useful when the high school was struck by lightning last year and when our system was upgraded this spring. It's used reluctantly—students complain they can't find the right books in the old catalog; librarians are annoyed by the time it takes to search manually.

CL-CAT, CLSI's acronym for its automated or online public access catalog, is the reason I'm sold on CLSI. There are many other advantages to automation, but the online catalog outweighs them all. CL-CAT is sophisticated, yet easy for students to use. With additional access points for each cataloged item, students are more successful in finding materials. They are no longer limited to the exact subject or title. In addition, since the collections of *all* Carmel libraries are now available, students usually find information on their topic.

Welcome to the Online Catalog of the Carmel Clay Public Library and the Carmel Clay School Media Centers.

The Collections of the Public Library and the School Media Centers are included in this catalog.

You May Search the Catalog Using Any of the Methods Listed Below. Choose By Pressing the Corresponding Number Key. You May Request Assistance at Any Time By Pressing the HELP Key.

TO SEARCH BY:

(1) SUBJECT
(2) AUTHOR
(3) TITLE
(4) AUTHOR AND TITLE
(5) ALL CATEGORIES

PRESS SELECTION NUMBER ☐

Fig. 1. CLSI Welcome Screen

The Welcome Screen leads users into the searching process on CL-CAT. At this point a student determines the context of his search by selecting among five options (Subject, Author, Title, Author and Title, or All Categories). Without instruction, most students elect to search by subject.

The search term is typed at the Subject Search Screen, and a choice is made between Browse and Keyword. Students usually select Browse—either because it's listed first or the concept is similar to the traditional card catalog. The Heading Browse Screen is a window into the database, giving an alphabetic listing of the items immediately preceding and following the search term.

HEADING BROWSE

SEARCH TERM(S): SUBJECT = STEROIDS
NO. HEADINGS   REFERENCES FOUND

No.	Heading	References Found
1.	Steroids	1
2.	Sterling (Seal)-Juvenile literature.	1
3.	Sterne, Laurence, 1713-1768.	3
4.	Steroids, Fiction.	1
5.	Stethoscope.	1
6.	Stettheimer, Carrie Walter, d. 1944.	1
7.	Stettheimer dollhouse.	1
8.	Steuben Glass, Inc.	1
9.	Stevens, Thaddeus, 1792-1868.	2

Press line Number(s) to Select One or More Headings.
Then Press BRIEF to See the Matching References.

Or PRESS:

NEXT Page.   SEARCH HISTORY to Enter Next Search.
PREV ious Page.   START OVER Completely.
HELP for Assistance.

Fig. 2. CLSI Heading Browse Screen.

By selecting the All Categories option from the Welcome Screen and then choosing to search by Keyword at the second screen, the student increases his/her chances of finding material. In our experience, the Keyword concept needs to be taught, at least until all students receive training before they reach us at the high school. The Brief Reference Screen lists the items (both print and AV) that match the search term(s). Items housed in our collection are highlighted. This is a welcome enhancement as more and more records are entered into our database.

BRIEF REFERENCES

SEARCH TERMS(S): STEROID OR STEROIDS
REFERENCES FOUND: 6   Page 1 of 1

NO.	AUTHOR	TITLE	DATE	FORMAT
1.	Dolan, Edward F.,	Drugs in sports/	1986.	PRINT
2.	Goldman, Bob,	Death in the locker room:	c1987.	PRINT
3.	Goldman, Bob,	Death in the locker room:	1984.	PRINT
4.	Mohun, Janet,	Drugs, steroids and sport	1988.	PRINT
5.	Miklowitz, Gloria D.	Anything to win/	1989.	PRINT
6.		How much is that body inc	1987.	AV

Titles at Carmel High School Main are Highlighted

Press Line Number to Select Your Choice:

Or PRESS:

HELP for Assistance   SEARCH HISTORY to Enter Next Search.

                                          START OVER Completely.

Fig. 3. CLSI Brief Reference Screen.

    The Copy Availability Screen includes a bibliographic citation. (Note how all the information students need for bib cards is right before them on the screen. And if you have a printer attached to a terminal, they quickly catch on to this shortcut.) Also listed is the Building (local agency listed first), Call No. (which can be agency specific), Notes (might list language, special collection, etc.), and Status (whether on shelf, lost, or due date if checked out).

    There are actually three modes of searching in CL-CAT: Browse, Keyword, and Command. Browse can be a starting point, as users always get results. It seems to be intuitive for students, as there is crossover from the traditional card catalog. One can actually browse forward and backward through the alphabetic window. If exact terms are known, such as author's name, Browse is simpler. When students are not sure of spelling, they can browse until the right word is discovered.

    With Keyword students don't need to know the exact search term or the right order of words within the title or phrase. Terms can be linked together with Boolean operators. This mode allows searches on a word stem (truncation) or for alternate spelling. This search can be limited by format, date, or language. Keyword is especially useful when students are not sure of the Library of Congress subject heading but think the term might be in the title or notes field.

    The Command mode allows searches by bibliographic identifier (LCCN, ISBN, or ISSN) or by combining commands with regular search terms in one phrase, using Boolean logic. An example might be a search for current books on air pollution. From the Search Screen one could search in All Categories for [Air Pollution and pubyr = > 1985]. This Keyword search would retrieve only those books on air pollution published in 1985 or later. Another useful command is [format = med] (media), which retrieves audiovisual items.

COPY AVAILABILITY

SEARCH TERM(S): AIR POLLUTION AND PUBYR = 1985
REFERENCES FOUND: 11

AUTHOR: Gribbin, John R.
TITLE: The hole in the sky : man's threat to the
IMPRINT: Toronto ; New York : Bantam Books, 1988

Page 1 of 1

BUILDING	CALL	NOTES	STATUS
HIGH SCHOOL	MA363.73 GRI		Due 6/27/90
CARMEL JUNIOR	363.73 GRI		On Shelf

PRESS YOUR CHOICE:

SEARCH HISTORY to Enter Next Search
FULL Record.
RECORD to BRIEF REFERENCES.
HELP for Assistance   START OVER Completely.

Fig. 4. CLSI Copy Availability Screen.

We've found that you can teach the concepts of Browse and Keyword generically. Students at CHS are instructed in database searching—including our current CD-ROM titles (*Readers' Guide Abstracts, NewsBank, UMI ProQuest*, and *Grolier's Encyclopedia*), CL-CAT, Dow Jones News/Retrieval and DIALOG's Classmate. We see each sophomore for a four-day library instruction unit in English 10 and each junior in connection with his/her research for an English 11 composition. Seniors receive individual instruction in Command searching as needed.

I believe we're actually teaching critical thinking skills as we teach them to use an automated card catalog.

Students need to decide the context of their search at the Welcome Screen (categories of headings used as access points, i.e., Subject, Author, Title). They need to determine whether Browse or Keyword is best. They may need to modify or limit their search, to interact, depending on results.

If an item is unavailable at CHS or is checked out, the student has several options. He/she may request an intrasystem loan. (Requested forms are FAXed between schools and CCPL.) Requested books are then delivered through the school system's regular courier service, usually by the next day. Or a student may decide to place an item on reserve, either at our agency or systemwide. When that reserved item is checked in, CIRC alerts us to the reserve, and the student is advised. A third option for high school students is to use the public library after school or on Sunday. CCPL has recently extended its hours of service to include Sunday afternoons during the school year. (The CHS Library remains open an extra hour three afternoons a week.)

High school intrasystem loan statistics demonstrate that we are filling a need for our community patrons. During the 1989-90 school year we loaned 416 books within our network, mainly to the public library. An equal number of fiction and biography titles were loaned. Travel and history have also proved popular with the public library patrons. The first book loaned was on the subject of prejudice—a book I had considered weeding as it hadn't circulated for several years.

These initial statistics surprised us. The assumption was that the schools would borrow more than they loaned. In actuality, in 1989 (the first year for intrasystem loan), the schools received 636 loan requests from the public library for materials and initiated 139 requests. (In other words, the schools loaned four and one-half books for each one borrowed from CCPL.) With more schools online in 1990, the number of requests also increased: CCS received 788 requests from CCPL and initiated 369. (Schools loaned two books for each one borrowed.) By the end of June 1991, the loan statistics show that the schools and public library are loaning almost on a one-to-one basis. The schools received 510 requests from CCPL and borrowed 449 items.

Our automation odyssey will never truly be completed. We're talking and dreaming of future enhancements to improve service. Dial-up access to CL-CAT for any student or patron who has a computer and modem was recently implemented. (I was one of the "beta" testers this summer and appreciated knowing in advance that a book or audio book was on the shelf before making a trip to the public library.) The possibility of loading the Wilsontape Database for *Readers' Guide Abstracts* onto our local database is being discussed. (Then the Welcome Screen would offer a sixth option—searching a magazine index.) In our renovated and expanded high school (targeted for completion in 1994), a CL-CAT terminal is planned for each department office.

So, even though the end of our odyssey of automation is in sight, the adventure is not yet over. With the speed at which technology advances, who knows what else our shared system will enable for the future. But I do know that it will continue to benefit not just the students at Carmel High School, but also our entire community. And that the voyage will be exciting.

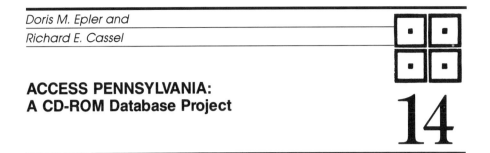

Doris M. Epler and
Richard E. Cassel

ACCESS PENNSYLVANIA:
A CD-ROM Database Project

14

Scenario

A woman moves among machines that collectively resemble the cockpit of a spaceship. The muted whir of spinning disks is punctuated by the clatter of printers and telefacsimile machines. The soft red glow of the LED displays on the computer, modem, and laser disk drives adds to the atmosphere. As the woman's fingers stroke the keyboard, one would almost expect it to catapult the spaceship into Warp Nine emergency speed. It would not seem out of place for Luke Skywalker (hero of the movie *Return of the Jedi*) to stride into the cockpit, blasters firing, to ward off invaders from the Empire.

But this is not a movie set. It is a library in a small school district in Pennsylvania. The woman is a librarian and she's in the process of accessing information on the holdings of libraries from all over Pennsylvania. The immediate focus of this immense technological power is the ruddy faced ninth-grader at the librarian's elbow who needs to complete a research paper by next Thursday.

Where did this librarian, who appears to be so comfortable with this technology, come from? Surely she must be a graduate of a technological university. No, she is not an MIT graduate, but she is a Pennsylvania school librarian who has embraced technology in order to be better able to provide resources to the students and teachers in her school.

This scenario is becoming more and more commonplace across Pennsylvania as the state launches its project—ACCESS PENNSYLVANIA—to manage the information needs of its citizens. A central component of this project is the School Library Catalog Program, which is a joint effort of the State Library, the Pennsylvania Department of Education, and

Source: Reprinted by permission from *Library Hi Tech* 5, no. 3 (Fall 1987): 81-88.

Brodart Company. The objective of this project is to harness the power of microcomputers and CD-ROM technology to create a union catalog.

One of the goals of ACCESS PENNSYLVANIA is to bring school librarians into the statewide system of resource sharing. In order to accomplish this goal, it is obvious that information about the holdings of the school libraries has to be converted into a machine-readable form.

With the help of consultants, various systems and technologies were examined to determine the technology that would be the most responsive to the needs of school library users. Technology chosen had to be easy to implement, cost-effective, and adaptable to the growth of the proposed database. The database had to provide students and teachers access not only to the collection of their own school library, but to those collections of other school, public, and academic libraries across the state or Commonwealth.

The compact disk was selected as the technology that came closest to meeting all the support requirements of the union catalog.

Major Objectives

The School Library Catalog Program was designed to accomplish two major objectives:

1. Provide all library users with access to the books, journals, media, and other information they need, whether contained in their own library or in any participating school, public, or college library in the Commonwealth.

2. Provide a way to facilitate the automation of many time consuming library management functions, such as cataloging, circulation, and inventory control, so that librarians will have more time to use their special skills in working directly with teachers, students, and other patrons.

Why CD-ROM?

CD-ROM is an optical technology that allows a tremendous amount of information to be stored on a small disk. Pennsylvania used this technology to merge 653,000 unique catalog records from 153 participating libraries, and to produce a union catalog that was made available to libraries in September 1986. An inexpensive ($500) laser reader is connected to a standard IBM microcomputer. The microcomputer is used to control the disk drive and to search and locate a single record, within the 653,000 records, in just a few seconds. This system has provided a quantum leap in the ability of librarians and library patrons to locate and manage information.

Changing from a "linear" searching method (thumbing through card catalogs) to a "logical" searching structure allows a user to enter several key subject words simultaneously. The computer will then find all records containing those words. This means a user no longer needs to know the actual title and author of a specific work, but will be able to locate it from the "clues" that are known. The system can locate items, identified only by key words and vague subject terms, even if those items reside in other libraries across the state. (It has been observed that CD-ROM technology may be as significant to locating and accessing information as Gutenberg's technology was to producing and storing it.)

CD-ROM eliminates the expense of long distance telephone charges that were previously incurred in performing online searches for the same information. The use of CD-ROM (1) provides administrators with a predictable budget line, (2) eliminates the concern over "how fast the clock is ticking" when a student or teacher conducts a lengthy search, and (3) eliminates costs associated with the downloading or off-line printing of citations.

Currently, Pennsylvania is updating the CD-ROM union catalog annually and will be pressing new disks by September 1990. The next edition of the database will contain approximately 2.6 million unique records and will require four CD-ROM disks. Enhanced search software will provide transparent access to the information contained in the two disks, and will provide additional search and telecommunication options.

The next edition will also make other databases available to libraries, particularly small libraries, that did not previously have access to them.

Features of the ACCESS PENNSYLVANIA Project

The combination of numerous objectives and features make ACCESS PENNSYLVANIA an innovative project. The project is statewide in scope. Even though Pennsylvania has a large population, much of the state is mountainous and geographically isolated. This factor contributes a significant challenge to the objective of meeting the goal — making all information available to all citizens of Pennsylvania.

Participation

The project is comprised of library consortiums, which usually consist of a variety of library types. Libraries that comprise the consortiums have agreed to function as a unit, providing inter-library loan access to each others' collections. In order for a consortium to become part of the ACCESS PENNSYLVANIA project, it has to submit a competitive proposal indicating what it hopes to accomplish by becoming part of the project.

Figure 1 indicates the various ways that different types and sizes of libraries, including public, academic, school, and special libraries may participate in the project. However, one unique feature of the project is that it is based in school libraries. Libraries requesting participation in the project must be associated with a school library; and it is the school library that submits the proposal requesting acceptance into the project. Placing such emphasis on the school library has resulted in catapulting school libraries into the automation age.

Funding

The State Library administers the project within the Pennsylvania Department of Education. The project is funded by a combination of state, federal, and local funds. Starting in 1986, the Pennsylvania State Legislature approved a fiscal line item in the governor's budget to support the project. In addition, the State Library has allocated some Library Services Construction Act (LSCA) monies to support certain aspects of the project. The state's financial participation includes retrospective conversion (primarily for school libraries), extraction of previously converted records (primarily for public and academic libraries), creation of a composite database, and mastering and pressing of the CD-ROM disks. The state also supports technical services and training for the participating libraries.

The financial responsibilities of individual schools fall into several categories. One requirement for a school to participate in the project is the implementation of an automated library management system, including such functions as inventory, circulation, or overdues control. This means that schools must fund the cost of

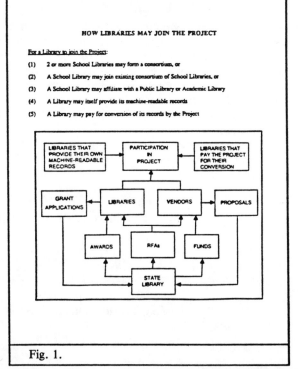

Fig. 1.

management software as well as the microcomputer and related hardware needed to implement the system.

All libraries must agree to support the cost of updating the database for a minimum of five years, and must purchase all additional hardware associated with the project, including CD-ROM drives, modems, and printers. In addition, libraries must absorb the costs involved with interlibrary loan telecommunications and the delivery of materials. Release time also must be provided librarians so that they can attend training sessions and workshops.

Technical Support

A technical service unit at the state level provides a number of important functions. These include (1) quality control for retrospective conversion and database creation, (2) testing of the compatibility of specific software and hardware, (3) testing of the compatibility of specific hardware components, (4) testing library management software packages, (5) evaluating commercially published CD-ROM products, and (6) dissemination of newsletters, provision of assistance in research data gathering, training, and updating of pricing information.

The State Library holds periodic meetings with various vendors, including vendors of retrospective conversion services, hardware, databases, CD-ROM products, and database maintenance and circulation software. The focus of these meetings is to learn about current capabilities and planned development efforts that are relevant to the various elements of ACCESS PENNSYLVANIA.

Pricing information and price guarantees obtained through competitive bidding for any of the products and services that are part of ACCESS PENN-SYLVANIA are also made available to nonproject libraries in the state. Because individual institutions do not need to conduct an independent bidding process, many additional school and public libraries have been encouraged to absorb the cost of their own retrospective conversion or the cost of acquiring support equipment.

The Database

The project accepts records from a variety of sources, including records derived from retrospective conversion undertaken as part of the project and records obtained as a result of conversion done by third party vendors. All records that are entered into the database are full MARC records.

One major component of the contract negotiated with the Brodart Company was that all keying of records had to be done by the vendor, not the librarian. The shelf lists were packed by librarians, with the assistance of a representative from Brodart, and taken to Williamsport, Pennsylvania, where the conversion process was started. This requirement was a major key to the success of the project. School librarians did not have the time to undertake the keying since they are heavily involved in teaching library skills to students. In addition, it is vital that the consistency and the quality of input be maintained since the database will comprise the holdings of hundreds of libraries. The need for quality control and adherence to standards is much greater in a collective project of this size than when a single library creates a database for its own in-house use.

CD-ROM Information Station

The technology used to manipulate and display the records is a micro-computer/CD-ROM information station. It utilizes the 4.75 inch CD-ROM laser disk that has the capability to hold 700,000 to 900,000 unique records per disk. The search software resides on a floppy disk and is available in two versions of operating systems, Bro-DOS and MS-DOS. The software allows Boolean logic searching using EITHER, AND, and OR logic operators. The use of NOT and adjacency operators is currently unavailable.

Each information station is relatively inexpensive, and is affordable even by medium and small size libraries. The system allows searching without telecommunications costs and provides response times under five seconds when a single search criterion is entered. Response time can be controlled by the user, and depends on the number and type of search terms entered. Screen displays are easy to read and understand. Each record includes local information such as location code and call number. The searcher can print out the bibliographic data about each item found.

The search software contains a "location" prompt that allows the user to isolate the geographical location of the collection to be searched. Collections can be isolated by entering a location code for any of the following:

1. Individual library

2. Consortium

3. Intermediate unit (regional school grouping)

4. District library center (public libraries)

5. Library system

Search terms can be entered in any or all of the following input fields:

TITLE
AUTHOR
SUBJECT
ANYWORD
LOCATION

The ANYWORD input capability adds tremendous power to the searching process. All fields in the record, with the exception of the notes field, are indexed. By use of ANYWORD, all records can be found that contain any specified search term or terms located in any portion of the record.

Currently, the database of 2.6 million unique records resides on four CD-ROM disks. The next CD-ROM database (to be delivered September 1992) will contain approximately 3 million records and will reside on four CD-ROM disks daisy-chained together. Search software will make the two drives appear transparent and the user will see a single large database.

The hardware can be used to support a number of library applications and databases, such as: other commercially produced CD-ROM products, circulation and other library management systems, word processing, online searching, and electronic mail. At most installations, a 20-megabyte hard disk drive is part of the hardware configuration, particularly in school libraries that maintain their circulation system on the microcomputer. The CD-ROM search software can be loaded on the hard disk, greatly facilitating use of the CD-ROM system.

Impact of the ACCESS PENNSYLVANIA CD-ROM Project on Various Types of Libraries

As could be predicted, the impact of the project varies by the type and size of the library involved. The larger public libraries tend to designate the CD-ROM system for staff use, primarily for the processing of ILL requests. The smaller public and school libraries use the CD-ROM database for both ILL and patron access.

Although the impact data for the first nine months is currently being analyzed by RMG Consultants, Inc., consultants for the project, a significant generalization can be made. Most participating librarians feel that ACCESS PENNSYLVANIA has had immense positive impact on the operation of their libraries, and that the initiatives sponsored by the project will have even greater impact in the future.

TABULATION OF SURVEY RESPONSES

(1) CATEGORIES OF USE	(2) NO RESPONSE 0	(3) MOST IMPORTANT 1	(4) 2	(5) 3	(6) 4	(7) 5	(8) LEAST IMPORTANT 6	(9) TOTAL
(6.1) Referral of Patrons to Other Libraries	4	1	4	3	5	3	1	21
Single Category Distribution	19.05%	4.76%	19.05%	14.29%	23.81%	14.29%	4.76%	
Cumulative Distribution		4.76%	23.81%	38.10%	61.90%	76.19%	80.95%	100.00%
(6.2) Local Interlibrary Loan	0	14	4	1	1	0	1	21
Single Category Distribution	0.00%	66.67%	19.05%	4.76%	4.76%	0.00%	4.76%	
Cumulative Distribution		66.67%	85.71%	90.48%	95.24%	95.24%	100.00%	100.00%
(6.3) Statewide Interlibrary Loan	6	2	3	4	4	1	1	21
Single Category Distribution	28.57%	9.52%	14.29%	19.05%	19.05%	4.76%	4.76%	
Cumulative Distribution		9.52%	23.81%	42.86%	61.90%	66.67%	71.43%	100.00%
(6.4) Staff Access Catalog	1	3	5	4	3	5	0	21
Single Category Distribution	4.76%	14.29%	23.81%	19.05%	14.29%	23.81%	0.00%	
Cumulative Distribution		14.29%	38.10%	57.14%	71.43%	95.24%	95.24%	100.00%
(6.5) Public Access Catalog	6	2	5	5	2	0	1	21
Single Category Distribution	28.57%	9.52%	23.81%	23.81%	9.52%	0.00%	4.76%	
Cumulative Distribution		9.52%	33.33%	57.14%	66.67%	66.67%	71.43%	100.00%

Survey Participants Responded to:
Rank in importance to your library the following uses for the ACCESS PENNSYLVANIA disc on a scale from 1 to 6 with 1 being the most important and 6 the least important. You do not need to rank all 6.

Fig. 2.

Figure 2 indicates the specific responses of libraries to a question that measures the level of impact the union catalog database has had on (1) referral of patrons to other libraries, (2) local interlibrary loan activity, (3) statewide interlibrary loan activity, (4) staff use of the catalog, and (5) public use of the catalog.

It is not yet possible to determine the impact of the project, and the database in particular, in such subjective areas as: its effectiveness, its impact on political and philosophical attitudes, and other related areas that may critically affect the future of automation efforts. However, initial observations suggest that the impact in these areas will be positive and significant.

Changing Patterns of Library Use

Patterns of library use will change dramatically in the years ahead, due to the introduction of this type of equipment and database. Try to imagine, for example, a student in a small school district in rural, mountainous northeastern Pennsylvania, sliding into a worn chair in front of a desk bearing decades of scratches and carved communications placed there by prior generations. Unlike the past generations that used the chair and table to examine a few of the several thousand books that constitute that school's library, our student enters a few keystrokes on the microcomputer in front of her and begins to browse the records of the 300,000 item collection of the Pittsburgh Carnegie Library, which is located 300 miles away. She's doing this as casually as she had browsed the lunch cafeteria menu. Another keystroke and the records she found to support her current research paper are printed out. She knows where the items are located as well as the appropriate call numbers for each one.

The school librarian, by connecting with a communications and delivery system, will then request that the items be retrieved and delivered to the library for use by the student.

This is not a scenario of some futuristic transaction. This is becoming a commonplace occurrence all across Pennsylvania.

Interlibrary loan transactions are not new to a large public library, but for a school library that has never loaned a book in the history of the school, conducting an ILL transaction is a momentous experience. The availability of the CD-ROM database makes it possible for libraries that never previously requested an ILL, to do so, and to request the item from a library that never previously lent an item. Suddenly, even the small isolated library, which previously could not afford online searching of databases, can see the holdings of any participating library in Pennsylvania. The consultants for the project have reported that all types of libraries have indicated an average increase of 68 percent in interlibrary loan transactions since the project began.

With the introduction of the microcomputer/CD-ROM information station, libraries, and particularly school libraries, have indicated an enormous increase in the circulation of their *own* resources. Most indicate a 300 to 500 percent increase in the circulation of their own books by their *own* patrons.

The cause for this increase in circulation is directly attributable to the increased ease with which items can be located. To effectively use a card catalog or computer output microfilm (COM) catalog, patrons must know the exact title of an item and its precise spelling. Patrons must search for items sequentially, by complete words. They must know all the letters that comprise each word, and the alphabetizing and filing rules that control the location of those words in the catalog. They must understand filing conventions for handling abbreviated words. For example, when searching for the book *Mr. Roberts*, patrons need to know whether the first word is filed as abbreviated or as spelled out, or take the time to look under each possibility (assuming the first guess fails).

The need to seek information in a linear process is taken for granted by most library users, and some have become quite adept at it. However, such a search process is very time-consuming and distasteful for most library users, and contributes to a *low success* rate in the search for library materials. Just the anticipation of the effort involved to locate information is enough to discourage some persons from using the library.

In contrast to the laborious and time consuming linear searching of the traditional card catalog are the enhanced searching capabilities provided by a CD-ROM system. Using a CD-ROM system, a patron needs only to type a few words that are related to the title or subject of interest. These words can occur anywhere in the record. The computer then performs a "logic" search, eliminating the physical necessity to move from location to location in the card catalog, the time-consuming process of double-checking spellings and blind leads, the mental gymnastics needed to understand filing rules, and other frustrating steps associated with locating information. The CD-ROM database makes library resources accessible to persons who never had the patience or skill to locate them before; in fact, the new technology makes libraries fun to use.

The size of the library no longer needs to be measured by the size of its own collection. The ability to access the collections of many libraries essentially extends the walls of the library. This also extends the usefulness and the effectiveness of the library. The probability that a patron can find a needed answer or resource is greatly increased, regardless of the size of the library. For example, a student at Mansfield University asked for information on guide dogs. He was told that there were no known books about guide dogs in the library's collection but was instructed to use the CD-ROM database where he found twelve items. This success has repeatedly brought him back to the library to locate other types of information. As the Mansfield librarian commented, "When people have genuine success in finding needed information, they *will* be back." (Incidentally, do you know if "guide dogs" is a Library of Congress subject heading? With a CD-ROM database and keyword searching capabilities, it doesn't make any difference if you know or not.)

The Image and the Reality

The CD-ROM system adds a positive image to the library; as one person observed, it adds "glitz." It promotes the fact that the library is using modern technology, which increases the ease and effectiveness of finding needed information. With minimal instruction, most users tend to enjoy personally using the CD-ROM system. In fact, the personal use of the system generates a sense of pride when techniques have been mastered. Many patrons experience a real sense of satisfaction—indeed, even joy—when they find needed information on their own.

Academic libraries that are equipped to support ILL requests from participating schools feel that this is an important public relations and outreach service that will hold significant benefit for their institutions. They feel that when students from high schools see a university's name and logo on the books they are using, the high school students will be more likely to consider the institution as a candidate for their higher education.

Public librarians also have indicated that their involvement in the project has enhanced their image in the eyes of school age youth. A librarian from a modest-sized library recently reported that students from six different school districts were all seeking resource materials in her library on the same day. (She was able to identify their school affiliations from the different school logos on the backs of their jackets!) These students had a positive experience using the public library, thanks, in part, to the CD-ROM system that the public library and a number of the school libraries had. This librarian and others believe that students who have successful experiences using the public library will carry these experiences with them. It is hoped that persons who have had these positive experiences, beginning early in life, will be supporters of their public libraries as taxpaying adults.

The Project as a Catalyst

The CD-ROM project has been a great catalyst for the automation of school libraries. Because the CD-ROM technology is easy to install, easy to use, and an effective tool, it has encouraged school librarians to implement other automation projects, and to use computers in a variety of additional ways. Schools are encouraged to use the MARC records created by Brodart for this project as input for their circulation systems. This eliminates countless hours from the process of automating a circulation system. To date, only a few library circulation system vendors that provide microcomputer-based systems for small libraries can extract the MARC records from the union catalog and load them into their systems. Among these are Follett and Winnebago.

The project has also been a catalyst for motivating librarians from different types of libraries to "mix." Typical Pennsylvania library meetings, where major library issues are being considered, are now attended by librarians from public, academic, and school libraries. Persons from various types of libraries now are more willing to share ideas and needs, and to work with each other, creating a large (and increasingly influential) group of persons dedicated to common objectives.

Librarians indicate that the project has increased their "standing" in their communities. The fact that needs of patrons can be effectively answered, that remote resources can be quickly identified and obtained, that local resources can be effectively searched and retrieved—in short, that library services are greatly improved, has enhanced the reputation of the libraries. Librarians, due to the increased effectiveness of their services, are viewed as being "more professional."

The project has also been a driving force in the development and sharing of telecommunications and document delivery systems. Initial lending policies, which contained many restrictions on lending to libraries within each consortium, have been greatly relaxed. In many circumstances, restrictive policies have been eliminated, resulting in the free exchange of resources among libraries. In fact, libraries that had never loaned books before now take pride in the number of ILL loans made by their institutions.

The enhanced capabilities of the libraries have resulted in greater respect for both the libraries and the staffs of the libraries. As a result, librarians feel better about being in the library. Because users can now find desired information with less help from the librarians, it allows the librarians to do more higher-order, professional work with their patrons.

Librarians repeatedly comment that they have never experienced so many positive activities related to the library. Politicians are actively involved in providing increased funding for libraries. Library and school administrators are extending strong support to librarians to help them install and use the new technologies. A common observation, which is particularly prevalent among librarians from schools and small libraries, is: "We are really starting to feel as though we are performing important functions."

The project has had another significant impact on libraries. There is an increased awareness of the importance of maintaining collections through weeding and joint collection development. Libraries that for years had avoided weeding their collections have now "cleaned house" and made their collections much more responsive to the needs of their patrons. Likewise, schools that never had supported cooperative projects are now planning and promoting joint collective development policies.

A Companion Project

A sister project called LIN-TEL (Linking Information Needs—Technology Education Libraries) is currently under way. It is a state-funded project that trains librarians to conduct online searches using BRS. The librarians subsequently integrate online searching skills into the secondary school library media curriculum. A large number of students have developed the skills needed to access online information.

Because much of the hardware used with the CD-ROM project (computer, modem, and printer) can be used for online searching, many libraries are simultaneously participating in both projects. As a result, students and librarians not only can access the holdings of countless libraries in Pennsylvania, they can also search and retrieve the latest information available in commercial databases.

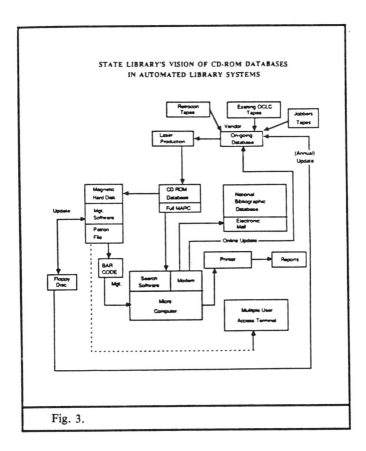

STATE LIBRARY'S VISION OF CD-ROM DATABASES
IN AUTOMATED LIBRARY SYSTEMS

Fig. 3.

Figure 3 depicts the interrelationships of technologies and functions, including local CD-ROM databases and online searching, that will become critical components of most libraries, including small public and school libraries.

ACCESS PENNSYLVANIA has been an exciting and rewarding project. Expressed in a contemporary vernacular, one might say "it has been a real trip!" So many positive benefits have been obtained and defined during the 60 months of the project, that in reality it *has* been a trip—a long one, to a destination from which we never want to return.

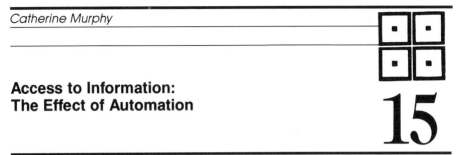

Catherine Murphy

Access to Information:
The Effect of Automation

15

Introduction

This paper focuses on the impact of OPAC upon subject access to information. The OPACs found in school library media centers are more likely to be microcomputer systems, although a number of larger school districts have implemented mainframe online systems, sometimes in cooperation with the local public library. At the present time, there are perhaps 12,000 microcomputer systems in schools, most of them circulation systems, but increasingly these programs are integrated with an online catalog. These figures are estimates from vendors, which I have requested in surveys for other reports published recently (Murphy, 1988, 1989).

The history of microcomputer OPACs in school library media centers dates from 1981, when COMPUTER CAT was developed for Mountain View Elementary School in Colorado. In the next few years, about a dozen vendors entered the school market. This number has remained the same although the list of companies fluctuates. Follett is the front-runner in sales of microcomputer systems to schools, followed by Winnebago; Utlas, Library Corporation, Columbia, and Data Trek, and other vendors also have school users.

In 1985, when I surveyed microcomputer systems users as part of my doctoral dissertation research (Murphy, 1987), only about 160 sites could be identified by vendors. There has been a strong and steady growth in automation in school library media centers since then, evidenced by my estimates of installations given above, and by the latest figures in *School Library Journal*'s (*SLJ*) annual report of school library media center expenditures (Miller and Schontz, 1991). Of the 644 respondents

---

Source: Reprinted by permission from *The Research of School Library Media Centers*, ed. Blanche Woolls (Castle Rock, CO: Hi Willow Research & Publishing, 1990): 163-74. Copyright 1990 Catherine Murphy.

to their survey of 1989-1990 resources (which was mailed to randomly selected *SLJ* subscribers), 30 percent had access to an automated circulation system, 45 percent planned to develop such a system, 7 percent had access to an automated card catalog, and 40 percent planned to develop an automated card catalog. In the two years since this data was collected, I believe that the percentages have increased again as they have done in each of the subsequent *SLJ* expenditures surveys.

The school library media professionals implementing these systems are beginning to regard them as more than library management tools. The OPAC database with full catalog records and a system enhanced for public use can revolutionize subject access to collections and provide an instructional tool for critical selection and analysis of information.

In order to consider the actual or potential impact of automation, it is necessary to define the components of subject access. One researcher included the design of the system itself, the bibliographic record, the user, and the additional tools we load into the system to improve access to the record, such as authority file, indexes, and class schedules (Mandel, 1985). Another writer described the parts of an online system that influence access as the files, functions, and communications of the system, and stated that it is the user interface, that reacts with all three components, which is the most important aspect of the system (Hildreth, 1985).

Others have analyzed what can be done to improve access by focusing on the difficulties encountered by subject searchers in online catalogs. For example, these major problems in subject access have been cited: finding the right subject term, knowing what is in the catalog, increasing and decreasing searching results, entering commands, and scanning long displays (Markey, 1986c). All observers have stressed the interaction between user and system as the major difference between online and card catalog searching.

This paper considers the areas suggested by these writers from the perspective of the state-of-the-art microcomputer OPACs, with a focus on the special needs of the school user. Catalog database development and enhanced subject access are not as well developed in microcomputer systems, nor have they been studied or theorized about to the extent that have big OPAC systems in academic and special libraries. Nor have the needs of online searchers who are children or students received much attention. The next section, about published research and/or theory, therefore includes relevant writings about children's access in the card catalog and studies or theoretical writings related to the big OPAC systems, in order to project implications for access in school OPACs. Early in the history of the OPAC, two phases of development were described, the minimal and the enhanced access stage (Gorman, 1982). The findings reported next are divided into these two stages.

Bibliographic Records for Children's and School Library Materials and the Nature of Access

It has been an accepted theory that simplified cataloging is appropriate for children's materials. This special treatment may provide descriptive cataloging that is both limited and enhanced. At its best, simplified cataloging means conformity to a standard adapted to the needs of children and school users. Adhering to a standard means that records can be shared among systems. At its worst, simplified cataloging implies that local rules substitute for a standard under the assumption that local needs are unique. If a standard is not followed, the catalog cannot be networked.

Following are some developments, issues, and research that have been selected as particularly important in the history of cataloging children's and school library materials. The list is not intended to be exhaustive.

Catalog Use Studies

Prior to the Council of Library Resources (CLR) studies beginning in 1981, the research indicated that it was more common to conduct a known-item (author or title) search than a subject search. In Matthews's (1984) summary of this research, known-item searching was also found to be more successful (66 percent) than subject searching (50 percent). The emphasis on subject access since the CLR studies is not as surprising to staff in children's and school libraries because they commonly assign more subject headings for fiction as well as nonfiction than do staff in other kinds of libraries.

The reports of card catalog use studies do not include many references to school and children's library participation. An important evaluation of students' searching in both card and online catalogs was funded by the first Baber research award (Edmonds and Moore, 1988). The results show that success in searching is developmental in both the online catalog and the card catalog, the eighth grade students having performed better than the sixth and fourth grade students in searching for author, title, and subject cards in identifying call numbers. Surprisingly, all participants in this study were not only more successful in searching the card catalog than the online catalog, but they preferred the card catalog over the online catalog.

Library of Congress and the Annotated Card Program

This program was established in 1966 to provide modified Library of Congress Subject Headings and some special classification numbers, as well as annotations, for children's materials. Despite the availability of this standard, school library media specialists appear to prefer the Sears supplementary list. Other less well known subject heading lists such as the Hennepin County, Minnesota Public Library's list (Berman, 1986) have been developed to reflect children's topical vocabulary. De Hart and Meder (1986) also note the Yonkers, N.Y. Public Library and Carolyn W. Lima's *A to Zoo* list of subject headings for special concepts in children's picture books, as well as earlier American Library Association (ALA) publications of subject headings to describe children's literature. Theoretical analysis of cataloging of children's materials centers on the relation of children's to adult cataloging. Should it really be so different that other cataloging tools, classification systems, and subject heading lists are used? Practice indicates that even into the age of automation, the approaches to improved subject access in children's cataloging vary from adult's cataloging. There are now some CD-ROM databases of MARC records that offer Sears headings as an alternative to LC headings, in response to the school market demand. Ideally, the full LC record, complete with annotations, can coexist with the more appropriate Sears and local headings.

Minimal Level Cataloging

In 1982 the Cataloging of Children's Materials Committee (CCS) of the Resources and Technical Services Division (RTSD) of the ALA, in conjunction with the Children's Literature Section of the Library of Congress, developed special guidelines for standardizing the cataloging of children's materials (works intended for use by children through junior high level, high school level optional) reported in "Guidelines for Standardized Cataloging of Children's Materials," *Top of the News* (Fall 1983). These guidelines recommend adherence to Level 2 descriptive cataloging, which requires that more detail be included, provided for by the AACR2, because of the potential for sharing MARC in all kinds of libraries. Yet many school practitioners are still developing Level 1 records, which exclude elements such as dimensions, other statements of responsibility (such as illustrator), and series information. *Commonsense Cataloging* (Miller and Terwilliger, 1983), a text in use in many school and other small libraries, recommends Level 1 under certain guidelines for materials and when the cataloging staff is limited. A recent report of networking activities (Van Orden and Wilkes, 1989) indicated that slightly more than one-third of the survey participants were following Level 1 guidelines (and the majority also used Sears as the subject authority).

Audiovisual, Software Cataloging

Catalog records for audiovisual materials have not been as readily available in MARC databases. Because these materials are a significant part of school library collections, the lack of MARC records is a major issue. If "homemade" card catalog records for these materials are replicated in the online catalog, important detail may be missing (e.g., running time, content notes). According to the BIBLIOFILE vendor, users in school districts in Montgomery County were sharing original cataloging for audiovisual materials by sending the catalog records to Library Corporation, where the files were combined on a floppy disk and returned to the districts for downloading to the local catalog. Bibliographic Access Network (BAN) is another project generated to share catalog records for materials (including books and other media) not located in the Library of Congress MARC record database. The BAN fiche database, to which a number of state school library systems are contributing and that will be available on a compact disk when it has reached a large enough size, was initiated by the developer of MITINET, a software program that creates records in MARC format (Epstein, 1988).

Research in Conformity to Standards
in the Card Catalog

Earlier studies of practices of school library media professionals in cataloging confirm their lack of adherence to standards. In 1977 Rogers (1979) investigated state supervisors' endorsements of AACR2 for nonprint materials and found that there was a lack of awareness of existing codes and guidelines that were accepted by other professionals. She did a follow-up study in 1982 and determined that there was some progress toward standardization (Rogers 1984). Truett (1984) did a study of the cataloging practices of Nebraska school library media specialists and also found that there was a lack of standardization in the use of rules for choice of main entry. Rogers and others have attributed the school library media specialists' lack of awareness of standards to their isolation from other professionals, lack of clerical help, lack of training in technical services, and the priority of instruction over library management.

Research in Conformity to Standards
in the Online Catalog

In my dissertation investigation of cataloging practices of school library media specialists in microcomputer systems (Murphy, 1987), it appeared that these nonstandard practices were continued into the online age. The majority of the survey respondents were not aware of MARC, AACR2, or RTSD cataloging guidelines for children's materials. This survey was replicated with the Follett circulation system users, and there was an increase in the number of respondents who endorsed the AACR2 and MARC standard, although the majority were still not aware of the RTSD guidelines (Follett, 1986). Follett's efforts to educate their users and the distribution of the survey almost a year later may account for the increase in awareness. (The author's survey was distributed in 1985, although the dissertation was not completed until 1987.)

Cataloging for Developmental
and Curriculum Needs

At the same time that the respondents to the author's survey (Murphy, 1987) were not conforming to AACR2 and MARC, they were creating special headings and notes in the catalog records. The major reason for creating special headings was to access curriculum materials; entries in the notes field were primarily made to indicate the reading level of the material. When this survey was replicated with the Follett circulation system users, the results were exactly the same (Follett, 1986). The use of special terms to catalog curriculum materials in school districts has been noted (Wehmeyer, 1976; De Hart and Meder, 1986). The content of catalog records for curriculum materials in OCLC has also been reported (Kranz, 1987-1988).

Upgrading Circulation Records to Catalog Records

Can a case be made for upgrading brief, non-MARC records in circulation systems to a full MARC catalog database? Some recommend against it, believing that retrospective conversion of the shelf list should be a one-time process to implement an integrated system. However, there are thousands of circulation systems now in school library media centers that were implemented with brief records entered manually because the cost was less than a full scale conversion. If these records have an LCCN or ISBN key, they can be matched against a MARC database for an upgrade to standard records (Crawford, 1987). In the case where there are no MARC records available for an item (and the "hit" rate for school library catalog records is not well established), some vendors may create records in MARC format but without descriptive detail. These records will need a second upgrade, which adds significantly to the cost of conversion. Meanwhile, circulation systems are providing users with limited subject access (which Crawford says is better than no access) via "category" fields identifying curriculum units, genre, and other headings.

The Influence of the Technology Standards

The development of new technology, the system itself, appears to be one of the most positive influences on school library media professionals' adherence to standards. The improved capabilities of the hardware and the computer programmers' acceptance of the importance of standards, have increasingly affected conformity. Again, my research (Murphy, 1987) showed that the school library media specialists implementing OPACs that provided for MARC records and other standards were more disposed toward conforming to these standards than the respondents using systems that did not provide for the MARC format. Rogers (1984) also notes the influence of participation in networks upon the members' adherence to AACR2 conventions.

The development of compact disks containing MARC records from the Library of Congress or other sources has made the standard more available and affordable. Union and local catalogs can coexist on a compact disk, e.g., Western Library Network's LASERCAT, and can also be used for cataloging as well as for patrons' searches of library holdings.

The Influence of Networking upon Standards

The leadership in some state education departments has provided models for shared databases, collection development and interlibrary loan. The exemplary projects include WISCAT in Wisconsin, TIES in Minnesota, and ACCESS PENNSYLVANIA in Pennsylvania. School library media specialists in these states receive planning assistance and sometimes financial support for retrospective conversion of catalog records. Awareness of mainstream standards and the state-of-the-art in development of automation is communicated.

How Much Standardization Is Enough?

The issue of standards continues to be debated in the mainstream library community as well as among microsystem users. One of the realities that tends to be forgotten is that MARC is a communications standard, not a guarantee of content. There are reports about the poor quality of some records received from retrospective conversion vendors. The MicroLIF format for catalog records is a case in point. The format was cooperatively developed by the book and micro-computer system vendors, and although it falls into the category of MARC compatible (which may describe the internal records in many systems), MicroLIF has been rejected by many prospective buyers because it is perceived as less than the standard. (At the vendor's request I became a member of the MicroLIF Standards Committee, and they have made a recent commitment to provide a full MARC record format.) Crawford (1989) describes the acceptable MARC standard as that which can be imported, adapted if needed within the system, yet also exported. Yet some vendors strip the directory and content designators from the record, supplying generic values when they export records (Mellinger, 1989). The designers of the microcomputer OPACs, and to some extent the mainframe systems are included in this group, do not appear to have completely met the challenge of standards implementation because of technology's limitations, the cost, or other reasons. It is difficult to validate the claims of vendors who state that they do conform to standards.

Designing the OPAC System to Meet the Needs of School Users

The online catalog that has passed through the minimal access stage has a database with records in full MARC format, as much as that is possible, and the enhanced stage will provide new features. Enrichments within the MARC record are sometimes considered too costly or too difficult to implement; the features more often recommended to improve subject access are enhancements in system design and additional tools loaded into the system to link to the MARC record. Mandel, Hildreth, Markey, Matthews, Cochrane, and others have made recom-mendations for improvements in these areas based on the CLR and other studies.

The top four choices of the OPAC users in the CLR study, out of a possible thirteen features related to improving searching, were the ability to search a book's table of contents, summary, or index; the ability to view a list of words related to search words, the ability to print search results; and the ability to search by any word in the subject heading (Matthews, Lawrence, and Ferguson, 1983). Some of the recommendations made in earlier card catalog use studies, which Cochrane states have not been fully addressed, are similar to the CLR desired features, such as making available contents notes, in-depth subject analytics, and front and back entries from books; other suggestions are for reversed geographic headings, incorporation of classification schemes, and improved user training (Cochrane, 1985).

The developments, issues, and research related to enhancing subject access discussed below touch upon these user recommendations. The list is not intended to be exhaustive.

Integrated Systems

One of the major advantages of an OPAC over a card catalog, identified early in the history of its development, is the ability to provide status information for an item (Matthews, 1984). Because the circulation system is linked to the catalog, the catalog searcher knows instantly whether the book is in, or if it is out, when it is due to be returned. An integrated acquisitions module provides the status of items on order. Local area networks increase access from points outside of the library area; interfaces with union catalogs and full text databases (a development still in the experimental stage) enhance access to resources beyond the local collection. It is possible that some of the circulation systems recently developed may remain at that stage unless it is recognized that the true benefits in access are at the online catalog stage, which provides full MARC records.

Authority Files and Cross-References

The issue of responsibility for a standard in authority systems is still being debated. Most of the early microcomputer OPACs were without authority files, and their development is still uneven. Matthews (1984) states that prior card catalog use studies have suggested that catalog success rates are directly proportional to the number of *see* references, which tell the user to look elsewhere in the catalog; he and Markey recommend the development in online catalogs of *see* and *see also* references, which tell the user of the existence of related terms (Matthews, 1984; Markey, 1986b, c). The problem in creating cross-references, which are not state-of-the-art in microcomputer systems, is that they are not included in the MARC record and must be loaded separately in a file obtained from the Library of Congress or another vendor or utility. The headings or other entries must then be linked to the appropriate records. As an alternative, some microcomputer systems build the authority files as records are created.

Physical Environment of the Catalog

Some hardware features of the OPAC improve access. The young catalog user has less well developed language skills and is particularly in need of any assistance that replaces typed responses. Touch screens and the mouse/icon combination, even function keys, can make searching easier. The INTELLIGENT CATALOG uses an audio tutor for online help as well as providing a map showing the location of items in the library. Increasing the number of terminals in the library as well as in other areas of a campus or building also improves access.

Communication Features

Hildreth (1985) describes the difficulties of communication in the user interface. These include command and response protocols and display formats, which vary from system to system. The young user may have particular difficulty in moving through menu steps, reading and analyzing the detail of catalog records, identifying call numbers, and even using features that Hildreth declares desirable in system design, such as moving backward and forward among search results, browsing indexes, and retrieving search history.

Searching Strategies

Many of the microcomputer OPACs have now implemented keyword searching, although the fields indexed vary. Keyword searching increases access significantly, sometimes too much, but can be enhanced by Boolean operators to refine searches. Other indexing approaches include right or left truncation (part of the word) and string searching (adjacency). An exciting research study by Lester investigated the extent to which users' subject terms matched Library of Congress Subject Headings (40.1 percent of the time); she applied three search processes to see how they would have increased matches. When all three were applied, the success rate increased almost 100 percent (keyword and Boolean were the single most successful strategies) (Roose, 1988). Interestingly, Lester found that name and geographic authority files did little to augment searching by themselves, but were enhanced when keyword and Boolean searching were added. Lester also experimented with searching anywhere in the MARC record and adding a sounds-like spell checker, and results increased again.

Markey also studied subject searching in the online catalog at Syracuse, and found that of the 859 searches made by 188 users in one day, only 154 (18 percent) exactly matched LCSH, and 5 percent matched LCSH cross-references (Markey, 1986b).

Enhancing the MARC Record Contents

Matthews described a potential database called AUGMARC in which additional content could be added to MARC records (Matthews, Lawrence, and Ferguson, 1983). He described the possibilities of using automated data machines to scan the index and/or tables of contents; it is also suggested that the Cataloging-in-Publication office of the Library of Congress could solicit additional annotations from publishers, or that the library community might request input for certain important titles. The alternatives for enriching the MARC record contents, and there have been experiments such as Cochrane's Subject Access Project (SAP), are to create separate databases or special indexes, and then link them to the catalog record.

There has not been any significant effort to create enriched records for students and children. Some vendors have made efforts to enhance records and make them available (e.g., Follett's database includes grade and reading levels of titles). There are enhancements in school library network records (e.g., analytics created by individual school library staff) that would be valuable to share.

Adding Classification Schedules and Other Indexes or Thesauri to the Online Catalog

Research has been conducted in an experimental online catalog incorporating subject rich terms from the Dewey Decimal Classification Schedules and Relative Index into the subject searching capabilities of the catalog (Markey, 1986a). Earlier research has included the development of PRECIS in Aurora High School in Canada in the 1970s, which allows the catalog user to enter the alphabetical subject heading string at any point (Taylor, 1983). The Children's Media Bank, an online thesaurus that indexed subject subdivisions related to form, curriculum content, and use, was created in 1976-1977 (Hines and Winkel, 1983). Wehmeyer noted the development of computerized lists of terms in university educational systems to index objectives, content, and usage of curriculum materials (Wehmeyer, 1976). These models could provide, or be adapted to, prototype catalogs and be tested by school users.

Implications for Practitioners

1. Although AASL and AECT, and probably most state education departments, have endorsed the MARC communications format as the standard for school library media automated systems, there is no direction at the present time to guarantee minimal content in catalog formats acquired from different bibliographic sources. Minnesota is at least working on such guidelines for school library media centers undertaking a retrospective conversion project.

2. The major issue for building and district library media staff is to select and implement only a system that provides for full MARC cataloging and conforms to other mainstream bibliographic standards.

3. Building and district level library media staff must assume the responsibility for maintaining the integrity of the OPAC database. Editing of records must be in conformity with AACR2 conventions. Archival tapes or disks that reflect current records should be maintained outside of the system.

4. Sources for full cataloging of audiovisual materials should be developed and shared.

5. Enhanced records, which contain annotations, analytics, and other subject-rich information, should be developed and shared.

6. Networking of systems, including financial support for local implementation, needs to be developed by state education department leaders.

7. Training in MLS and school media certification programs, as well as in continuing education programs, should include education in technical standards and services.

8. Publications should be solicited that describe state-of-the-art OPAC development and retrospective conversion.

9. Conferences should provide settings for workshops on new technologies and reports about automation experiences. Publication of the proceedings of these conference programs should be encouraged, (e.g., the Retrospective Preconference at AASL in Dallas in 1989 proceedings will be published in a forthcoming *SLMQ* issue).

10. School library media specialists who are implementing systems have the responsibility to communicate to their vendors the ways in which the systems are not meeting the needs of users. Documentation of searches and other aspects of OPAC development will support claims made to vendors via users' group meetings, letters, etc.

Implications for Researchers

The Council of Library Resources established priorities early in the development of OPAC systems. A similar agenda for the school library media community should be prepared by a national group or association.

1. First, establish a foundation for research similar to the Council of Library Resources, which was financially supported by a granting agency and vendors. Identify potential grant-givers for such a foundation to assist the development of research in online catalog use by children and students.

2. Monitor OPAC development in schools by conducting state-of-the-art and evaluative studies of systems.

3. Test the behavior and analyze the user requirements and requests of children and student searchers. Some of the research conducted in the big OPAC systems, such as logs of searches matching searchers' terms and online indexes, with appropriate enhancements to improve access, could be replicated with young users. Research should be carried out in experimental models as well as in existing OPAC in use at school library sites.

4. Encourage school library media specialists to conduct simple research projects locally, such as keeping logs of search terms and successful and unsuccessful matches in the OPAC. These local projects could provide a large pool of information.

5. Investigate state networking systems and report successful models. Report the differences in financing. Evaluate the cost-effectiveness of interlibrary loan.

6. Experiment with interfaces between microcomputer systems and free text databases/distributed networks.

7. Investigate and report the most cost-effective and efficient methods of retrospective conversion, including the upgrading of circulation records.

8. Evaluate the quality of MARC records supplied from various sources.

9. Investigate the best means for instructing students in online catalog use.

10. Investigate the impact of the online catalog on the role of the library media specialist.

11. Investigate the influence of a computer programmer position in the school on the implementation of OPAC catalogs and networking.

References

Berman, Sanford. "A Selection of Hennepin County Library Subject Headings for Children's Material." In *Cataloging Special Materials: Critiques and Innovations*, 172-175. Phoenix, Ariz.: Oryx Press, 1986.

Cochrane, Pauline. "Classification as an Online Subject Access Tool: Challenge and Opportunity." In *Improving LCSH for Use in Online Catalogs*, edited by Pauline A. Cochrane, 148-149. Littleton, Colo.: Libraries Unlimited, 1986.

_____. *Redesign of Catalogs and Indexes for Improved Online Subject Access.* Phoenix, Ariz.: Oryx Press, 1985.

Crawford, Walt. *MARC for Library Use*, 2nd edition. Boston: G. K. Hall, 1989.

_____. *Patron Access: Issues for Online Catalogs.* Boston: G. K. Hall, 1987.

De Hart, Florence E., and Marylouise D. Meder. "Cataloging Children's Materials: A Stage of Transition." In *Cataloging Special Materials: Critiques and Innovations*, edited by Sanford Berman, 71-97. Phoenix, Ariz.: Oryx Press, 1986.

Edmonds, Leslie, and Paula Moore. "Fresh Findings: Catalog Use Studies." Author's notes from a report given at ALA Midwinter Conference, San Antonio, Tex., January 11, 1988.

Epstein, Hank. "Improving the Retrospective Conversion Hit Rate for School Libraries: The BAN Fiche." *School Library Media Quarterly* (Summer 1988): 255.

Follett Software Company. "Online Public Access Catalogs in Public and School Libraries." Report of survey results to the author, who developed the questionnaire for Follett Software Company, June 1986.

Gorman, Michael. "Thinking the Unthinkable: A Synergetic Profession." *American Libraries* 13 (July/August 1982): 473-474.

"Guidelines for Standardized Cataloging of Children's Materials." *Top of the News* 40 (Fall 1983): 49-55.

Hildreth, Charles R. "The User Interface in Online Catalogues: The Telling Difference." In *Online Public Access to Library Files: Conference Proceedings*, edited by Janet Kinsella, 111-132. Oxford, U.K.: Elsevier, 1985.

Hines, Theodore C., and Lois Winkel. "A New Information Access Tool for Children's Media." *Library Resources and Technical Services* 27 (January/March 1983): 94-105.

Kranz, Jack. "Cataloging of Curriculum Materials on OCLC: A Perspective." *Cataloging & Classification Quarterly* 8 (1987/1988): 15-28.

Mandel, Carol. "Enriching the Library Catalog Record." *Library Resources and Technical Services* 29 (January/March 1985): 5-15.

Markey, Karen. "Searching and Browsing the Library Classification Schedules in an Online Catalogue." In *Online Public Access to Library Files: Second National Conference*, edited by Janet Kinsella, 49-66. Oxford, U.K.: Elsevier, 1986a.

_____. "Subject Searching in Library Catalogs." In *Improving LCSH for Use in Online Catalogs*, edited by Pauline A. Cochrane, 243-256. Littleton, Colo.: Libraries Unlimited, 1986b.

_____. "Users and the Online Catalog: Subject Access Problems." In *The Impact of Online Catalogs*, edited by Joseph R. Matthews, 35-69. New York: Neal Schuman, 1986c.

Matthews, Joseph R. *Public Access to Online Catalogs.* New York: Neal Schuman, 1984.

Matthews, Joseph R., Gary S. Lawrence, and Douglas K. Ferguson. *Using Online Catalogs: A Nationwide Survey.* New York: Neal Schuman, 1983.

Mellinger, Michael J. "Automation Standards: Myth vs. Reality." *Library Journal* 14 (June 1, 1989): 72.

Miller, Marilyn L., and Marilyn L. Schontz. "Expenditures for Resources in School Library Media Centers, FY '88-'89." *School Library Journal* 37 (August 1991): 32-41.

Miller, Rosalind E., and Jane C. Terwilliger. *Commonsense Cataloging*, 3d edition. New York: H. W. Wilson, 1983.

Murphy, Catherine. "The Microcomputer Stand-Alone Online Public Access Catalog in School Library Media Centers: Practices and Attitudes Toward Standardization." Ph.D. dissertation, Columbia University, 1987.

_____. "A Primer on Automating the School Library Media Center." *Electronic Learning* 8 (May 1989): 34-37.

_____. "The Time is Right to Automate." *School Library Journal* 35 (November 1988): 42-47.

Rogers, Jo Ann V. "NonPrint Cataloging: A Call for Standardization." *American Libraries* 10 (January 1979): 46-48.

_____. "Progress in Access to Non-Print Materials." *School Library Media Quarterly* 12 (Winter 1984): 127-135.

Roose, Tina. "Online Catalogs: Making Them Better Reference Tools." *Library Journal* (December 1988): 76-77.

Taylor, Audrey. "Alternatives in Action: The Aurora COM/PRECIS Experience." *School Libraries in Canada* 13 (Winter 1983): 3-8.

Truett, Carol. "Is Cataloging a Passe Skill in Today's Technological Society?" *Library Resources & Technical Services* 28 (July/September 1984): 268-275.

Van Orden, Phyllis J., and Adeline W. Wilkes. "Networks and School Library Media Centers." *Library Resources and Technical Services* 33 (April 1989): 123-133.

Wehmeyer, Lillian. "Cataloging the School Media Center as a Specialized Collection." *Library Resources & Technical Services* 20 (Fall 1976): 315-325.

Robert Skapura

The Card Catalog and the Tower of Babel

16

No matter which automated catalog a person tries first, the immediate reaction by almost everyone is, "How easy." The speed of the search, the display of the "found" items, and the ease with which one can expand or narrow a search cannot fail to impress the user. To go back to using a traditional card catalog after any extended period is similar to using a manual typewriter after regularly using a word processor.

Although more and more libraries are installing automated catalogs, something interesting is happening in our profession that goes unnoticed unless a person has had the chance to search on a number of systems. Every company seems to be creating its own search terms and its own way of moving from screen to screen.

The public library in the community where I live has a computerized catalog (Auto-Graphics). The local junior college has one, too (Innovative Interfaces). UC Berkeley has two concurrent systems, one to search the entire UC system (MELVYL) and another to search only the UC Berkeley libraries (Gladis). I will avoid making any comment on the proliferation of names and acronyms for the various catalogs. However, between the systems in the Bay Area and the ones I've seen through the Technology Committee for AASL, a very disturbing trend seems to be developing. There seems to be little common terminology among the various automated catalogs.

No matter how cumbersome the traditional card catalog is to use, a student using the catalog drawers in different libraries could expect a great deal of commonality: drawers in alphabetical order, cards in alphabetical order by top line. There are some variations and exceptions in filing rules, but basically the card catalog presents the patrons throughout the United States with, to use a computer term, a common search interface.

Source: Reprinted by permission from *California Media and Library Educators Association Journal* 14, no. 1 (Fall 1990): 35-37.

That is no longer true in the automated world. What the user first sees on the screen and how the user responds to the prompts is very different depending on which system the student is using. A rose may be a rose, but a search by a different name can be simply confusing. For example, many systems automatically ignore the lead articles "The," "A," and "An" at the beginning of a title. The computer does what we tell our students to do, so the librarian never has to explain that one has to pretend that the lead articles are not there. I was in Cleveland this summer and used a system from one of the largest companies in the library automation market. After I came up with zero titles for a search I knew should produce something, I noticed a printed card taped to the right side of the computer keyboard. On the card, among other directions, was the admonition to drop the lead articles when typing in a title. Apparently a computer big enough to run an oil refinery could not ignore the lead articles in a title search. The point here is not what makes a good user interface. The point is that if a student regularly uses a system that drops the lead article, it is likely that he would assume the catalog in another library would also. My students would probably not look at a little printed card taped to the side of the computer.

Anyone who has had to learn *another* word processing program knows how hard it is to shift thinking, to learn how to move comfortably from screen to screen, and to "unlearn" familiar commands. The American Library Association has shown little interest in suggesting a standard search interface for the online catalog. I'm not sure at this point that anything can (or should) be done. I would, however, like to see my teaching have a carryover for my students no matter what library they are in.

The first step for librarians is an awareness that there is a problem. I feel strongly that the initial steps of a search should be the same no matter what automated catalog a student is using. The terms that a search screen uses should have common meanings. The problem becomes apparent when you realize that, depending on the system, students must choose among the following search terms: Find, Search, Browse, Keyword Search, Quick Search, Express Search, Full Search, Topical Keyword Search, and Extended Search. What is a *quick search* anyway? And is the opposite a *slow search*? It's not that these terms are incorrect or lack meaning. It's that their meaning is specific to the system being used. As professionals we, not the vendors, should create standards. We cannot blame companies for the confusion if we say nothing.

There will be a natural evolution over the next few years, with weaker systems falling by the wayside. During this time we should be very aware of what works and what doesn't work in helping our students search for materials.

In June 1990, 12 companies were selected by the members of the AASL Technology Committee to participate in an all-day preconference on "The Automated Catalog." The screens that follow show basically the choices a student sees when beginning as search. I do not wish to imply that one is better than another, simply that they are very different and that the difference will confuse students when they move from system to system. In fact, all the programs allow for expanded or Boolean searches. The opening screens in no way testify to the power of the search engine that, in a sense, powers the catalog. This is not an evaluation of systems or even features. It is only to illustrate the confusion of screens that is already out there in libraries.

For the sake of comparison, only the words from the opening search screens are duplicated here. Some systems use menu bars or arrows, others use function keys, and some require that you press a number or type in a letter. In reproducing the screens, everything but the words the student sees has been stripped off. The "look" of the screen is gone; only the choices remain.

Mandarin-Media Flex
MANDARIN

Search by:
1. Subject
2. Title
3. Author

General Research Corporation
LASER GUIDE

Search by:
1. Subjects
2. Authors
3. Titles

Winnebago Software
WINNEBAGO CAT

Search by:
1. Keyword (From Sub or Titles or Notes)
2. Change Boolean
3. Include Author
4. Browse Words

CLSI
CL-CAT

Search by:
1. Subject
2. Author
3. Title
4. Author and Title
5. All Categories
6. Call Number

Library Corporation
INTELLIGENT CATALOG

1. FIND ANYTHING: to find any word, words, or phrases
2. VIEW CATALOG: to see the library catalog arranged alphabetically
3. BROWSE TOPICS: to go directly to your area of interest

Auto-Graphics
IMPACT

1. Find by Author
2. Find by Title
3. Find by Subject
4. Find All
5. Find by Call Number
6. Find by Number
7. To Word Search

Columbia Software
CLS-OPAC

Search by Index:
1. Author Index
2. Subject Index
3. Title Index
4. Call Number Index

Search by Keyword:
5. Author Keywords
6. Subject Keywords
7. Title Keywords
8. Note Keywords
9. Mixed Keywords

Follett Software
CATALOG PLUS

Search by:
1. Title
2. Author
3. Call Numbers
4. ISBN/LCCN
5. Subject
6. Series
7. Keyword

Western Library Network
LASERCAT

Keyword Search:
1. Author
2. Title
3. Subject

Browse Search:
4. Author
5. Title
6. Subject

Brodart
LE PAC

1. BROWSE: Search through alphabetical lists of Authors, Titles, and Subjects
2. EXPRESS: Type in your search information

Nichols
MOLLI

1. Full Search
2. Quick Search
3. Call Number Search

Dynix
SCHOLAR

1. Search All
2. Subject
3. Title
4. Author
5. Other Searches
6. Quit Searching

Patricia A. Hooten

Online Catalogs: Will They Improve Children's Access?

17

Libraries are rapidly changing the methods used to gain access to library resources. Electronic access via online or CD-ROM systems is becoming the norm in using indexing/abstracting services and library catalogs. While most libraries continue to build collections that are predominantly paper based, many have shifted to technologically based access to these materials.

The OPAC Scene

Online public access catalogs (OPACs) are already in the second generation of development, with third-generation features beginning to surface. First-generation OPACs, many of which, although technologically obsolete, remain widely used, provide access to library holdings via traditional card catalog access modes: author, title, and indexer-assigned subject headings(s). First-generation online catalogs are often derived from circulation control systems based upon shortened MARC records.

While second-generation OPACs provide author, title, and subject search capabilities too, they include the additional ability to search keywords. Through keyword access, second-generation OPACs allow the user to search any word or words that come to mind in any indexed field. This capability relieves the user from the necessity of matching a subject search term with an indexer-assigned term or of knowing the order of terms in a title. Complex searches using Boolean operators (the terms "and," "or," or "not" to delimit topics in an automated search), truncation, and limitation by date of publication and language are possible in most second-generation OPACs today.

Source: Reprinted with permission of the American Library Association, from *JOYS*, Vol. 2, No. 3, "Online Catalogs: Will They Improve Children's Access?," by Patricia Hooten, pp. 267-272, © ALA, 1989.

Third-generation online catalogs will provide interactive search assistance, error-correction features, and additional information about the contents of materials. For example, catalogs of the future may include each book's table of contents. If today's innovations are indicative of trends, future users can expect to access library holdings and indexing and abstracting services, and libraries will negotiate with database vendors to load indexing and abstracting products directly onto the library's computer system.

What Online Catalogs Can Offer

From most evidence, automated bibliographic access appears superior to traditional card catalog access. Online access allows the user the potential for searching from physically remote sites. By telecommunications, libraries can relieve the user from physically coming to the library. By use of multiple terminals, different users can access the same online information simultaneously. Access is not limited by a queue of users waiting for a particular card catalog drawer.

As noted above, automated access provides the potential for increasing search efficiency. Users can limit or expand search terms through use of Boolean operators. Keyword access allows the user to search by terms in current and everyday usage.

Online catalogs can facilitate resource sharing among libraries, allowing users to access the holdings of nearby libraries and enabling libraries to practice cooperative collection development. As resources are shared, libraries can reduce unnecessary duplication and can build in each library specialized collection strengths that, when shared among several libraries, can strengthen each library's ability to meet the needs of its users.

Children's Bibliographic Access in the Online Environment

While access to information resources is generally improved by online catalogs, it is unclear if all users will benefit from OPACs. Most researchers who have examined online catalog use have chosen academic and public library environments, focusing on adult users. Only one study has been reported that has examined children's effectiveness in using online catalogs.[1]

Children and youth need access to information to find answers to problems, to pursue independent discovery of who they are and who they want to become, to obtain information that can assist them to overcome their weaknesses and enhance their strengths, and to allow them to build lifelong information-seeking patterns. Age should not be a barrier to the ability to access, receive, and utilize information.

How, then, are children and youth affected by libraries' decisions to automate access to library holdings? In the short term, children may be affected more than adults by the move to online catalogs, because they use multiple library systems (public and school libraries) that are frequently implementing quite different automation hardware and software systems at different rates. In the future, many children will likely be confronted with use of one type of access mode in the public library and another type in their school library. Initially, these different modes may consist of a traditional card catalog and some form of automated catalog and later two different kinds of automated catalogs.

While there is no study to support the assertion, it appears that public libraries are automating at a faster rate than school libraries. This assertion is especially true when elementary school libraries are considered. Furthermore, when school libraries do automate, they often opt for stand-alone automated circulation systems. School libraries rarely choose advanced integrated systems that link acquisitions, circulation and catalog functions—the systems most often chosen by public libraries. For example, in 1987, the latest year of published figures, the automation marketplace witnessed the installation of 78 integrated systems in public libraries compared with nine in school libraries.[2] School libraries have generally found the cost of integrated systems to be outside their budgets and have opted for simpler stand-alone systems, even though school library automation needs are no simpler than those of other types of libraries.

In the near future, then, youths will likely be confronted with one type of access system in the schools and another type in their public library. Even if both libraries are automated, youths will need to be proficient in the use of two different automated systems.

Skills Needed to Use Traditional and Online Catalogs

The intellectual and physical skills needed to use traditional catalogs and online catalogs differ. Traditional card catalogs require users to follow an alphabetical sequence, to know filing rules, to determine when a term falls between pairs of terms to position the search initially, to maintain order among a number of steps, and to identify individual information elements contained on a card.

The skills required for online catalog use are heavily dependent upon the terminal hardware (i.e., touch screen or keyboard) as well as the software chosen. Touch terminals require intellectual skills and an accessing sequence almost identical with the traditional card catalog. The user searches a touch terminal by browsing through a list of search terms and selecting the one desired (or, if it is not there, the one preceding it) from the alphabetical display. Through successive screens of terms, the system presents progressively narrower lists until the term sought is found. As with the traditional card catalog, the user must possess alphabetical skills and the ability to position the term successively between pairs or terms until the chosen one is located.

Touch-screen terminals can require many screens and multiple selections before reaching the chosen term. With CLSI/Pac 1, the user on the average must make between six and nine touches to get to a record.[3] Using touch screens can become quite tedious with large files. This difficulty in use is heightened when the system makes the user start the selection process over from the beginning if a mistake is made.

Touch-screen terminals may be more difficult for children than traditional card catalogs because they are less concrete. Each item in a card catalog is physically represented by at least one individual card. Children can see the number of drawers and cards between the terms "Badminton" and "Basketball" and estimate where "Baseball" would fall between them. With online catalogs, the user has no indication of the number of entries between any pair of terms.

Touch terminals require as many ordered steps as traditional card catalogs. Keeping track of where one is in the sequence of steps is more difficult with touch terminals since the screens change, erasing the preceding reference points. In contrast, the card catalog remains constant and the user can review steps by visually checking drawers already searched.

Keyboard terminals provide the user with keyword access, not available through touch screens. With keyboard access, the user keys in terms and chooses the categories (fields) in which the terms are to be searched. With keyword access, the order in which the user enters the terms does not affect the search success.

The intellectual skills needed for use of keyword access on keyboard terminals are quite different from browse access by touch-screen terminals. Keyword access on keyboard terminals requires accuracy in spelling, spacing, and punctuation when typing in terms. In addition, the user must decide which category—author, title, subject, or all categories—is appropriate for the chosen keyword. While it is logical to expect that children's physical dexterity may affect their success in the use of keyboard terminals, librarians in the field report children also have dexterity problems with touch screens, frequently aiming above or below the actual line they need to press.

The only study to date of children's effectiveness in use of online catalogs, a study based upon use of touch-screen terminals, concluded that children have difficulty in using OPACs.[4] A comparable study using keyboard terminals is under way at Orchard Park Elementary School in Carmel, Indiana. The Carmel study is examining children's effectiveness in accessing materials by author, title, subject, and all categories using keyword and browse modes on CLSI's CL-CAT online catalog system. Of particular interest is the question of whether children may be more successful in using keyboard than touch-screen terminals.

Libraries will continue to automate functions, including their catalogs, because of the overall benefits automation can provide. Access to information by children and youth will be affected as libraries introduce electronic forms of information access. What, then, can libraries and librarians do to assist children in the use of these new forms of access?

What Librarians Can Do

1. Many online systems allow individual libraries some flexibility in the design of search-screen and help messages. While no optimal format for messages has emerged, there are several standard guidelines that can make screens more readable for children and youth as well as adult users.

    Patrons can read and comprehend screens with low information density more rapidly than dense screens. Density of information is controlled by the length of message lines, vertical spacing between lines, and use of uppercase and lowercase letters. Narrow lines of text and a combination of uppercase and lowercase letters allow text to be read quickly. Vertical spacing providing blank lines between groups of elements make the groups more evident and messages more immediately understandable.

    While improved readability results from controlled spacing and information density, it must be balanced against making records so long that they require multiple screens. The goal should be to provide a maximum number of database records on a single screen in a format that utilizes layout features known to facilitate readability.

2. Libraries may also have the option of selecting the labels to be used in displays. Labels for MARC record fields should be spelled out fully so that the user is not forced to decode. Crawford suggests the following labels:

    AUTHOR for the main entry (100-130)
    TITLE for the title statement (245)
    EDITION for the edition statement (250)
    PUBLISHED for publication, distribution, etc. (260-262)
    MATERIAL for the physical description (300-305)
    SERIES for each series statement (400-490)
    SUBJECT for each subject added entry (600-699)
    OTHER ENTRY for each added entry (700-740, 796-798)[5]

3. Some online systems allow the use of multiple languages for menus and screen messages. This capability will support separate menu and screen terminology on terminals in children and adult areas. Such a capability allows library staff to develop screens and help messages tailored for youth and presents children searching options appropriate to their skill levels. If children are confused by complex Boolean searching, truncation, and limitation by date, instructions in the use of these features may be omitted from the terminals children will use. Children may be instructed to use those search features that they can master, while adult patrons may be provided instruction in the use of the complex searching features of sophisticated online systems.

4. In addition to designing readable screens and messages, librarians can press library administrators to specify in their requests for library automation proposals that vendors offer user-friendly features especially helpful to children, such as spelling checkers, a popular feature of word processing programs. Standard installation of spelling aids on online catalogs would be invaluable to children using keyboard-access terminals. Systems that disregard initial articles in search phrases would also be useful. The disregarding of initial articles will ensure that inputting "The Adventures of Alice in Wonderland" and "Adventures of Alice in Wonderland" in a title browse search will both provide successful results.

5. Librarians in public and school libraries can assist children by working cooperatively. Librarians in each institution need to be informed about the access modes used in the other institution. School librarians, who provide most of the formal instruction in traditional catalog use, may want to work with public librarians who already have online systems to introduce students to the use of such systems.

6. School and public librarians can press their administrations to explore cooperative automated systems. A growing number of model public and school joint automation projects are forming. Especially in small and

midsize communities, where the public library and school system can often find reasons to develop a joint database, students, teachers, and taxpayers can benefit from this efficient use of community resources.

Youth Deserve Consideration

Children have no direct representation in decisions about the choice of automated systems or the design of optional features for these systems. Children do, however, represent a significant portion of public library users and are the dominant users of the estimated 73,000 public school media centers in this country. Based upon sheer numbers, students represent a library population whose needs deserve to be examined.

While the card catalog provided imperfect information access, it was predictable and fairly consistent across libraries. The transition period from use of traditional card catalogs to online catalogs will be a period of inconsistency and diversity that will be especially problematic for children, who generally thrive on consistency. Librarians will need to muster all forces available to them to press for online catalog features and programs that will enhance children's effectiveness in the use of OPACs. There is too little evidence to say exactly what effect online catalogs will have on children or what the magnitude of their needs will be regarding these new access tools. Observations are needed from the field to provide a clearer understanding of needs and use.

Notes

[1] Leslie Edmonds, "The Birth of a Research Project," *Top of the News* 43, no. 3 (Spring 1987): 233-35.

[2] R. A. Walton and Frank R. Bridge, "Automated System Marketplace 1987: Maturity and Competition," *Library Journal* 113, no. 6 (April 1, 1987): 33-44.

[3] Nathalie Nadia Mitev, Gillian M. Venner, and Stephen Walker, *Designing an Online Public Access Catalogue: Okapi, a Catalogue on a Local Area Network* (London: The British Library, 1985): 108.

[4] Leslie Edmonds, Paula Moore, and Kathleen Mehaffey Balcom, "An Investigation of the Effectiveness of an Online Catalog in Providing Bibliographic Access to Children in a Public Library Setting" (unpublished report submitted to ALA in fulfillment of a Baber Grant, 1988).

[5] Walt Crawford, *Bibliographic Displays in the Online Catalog* (White Plains, N.Y.: 1986): 79.

Usage Patterns in a Middle School Library: A Circulation Analysis

18

The increasing availability and use of computerized circulation systems that provide for the collection and compilation of data in a convenient form make it possible for librarians, even in small libraries, to analyze collection use in a manner previously available only to university and special libraries.[1] The present study uses data accumulated by a commercially available computerized circulation system to analyze the usage patterns of a middle school library, and to suggest ways in which the data available may be interpreted and used to decide upon future collection management and acquisition policies.

Analysis of the Data

The circulation program used was Circulation Plus produced by the Follett Software Company (Chicago, 1986). Version 6.2 of this program was installed in September 1986 on an Apple IIe with a ProFile hard disk. Version 7.0 with expanded capacities for record searching and collection-use analysis was installed in June 1987. This program records the number of books circulated to each student, the number of times each book has circulated since the installation of the program and for a time period specified by the user, and calculates statistics on relative collection use in the form of collection composition percentages and related circulation percentages. Unless otherwise stated, all calculations in this study were based on counts compiled by the program during the 1986-87 school year.

This study was conducted at a suburban middle school with grades six to eight. The school opened in 1980 and is part of a district that has six elementary schools, three middle schools, and a high school. The average school population is 580 students.

Source: Reprinted by permission of the ALA from *School Library Media Quarterly*, (Spring 1988): 200-203. In "Current Research" by Jacqueline C. Mancall, Column Editor.

The library contains 10,606 books (18 books per student). This collection is typical of junior high schools and of schools of its size nationwide based on data collected by Miller and Moran.[2] They found a mean of 10,861 books per collection with 18 books per student for junior high schools and a mean of 10,014 books with 17 books per student for schools with 500 to 699 students. The collection is widely used by the students; during the 1986-87 school year, 96 percent of the students in the school checked out at least one book.

There are marked differences in the extent of use of the collection by the three grades (see table 1).

TABLE 1
Use of Library Materials by Students and Faculty

	No. of students	Items borrowed	Items/ student	% of total use
Sixth grade	225	5,287	24	53
Seventh grade	147	1,392	10	14
Eighth grade	181	1,101	6	11
Special-education classes	46	810	18	8
Faculty and other libraries	—	1,174	—	11
Miscellaneous	—	221	—	2

These result from three different patterns of use by the students and strongly support the findings of previous studies that the classroom teacher is the greatest influence upon the use of the library. Fifty-three percent of the circulation was to the sixth grade. The sixth-grade reading teachers brought their classes to the library at two-week intervals for a library skills lesson and to select books for book reports and for leisure reading. The teachers stayed with the classes and assisted with instruction and book selection. The sixth grade also contains all the sixth-grade gifted students in the school district (approximately 70), and these students were frequent users of the library materials for classroom assignments in social studies and science. Four special education classes with a total of 46 students contributed 8 percent of the library use. Two of these classes came to the library at two-week intervals to obtain materials, and teachers of the other two encouraged the use of the library by their students.

The seventh-grade students used the library mainly to obtain materials for leisure reading. This use contributed 14 percent of the total circulation and a mean use of ten books per student. These students did use the library for classroom assignments, but this use was principally of noncirculating materials.

Eighth-grade students obtain books for their reading class from a source other than the school library, reflected in their low contribution to the total circulation (11 percent). The eighth-grade reading class centers around the reading of young adult novels dealing with themes such as family relations, addictions, handicaps, aging, and death. These students read an average of 16 books during the school year. Most of these books are supplied by the reading teacher from an extensive classroom library, and the school library is used as a supplement for books that are not in her collection. The library is also used as a source of circulating materials for reports for social studies and English.

Materials circulated to faculty members consist primarily of audiovisual materials and collections of books to be used in the classroom. Audiovisual materials, including computer software, may be borrowed only by the faculty but are freely available to the students for use in the library. This in-house use is not recorded by the circulation system.

The Circulation Plus program compiles data on both collection composition and circulation so that the librarian knows both the size of the various components of the collection and the amount of use each receives (see table 2).

TABLE 2
Composition and Use of the Collection
Total Circulations from September 26, 1986, to June 10, 1987

Range	No. of Items	% of collection	Total circulations	% of circulation	Use factor
001–099	689	5.94	521	5.22	0.89
100–199	102	0.88	143	1.43	1.64
200–299	100	0.86	63	0.63	0.72
300–399	765	6.60	372	3.73	0.58
400–499	37	0.32	25	0.25	0.78
500–599	903	7.79	460	4.61	0.58
600–699	892	7.69	696	6.98	0.91
700–799	1,013	8.74	1,095	10.98	1.26
800–899	182	1.57	225	2.26	1.47
900–999	1,673	14.43	522	5.23	0.37
Hardcover fiction	2,389	20.61	3,085	30.92	1.49
Paperbacks	893	7.70	1,993	19.98	2.65
Short stories	81	0.70	53	0.53	0.76
Reference	778	6.71	93	0.93	0.14
Audiovisual materials	986	8.51	477	4.78	0.56
Other	109	0.94	153	1.53	1.63
Total	11,592		9,976		

In this library, the paperback range is primarily fiction with approximately 5 percent nonfiction books. Eighty percent of the paperbacks are in reinforced bindings; the remaining 20 percent are the softbound form. Biographies have been cataloged as 092 and are part of the 001-099 range. The only reference materials that circulate are several sets of older encyclopedias. Others contain mainly professional materials for use by the faculty and a few miscellaneous items. Periodicals and vertical-file materials were not circulated through the computer.

Use of the computerized circulation system allows the librarian to monitor the relative use of the collection with time and observe possible changes in collection use that could result from classroom assignments and changes in student reading interests. However, in this library, there was very little variation in the overall use of the collection with time. The basic pattern of circulation of library materials was established as early as two weeks after the opening of the library in September and varied little during the course of the school year (see table 3). There were marked changes only in the 001-099 range and the hardcover fiction ranges. These changes could be attributed to both an increased use of biographies instead of fiction for book reports and to the increased use of books on computers.

TABLE 3
Percent Circulation of the Ranges of the
Collection During the 1986–87 School Year

Range	October 8 (1,007 circula- tions)	November 5 (2,442 circula- tions)	January 12 (4,996 circula- tions)	March 30 (7,452 circula- tions)	June 10 (9,976 circula- tions)
001–099	1.69	2.01	2.90	4.84	5.22
100–199	1.19	1.19	1.26	1.29	1.43
200–299	0.10	0.12	0.40	0.44	0.63
300–399	3.67	3.03	3.50	3.53	3.73
400–499	0.10	0.20	0.34	0.30	0.25
500–599	4.07	4.87	4.34	4.29	4.61
600–699	6.65	5.90	5.76	6.25	6.98
700–799	11.62	11.47	10.47	11.47	10.98
800–899	1.09	1.15	1.20	1.29	2.26
900–999	6.65	4.50	4.72	5.37	5.23
Hardcover fiction	33.47	35.38	34.95	32.03	30.92
Paperback fiction	18.07	18.35	21.12	20.85	19.98
Short stories	1.09	1.31	0.84	0.60	0.53
Reference	0.40	0.98	0.70	0.82	0.93
Audiovisual materials	6.85	6.35	5.04	4.78	4.78
Other	3.28	3.19	2.44	1.84	1.53

It could be anticipated that the percent of circulation of a range of a collection would be in direct proportion to the percent of the collection comprising that range. However, in almost all ranges of the collection, there is a variation between the percent of circulation of the range and the percent of the collection comprising that range. The 900-999 range comprises 14.43 percent of the collection but yields only 5.23 percent of the circulation, while the paperbacks comprise 7.7 percent of the collection but yield 19.98 percent of the circulation.

The number obtained by dividing the percent of circulation by the percent of the collection responsible for that circulation has been named the "use factor" by Bonn.[3] A high use factor will indicate that that range is being very actively used, while a low use factor will indicate little use of a collection range. The exact interpretation of the value of the use factor as a guide to collection management has not been clearly established. Lancaster has designated areas with a use factor less than one as underused.[4] Underused materials could no longer be relevant to the curriculum or to the interests of the patrons, and further purchases would not be warranted; or they could be so dated as to be unusable, and weeding and purchase of new materials would be necessary. He designated materials with a use factor greater than one as overused. These are areas that may need addition of new materials to meet present and future demands by patrons.

To obtain a better correlation between the value of the use factor and the actual use of the materials in the range, the percent of the range actually circulating and the frequency of that circulation were determined. The number of circulations for each book was determined from the computer printout of titles in the designated range. The percent of the range circulating is calculated by dividing the number of books that have circulated during the time period by the total number of books in the range. The mean circulation rate is obtained by dividing the total circulation for each range by the number of books in that range that have circulated (see table 4).

TABLE 4
Use Factor, Mean Circulation Rate, and Percent of Range
Yielding 100 Percent of Circulation for That Range
from September 26, 1986, to June 10, 1987

Range	Use Factor	Mean circulations per book	% of range giving 100% circulation	% of range circulating 9 or more times
900–999	0.37	1.55	21.0	0
300–399	0.58	1.78	27.3	0.4
500–599	0.58	1.65	30.3	0
200–299	0.72	1.65	37.6	0
Short stories	0.76	2.14	35.8	0
400–499	0.78	1.56	43.2	0
000–099	0.89	2.00	38.0	0.1
600–699	0.91	2.06	37.8	0.2
700–799	1.26	2.45	44.2	1.1
800–899	1.47	2.09	59.9	1.1
Hardcover fiction	1.49	2.81	45.0	1.9
100–199	1.64	2.70	51.9	1.0
Paperbacks	2.65	3.45	64.0	4.1

A direct relationship exists between the use factor and the percent of the range giving 100 percent circulation, the mean circulation rate and the percent of the range circulating nine or more times. The value of nine has been chosen arbitrarily as the point at which a duplicate copy of the book should be obtained for this collection based on observation of use and patron requests. This, of course, will vary from library to library, and with the time period under consideration. The values for the 800 range vary from those that would be anticipated from the value of the use factor. This range was widely used for a short period of time when several classes did poetry units at the same time. The high demand over a short period of time resulted in a high percentage of the range circulating with a low mean circulation rate.

These measures are time-dependent and will vary during the course of the time period being observed. They provide a measure of the relative use of the collection not the absolute use. The percent of range used is a time-dependent factor, but for the paperbacks, at least, it is not a linear function. Eight weeks after the beginning of school, 38 percent of the paperback range had circulated, and 56 percent had circulated after 16 weeks. After 38 weeks, 64 percent of the range had circulated. In other words, the increase in range use decreased with time and appears to be slowly approaching a maximum value. This indicates that only a certain number of books in the range may ever be used and that the remainder may not circulate no matter how long they remain upon the shelf.

Hardcover fiction and the paperbacks together compose 28 percent of the collection and 50 percent of the total circulation. They both have use factors greater than one (1.49 and 2.65, respectively) that could indicate the need for future purchases to supplement the present material. Indeed, given the high use of these materials, a considerable expenditure might be needed to bring the number of books in line with the amount of use they are receiving. Since both are fiction with almost no in-house use, circulation analysis seems an excellent method for evaluating their use.

Shelf samples were collected to determine the past use of the books in these two ranges that had not circulated during the 1986-87 school year. Sample sizes were chosen to achieve 5 percent error and 90 percent confidence.[5] The hardcover sample contained 241 books, and the paperback sample contained 138 books. Books for the sample were selected by choosing titles at an appropriate interval chosen to give the desired number of books from an alphabetical list of titles printed by the computer. The last date of circulation was determined from the date slip in the book. The number of missing books was obtained from an inventory conducted in June 1987. The shelf samples gave quite similar numbers of missing books, and an inventory is not necessary to obtain this data. The combined data from the 1986-87 computer records, the shelf sample, and the inventory are presented in table 5.

TABLE 5
Use History of the Hardcover Fiction and Paperback Ranges
for the Seven School Years in Which the Library Has Been Open

Date of last circulation	% of hardcover fiction (n = 2,388)	Cumulative % of hc. fiction	% of paperbacks (n = 896)	Cumulative % of paperbacks
1986–87	45.0	45.0	63.9	63.9
1985–86	11.8	56.8	9.9	73.8
1984–85	12.0	68.8	4.6	78.4
1983–84	5.7	74.5	4.6	83.0
1982–83	3.5	78.0	2.6	85.6
1981–82	1.5	79.5	1.4	87.0
1980–81	0.9	80.4	1.2	88.2
Never circulated	17.3	97.8	3.2	91.4
Missing	2.4	100.2	8.8	100.2

These data present a picture of how the books in these two ranges have been used during the history of the library. The number of missing books has been included in the calculations because they were included in the calculation of collection use by the computer during the year. Seventeen percent of the hardcover fiction has never circulated compared to 3 percent of the paperback fiction. Although this figure is lower than that of 40 percent reported for the number of uncirculated books in the collection of one university library,[6] it still represents an expenditure of funds for unused items.

It has been observed that library materials that have not circulated within a certain time period have little probability of circulating again.[7] In June, sampling was used to determine the date of the next to last circulation for both hardcover and paperback books that had circulated during the 1986-87 school year. It was found, for both ranges, that 99 percent of the circulation during the year came from books that had circulated during the 1983-84 school year or later. In other words, those books that have not circulated since the 1982-83 school year have about a 1 percent chance of circulating again. This data could be used as a criterion for weeding these ranges, and at least 6 percent of the hardcover fiction and 5 percent of the paperbacks could be removed from the collection without decreasing the circulation of these ranges.

How can all the parameters examined so far influence future purchase decisions for the hardcover fiction and paperback ranges? For the hardcover fiction, 6 percent has only a small probability of circulating again and 2 percent is missing. This means that 92 percent of the books have the probability of circulating in the future. Of these books, only 45 percent did so during the current school year; 47 percent (1,122 books) of the collection was not used during the 1986-87 school year. Assuming that future use will not vary excessively from past use, it would seem that the present collection with a use factor of 1.49, and 3.7 books per student is adequate for the needs of the school population for the coming year with duplication of highly circulating titles, replacement of missing titles, and routine addition of newly published materials.

The data for the paperback books show that 9 percent are missing, and 5 percent have only a small chance of circulating again; thus 86 percent of the collection has a probable chance of circulation. Of this, 63 percent circulated during the present school year. Only 23 percent of the range (206 books) that has a probability of circulating was not used at all during the year. This range with a use factor of 2.65 and 1.36 books per student may not be able to meet future demands, and a significant number of new books seem to be needed to meet future demands of the patrons though the exact size of the number cannot accurately be determined from the available data.

The use of the paperbacks compared to that of the hardcover fiction suggests that the paperback format alone is more appealing to the students. To test this, the total number of circulations for each of 132 titles available in both paperback and hardcover in the library were compared using the student's t-ratio test. The results of this test support the hypothesis that there is no difference in the circulation rate of the two forms ($t = 0.719$, $df = 132$, significance $= 0.01$).

Other factors besides format are influencing student choices of one form or another. Analysis of the "best-seller" titles for these two ranges (those titles circulating seven times or more during the nine-month school year) shows that student interests and ease of location may be the strongest determining factors in their selection of either the paperback or hardcover form. Of the paperbacks that circulated seven or more times, 55 percent were from popular paperback series such as *Sweet Dreams* or *Choose Your Own Adventure*. The remainder were teenage romance novels, science fiction, TV and movie tie-ins, and books on rock music. In other words, titles that are primarily available only in paperback.

The "best-seller" list for hardcover fiction books was composed primarily of books by well-known authors such as Lloyd Alexander, Judy Blume, Beverly Cleary, and Paula Danziger along with Ellen Raskin, Scott O'Dell, Katherine Patterson, and Louise Fitzhugh. Thirteen titles by Alexander, Blume, Cleary, and Danziger are available in both paperback and hardcover forms. Comparison of the number of circulations for these titles using the student's t-ratio test showed a strong preference for the hardcover forms of these books ($t = 4.23$, $df = 12$, significance $= 0.01$). Paperback books are shelved in no order in this library. Obviously, students find it more convenient to locate a hardcover book by an author whose name they know than to go rummaging around the paperback shelves to locate it.

These results suggest but do not prove that the students do not select reading materials from one format to the exclusion of the other. They indicate that students are selecting paperback books for topics mainly available in paperback. When they know the author of the book, they choose the hardcover because it is easier to locate. A better test of their preference for format could be done if the paperbacks were arranged alphabetically by author as the hardcover books are.

Conclusion

The use factor serves as an indicator of the relative use of the collection, but no exact value may exist denoting a sharp dividing point between overuse and underuse. The results presented here are more consistent with a range of values that indicate normal collection use with overuse and underuse represented by high and low points at the ends of the range. Dowlin and Magrath have proposed that one standard deviation below the mean use factor represents underuse and one standard deviation above the mean represents overuse.[8] If this measure is applied to the present collection, underuse would be indicated by values lower than 0.42 and overuse by values higher than 1.64. This would agree with the observation that the paperbacks with a use factor of 2.65 is an overused range.

The use factor alone cannot serve as a guide to collection management decisions. Aguilar has used a combination of the use factor and a measure of interlibrary loan requests as a guide to decision making.[9] The present study has shown that a direct relationship exists between the use factor and both the percent of the range circulating and the percent of the range circulating at a very high frequency. These two measures, more than the use factor itself, may form a basis for the determination of the need to add new materials to the collection and for determination of the most effective collection size in terms of books per student. No quantitative values can serve as the sole basis for decisions on building a collection; they must be coupled with considerations of the needs of the curriculum and qualitative evaluation. Conversely, the latter two parameters should be coupled with quantitative measures to be most effective in making decisions about the collection.

The results presented here give only an initial look at the type of analysis that can be conducted with the data accumulated by a computerized circulation system. Several comprehensive reviews of the literature are available to assist those who are interested in conducting circulation analysis studies.[10] Similar analyses could be applied to nonfiction. The Circulation Plus program provides for the grouping of items into categories that can be used to study the circulation of materials in subject area ranges such as medieval life or drug abuse where materials can be found in more than one class of the Dewey decimal system. Analysis of this type of use could be more informative to the school librarian than the study of the rather arbitrary divisions of the Dewey system.

Circulation analysis has its limitations. It cannot evaluate the quality of a collection. It cannot measure the in-house use of materials nor can it measure which materials were actually used by the students as opposed to being merely checked out. It cannot predict which materials will definitely circulate in the coming year, but it can identify items that will probably not circulate again. It can give a quantitative picture of how a collection has been used. It can serve as an evaluation tool for past acquisition decisions and provide in quantitative terms a justification for both past and future expenditures. And, to whatever extent past use predicts future use, it can be part of the decision-making process for formulation of future collection management and acquisition policies.

Notes

[1]Allen Kent and others, *Use of Library Materials: The University of Pittsburgh Study* (New York: Dekker, 1979); Adelaide A. Del Frate, "Use Statistics: A Planetary View," *Library Acquisitions: Practise and Theory* 4:248-53 (1980).

[2]Marilyn Miller and Barbara Moran, "Expenditures for Resources in School Library Media Centers, FY 85-86," *School Library Journal* 33:37-45 (June/July 1987).

[3]George S. Bonn, "Evaluation of the Collection," *Library Trends* 22:265-304 (Jan. 1974).

[4]F. W. Lancaster, "Evaluating Collections by Their Use," *Collection Management.* 4:15-43 (Spring/Summer 1982).

[5]Herman Burstein, *Attribute Sampling: Tables and Explanations* (New York: McGraw-Hill, 1971).

[6]Allen Kent and others.

[7]Stanley J. Slote, *Weeding Library Collections-II.* 2d ed. (Littleton, Colo.: Libraries Unlimited, 1982).

[8]Ken Dowlin and Lynn Magrath, "Beyond the Numbers: A Decision Support System," in *Proceedings of the 1982 Clinic on Library-Applications of Data Processing* (Urbana: Univ. of Illinois, Graduate School of Library and Information Science, 1983).

[9]William Aguilar, "The Application of Relative Use and Interlibrary Demand in Collection Development," *Collection Management* 8:15-24 (Spring 1986).

[10]Dorothy E. Christiansen, C. Roger Davis, and Jutta Reed-Scott, "Guide to Collection Evaluation through Use and User Studies," *Library Resources and Technical Services* 27:432-40 (Oct./Dec. 1983); F. W. Lancaster, *The Measurement and Evaluation of Library Service* (Washington, D.C.: Information Resources Pr., 1977); Rose Mary Magrill, "Evaluation by Type of Library," *Library Trends* 33:267-95 (Winter 1985); Jacqueline C. Mancall, "Measurement and Evaluation of the Collection," *School Library Media Quarterly* 10:185-89 (Winter 1982); Paul H. Mosher, "Quality and Library Collections: New Directions in Research and Practice in Collection Evaluation," in *Advances in Librarianship*, V. 13, (Orlando, Fla.: Academic Pr., 1984).

Catherine Murphy

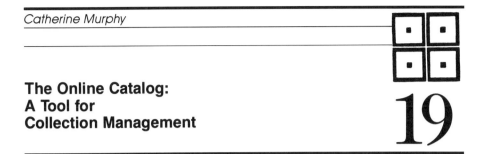

The Online Catalog: A Tool for Collection Management

19

Introduction

Collection management in all libraries involves a series of cyclical tasks. It is not a once-a-year process of inventory, weeding, and ordering of materials. The overall objective of collection management is to provide materials that meet the specific needs of library users. This objective can be broken down into individual tasks of identifying the collection materials, monitoring their use, and identifying what might be removed from or added to the collection. Some problems associated with this evaluative process might be addressed more effectively if an online public access catalog (OPAC) has replaced the library's card catalog and shelf list. Ideally the OPAC will be integrated with a circulation system and/or an acquisitions module, providing the optimum benefits for collection management.

This article will review some collection management problems that have been documented in the literature and will discuss how OPACs are used to assist the school library media specialist. Collection management issues that are not as readily affected by automation will not be addressed in this paper.

The differences in automated systems will also be discussed, since the influence of the OPAC on collection management depends to some extent on its sophistication — although even the simplest database program can be used as a tool for access to a part of the collection and analysis of its use. The OPAC or any automated system is not a panacea for all collection management problems, nor is it recommended for every school library media center. First, it must be determined that installing an OPAC meets some desired objectives that are not being met by manual systems. Second, the library professional must have the motivation, the energy, and the expertise to undertake a project

Source: Reprinted by permission of the ALA from *School Library Media Quarterly* (Spring 1987): 154-57.

project of this size. Third, institutional support from the school administration and staff is needed to see the project through.

Using OPACs to Address Collection Management Problems

Accessibility of the Collection

The primary goal of the school library media program is to provide materials that support the instructional objectives of the curriculum. Achieving this goal is often hampered by access problems due to inadequate cataloging of materials, user's difficulties in locating materials in the card catalog, and backlogs of unprocessed or uncataloged materials. Automated cataloging may increase retrieval of material by improving the quality of the catalog record and by speeding up processing.

Improving Access to the Collection

The extent to which access can be improved will depend on the features available in the OPAC system. Here are some ways that access to materials can be made easier and more specific.

1. Online help menus, browsing screens with author, title, subject, or call-number ranges, and keyword or Boolean search strategies, will increase the chances of a successful search. If the catalog record is detailed (preferably MARC [machine-readable cataloging] format) and appropriate fields of the record are available for online searching, the search range is extended. Research is under way or recommended in two directions—enhancing the record beyond the present contents of the MARC format and considering alternative strategies for internal indexing structures to improve retrieval of more specific information about materials in the collection.

2. If the OPAC is integrated with circulation and/or acquisitions, the status of the material can be provided to the user (on the shelf, borrowed, on order). This process saves time for the user and may suggest that another search be made.

3. Vendors are now providing books and other media compatibly processed for the library's automated system. Bar codes are applied to the media for circulation purposes and these data are entered on a floppy disk to download onto the hard disk at the local OPAC site. The complete catalog records might also be acquired on floppy, tape, compact disk, or via modem, and downloaded into the local system. If the entire process of entering data is automated, the media is placed on the shelf without any delay.

Availability of the Collection

No library can house all of the materials requested by patrons because of budget and space constraints. Borrowing materials from other libraries was a time-consuming, cumbersome, and limited process before the automation of cataloging and catalogs. Networking systems enhanced by technology can enlarge collections beyond the walls of the individual school library media center and can systematize the interlibrary loan process.

Improving Availability of the Collection

The extent to which library material is available to meet immediate needs in the local library depends on both the network system set up to borrow and return materials from member libraries and the technology available to process the request (development being more evident in some states than in others). These are variations of networking currently available to some OPAC users, all of which include school library media centers as participants.

1. Electronic Bulletin Board. If several libraries in a district or region have OPACs that are not connected by hardware (or even if they have card catalogs), and if they have a modem that can access a bulletin board, requests can be left for material not available in the local library. Each participating library would have to check the bulletin board daily and leave a response if the request can be met.

2. Local Area Network (LAN). If there is more than one library site in a building or on campus, terminals at each site can be cabled together. Users at different sites can access the union catalog in one location to determine what is available in other libraries.

3. Multilibrary Network. Libraries with memberships in bibliographic utilities, e.g., OCLC, can access the collections of remote libraries participating for interlibrary loan purposes. Members of regional or branch networks that have a turnkey system can receive the same service. Some states have developed interlibrary loan systems using COM (Computer Output Microform) catalogs, e.g., Wisconsin or compact disks, e.g., Pennsylvania, to develop a union catalog that can be duplicated and placed at each site. Networking also encourages the planned development of special collections in local sites.

Balance of the Collection

Phyllis Van Orden has stated that quantitative recommendations from standard sources for the acquisition of materials in different formats and subject areas must be balanced with the needs for materials to meet instructional objectives of the school which the school library media center serves.[1] If the catalog is automated and integrated with a circulation system, the maintenance of statistical records will be greatly facilitated, and relationships between the content of the collection and its use can be revealed.

Adjusting the Balance of the Collection

The collection mapping techniques recommended by David Loertscher can provide comparisons between what is in the collection and what is recommended by standard references, and between what is in the collection and what is being circulated.[2] A simple database and spreadsheet program such as Appleworks can computerize the record-keeping, he suggests. If the stand-alone microcomputer OPAC is integrated with a circulation or acquisitions module, the same type of statistics can be gathered for collection development and management purposes. The turnkey OPACs provide the most sophisticated record-keeping possibilities for these purposes.

1. A database inventory printout by Dewey ranges can immediately provide the numbers of books and other media in each subject category. Loertscher suggests making a chart using bar graphs to demonstrate the comparison between quantitative recommendations from several standard sources and what is contained in the local collection. This exercise may indicate that additional funds are needed to increase materials in the local collection; the statistics generated are used to support the request at annual budget time, as was reported at a recent conference.[3]

2. Also illuminating is the comparison between what is in the collection and what is being used. If circulation statistics are printed out by the same Dewey ranges, and bar graphs are used to compare the percentages of materials circulated and the percentages of materials held, it may reveal that some subject areas are being used more than others that a collection balance adjustment needs to be made. One high school librarian found that within the 500 classification, books about insects had the highest circulation figure. Although it is likely that such statistics will vary from school to school, if computerized statistics were to be kept in a number of school library media centers, an important profile of school library media collection use could be developed.[4]

3. A third chart, showing the numbers of unsuccessful searches in the OPAC by subject categories, would be another indicator of a needed collection adjustment balance. Not all OPACs keep track of unsuccessful searches, but if the OPAC does have this capability, comparisons could also be made between acquisitions recommended by faculty, acquisitions recommended by students, acquisitions for replacements, and the circulation figures for these groups.

Alternatives for OPAC Development

The history of OPACs in libraries is only about ten years long. The development of MARC on magnetic tape in 1969 made possible the development of online networks for cataloging and interlibrary loan, e.g., the Online Computer Library Center (OCLC). By the early 1970s turnkey circulation systems were provided by vendors, e.g., CL Systems, Inc. (CLSI), which led to the next development, expanding circulation records to provide a public access catalog. The advent of the microcomputer in the late 1970s provided a less expensive means for automating cataloging, catalogs, and other technical services. Software programs to produce catalog cards were early products developed for microcomputer use in school library media centers. Simple programs for overdues and general database software adapted to library applications became more common. The introduction of Computer Cat by Betty Costa in 1981 at Mountain View Elementary School in Colorado was a pioneer OPAC development in a school library media center.[5]

There are now a number of other microcomputer programs marketed and sold to an increasing number of school library media centers. These programs have different features, and the interested buyer must plan carefully to purchase a system that will meet the needs and resources of the individual school. Figure 1 outlines the different types of systems with examples: general database programs may be as simple as Appleworks or as complex as Inmagic; stand-alone microcomputer software also varies in system design; the turnkey OPACs are the most powerful and costly systems available for minicomputers as well as microcomputers and as such are not found in as many school library media centers. The development of the compact disk has provided options for online cataloging and union catalogs that reduce or eliminate telecommunication costs, and this technology is being interfaced with the turnkey systems as well as the stand-alone systems.

Microcomputer, stand-alone general database software; e.g., Appleworks, Microsoft Works	Microcomputer, standalone special application software; e.g., Intelligent Catalog, CAT PLUS	Turnkey system, includes hardware, software, maintenance, training, support; e.g., CLSI
Usually limited to a special collection; manual data entry	Total collection of local records stored on hard disk or CD possibly with CD interface	Various options for access to local records, union catalog, online ILL/cataloging
Less expensive, usually uses available hardware, software; may need hard disk	Moderate expense for extended RAM/hard disk. Added costs possible for conversion and interfaces, support	Most expensive, package includes everything, monthly charges by vendor/telecommunications
Easiest to implement	Moderately difficult to implement, support not as readily available	Most extensive to implement but vendor provides installation, training, and support
If integrated with spreadsheet can increase functions	Should be integrated package providing circulation, catalog, and cataloging, perhaps acquisitions and serials	Integrated with other services, by same or different vendor

Fig. 1. Alternatives for OPAC development.

A Summary—Considerations
Before Automating

It is not the intent of this article, nor is it possible in this space, to cover all of the prerequisites for undertaking an automation project. It was stated earlier that the school library media specialist should have a clear goal for computerizing the catalog, personal commitment to the project, and institutional support for it. These are a few other considerations.

1. Develop technological literacy. It is important for the professional to read the general literature about online catalog development to acquire a broad perspective of the possibilities and the problems of automation. An important way of acquiring information is to attend conference programs and visit the vendors' exhibits at these conferences. Some vendors offer demonstration disks of products, either free or for a small charge. Before making a decision about a particular product, a request should be made to the vendor under consideration for names of current users. These users might be contacted in order to answer questions or to arrange a site visit. To develop awareness, as many opportunities as possible should be explored.

2. Do a needs and resources assessment. After a general awareness level has been established, school library media specialists can zero in on their local situations. What are the specific benefits that can be expected if the catalog and/or circulation system are computerized? Some schools decide not to automate when their manual systems are judged adequate. Look to the future, however, and assess what is happening with automation in the local region or at the state level. Networking possibilities will affect choices and benefits. How much money is available to implement an OPAC? All professionals should experiment with general database applications to experience firsthand what automation can or cannot do. What other resources are available to develop automation, both personally and within the institution? It takes more than money to develop an automation project successfully. When products on the market have been previewed to meet institutional goals and resources, a plan and time line for implementation can be developed.

3. Consider retrospective conversion options carefully. One of the biggest concerns in developing an OPAC is how the shelf list will be entered into the computerized catalog, complete with up-to-date cataloging information. There are a number of options: entering an identification number on a floppy disk that will be sent to a utility or other provider of complete catalog data and returned on some medium for transfer into the local system, contracting with a vendor to pick up the shelf list and handle the entire electronic conversion, searching a compact disk by identifying number or title and transferring the record to the OPAC hard disk, or a combination of these methods. The kinds of conversion available will vary according to the OPAC vendor's provision of services and interfaces with other products. The issue of cataloging standards is

paramount. If an OPAC is developed with nonstandardized records, it will be more difficult and costly to upgrade and transfer these records at a later date.

4. Evaluate what the vendors can provide in ongoing support. The prospective purchaser of an OPAC should carefully investigate the kinds of support that vendors can provide after the OPAC software and/or hardware is purchased. The vendor's share of the market, and the availability of support mechanisms such as a toll-free hot line, local area representatives, a newsletter, and organized users groups should be appraised.

Notes

[1]Phyllis J. Van Orden, "Issues about Collection," in *The Collection Program in Elementary and Middle Schools*, (Littleton, Colo.: Libraries Unlimited, 1982): 49-56. The same discussion is in the Van Orden book about high school collection programs.

[2]David Loertscher, "Collection Mapping," in *Appleworks for School Librarians* by May Lein Ho (Fayetteville, Ark.: Hi Willow Research & Publishing, 1985): 109-21. A more complete treatment of collection mapping appears in a subsequent volume by David V. Loertscher and May Lein Ho, *Computerized Collection Development for School Library Media Centers*, Hi Willow Research and Publishing, 1986.

[3]"Collection Development 1990s and Beyond," presented by the AASL Supervisors Section at the American Library Association Conference, New York, N.Y., June 1986.

[4]Bob Hammill, "Improving Collection Development through Low Cost Automation," *Computers in the Media Center News* 6:5 (Spring 1986): 6.

[5]Betty Costa and Marie Costa, "Microcomputer in Colorado — It's Elementary," *Wilson Library Bulletin* 56 (May 1981): 676-78.

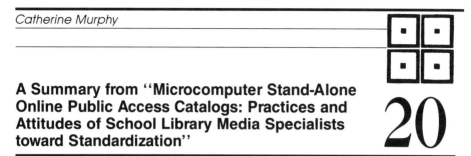

Catherine Murphy

A Summary from "Microcomputer Stand-Alone Online Public Access Catalogs: Practices and Attitudes of School Library Media Specialists toward Standardization"

20

Studies by JoAnn Rogers and Carol Truett have demonstrated that the standard format established by the *Anglo-American Cataloging Rules,* 2d edition (*AACR2*) was not accepted nor practiced by the majority of school library media specialists.[1] Various reasons—the pressure of both managerial and instructional duties, not enough clerical assistance, and lack of training in cataloging—have been offered in the literature as explanations for this nonconformity.

In light of the research just cited, I theorized that school library media specialists would also develop and maintain microcomputer catalogs in the same nonstandard fashion as they have kept the card catalogs.[2] This seemed likely to occur even with development of larger automated systems because there was not a consensus or standard in design. Furthermore, the microcomputer technology of the early 1980s did little to promote adherence to the MARC standard.

To test my hypothesis, two checklists were developed to use in evaluating currently available online public access catalogs. One checklist (see figure 1) covered points that indicated the degree to which the program supported a standard record. The second list covered points related to one's ability to locate subjects.

In addition to the question of standard records, a major issue in automating catalogs is subject access. This is a critical issue because enhancing the limited availability of traditional subject access is the real goal in automating catalogs. The average searcher will be able to access multiple, interrelated subjects almost instantly in an OPAC. Based on recommendations in the literature, I devised a checklist to measure access (see figure 2).

Source: Reprinted by permission from *School Library Media Annual* 6, ed. Jane Bandy Smith (Englewood, Colo.: Libraries Unlimited, 1988): 154-59. Copyright 1988 Libraries Unlimited.

1. Access points automatically created according to AACR2

2. Full or at least a brief MARC record format with tags

3. Authority control for at least name files

4. An ISBN/LCCN identifying field

5. A bibliographic utility link or record transfer program

Fig. 1. OPAC's minimal features to conform to standards. Adapted from Judy McQueen and Richard W. Boss, "Selecting Sources of Machine Readable Bibliographic Records and/or Cataloging," *Library Technology Reports* 21 (November-December, 1985): 622-23.

Online enhancement of subject access would go beyond these basic levels to provide improved searching or indexing features and/or add information to the bibliographic record itself.

1. Catalog records up-to-date

2. Online searching by first word to access conventional fields conforming to AACR2

3. Authority file for at least names

4. "See also" references indexed

Fig. 2. Minimal features that provide traditional subject access. Adapted from recommendations in Michael Gorman, "Thinking the Unthinkable: A Synergetic Profession," *American Libraries* 13 (July-August, 1982): 473-74.

Fifteen microcomputer online catalogs marketed in 1985 were evaluated. Most software programs (12) were nonstandard in design; that is, records they produced did not conform to standards. These nonstandard OPACs were labeled non-MARC; the other three were described as MARC systems because they had most of the standard features. In terms of subject access, the non-MARC systems did not provide authority control or cross-referencing. These are serious deficiencies that result in limited subject access and search performance.

A second aspect of this study was to survey 161 sites involved with OPACs, either currently OPAC users or in the planning stages of OPAC development. The survey form (first reviewed by five experts in the field) included demographic and personal questions as well as questions investigating bibliographic practices and attitudes related to standards and access.

Findings of the Study

Responses to the questionnaire (see table 1) indicated an overall lack of awareness by the respondents of cataloging standards. There appeared to be both a lack of understanding of related acronyms (although those used in the questionnaire were defined) and a lack of knowledge of cataloging guidelines. In fact, there was a nonconforming stance against established guidelines that was evidenced by the number of missing responses and marginal notes. There was more support for using the standard MARC format than there was a belief that there should be a brief or special MARC format for schools. However, actual practice of participants did not conform to this support for standard MARC.

Table 1.
Responses for standard bibliographic practices and attitudes.

PRACTICE	YES	NO	MISSING
Use AACR2 guidelines	47.0%	29.0%	22.9%
Record ISBN or LCCN	34.4%	49.0%	16.7%
Use special guidelines for cataloging children's materials	28.1%	52.1%	19.0%

ATTITUDE	AGREE	DISAGREE	MISSING
Endorse MARC format	49.0%	34.3%	16.7%
Endorse brief MARC record	37.5%	45.8%	16.7%
Endorse school MARC record	43.8%	40.6%	15.6%

When variables in the study were reviewed for their influence upon practices and attitudes toward standards, the OPAC system itself was found to be the most influential variable. Those respondents using the more standard systems were generally more conforming. Interestingly, these participants were generally from larger, more urban school districts.

Responses to questions about subject access (see table 2) revealed there seem to be special cataloging needs in a school library media center. Unlike other types of libraries, the majority of study participants reported using Sears over LC (although incredibly, almost 15 percent either did not respond or were using some "other" subject heading list). Over one-half of the respondents found traditional subject access less than adequate, which may indicate that other factors prevent implementing a desirable cataloging treatment.

Table 2.

Responses for subject access practices and attitudes.

PRACTICES REPORTED MOST OFTEN	PRACTICES REPORTED LEAST OFTEN
Use of Sears Subject Headings	Use of LC and "other" heading lists
Added entries: analysis, nonprint	Added entries: illustrator
Subject enhancements: curriculum units	Subject enhancements: maturity of readers
Notes enhancements: reading level	Notes enhancements: learning objectives

ATTITUDES	AGREE	DISAGREE	MISSING
Cataloging of children's materials should be simplified	54.2%	38.5%	7.3%
Traditional subject headings are adequate	40.6%	52.1%	7.3%
Added entries to record are essential	73.9%	21.9%	4.2%

The majority of respondents did *not* report making added entries or subject or note field enhancements, although 73.9 percent agreed that making enhancements was essential. When enhancements were made, they were mostly school-focused (e.g., curriculum units, analysis, reading level). The users of MARC (i.e., standard) OPACs were less likely than the non-MARC users to create enhancements to the record. It might be theorized that either the adequacy of the MARC record for MARC users or deficiencies of non-MARC OPACs (including the need to key in all data) influenced this practice.

In general, the most important variable in terms of practice and attitude toward standards and subject access is the OPAC system itself. While library media specialists in the survey and opinions cited in the literature favor catalog systems that use a MARC format for each record, in 1985 most of the OPACs available did not conform to the MARC standard. (In 1991, there is fairly universal conformity to the MARC standard.)

Notes

[1]JoAnn V. Rogers, "Progress in Access to Non-Print Materials." *School Library Media Quarterly* 12 (Winter 1984): 133; Carol Truett, "Is Cataloging a Passe Skill in Today's Technological Society?" *Library Resources & Technical Services* 28 (July-September 1984): 268-75.

[2]Catherine Murphy, "Microcomputer Stand-Alone Online Public Access Catalogs: Practices and Attitudes of School Library Media Specialists toward Standardization," Ph.D. dissertation, Columbia University, 1987.

Kathleen W. Craver

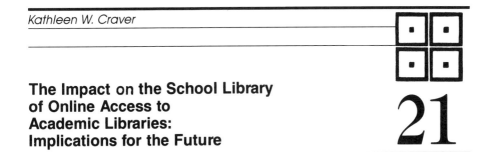

The Impact on the School Library of Online Access to Academic Libraries: Implications for the Future

21

Introduction

The purpose of this article is to discuss the results and implications of a study concerning the impact of online access to neighboring academic libraries by college-bound high school students to determine the following: (1) the degree of academic library use in connection with college-bound high school senior research projects, and (2) the nature of academic materials used. The primary focus was to determine if an increase occurred in the use of academic libraries based upon the availability of an academic online catalog in a school library. Two relational hypotheses were proposed: (1) access to an academic online catalog in the school library is directly related to the number of bibliographic citations obtained from academic libraries, and (2) access to an academic online catalog in the school library is directly related to the diversity of library materials cited.

To test these hypotheses, a database was constructed which consisted of 153 bibliographies compiled by high school seniors during the years 1983 through 1986, in conjunction with debate projects. The classes of 1983 and 1984 were represented by 73 bibliographies from students who had no school library access to an academic online public access catalog (OPAC), whereas the 80 students in the classes of 1985 and 1986 had an OPAC available to them at the school. In each of the four years, the bibliographies were comprised of between 25 and 50 citations.

Source: Reprinted by permission from *Catholic Library World* 60, no. 4 (January/February 1989): 164-68.

Previous Research

A comprehensive search of the literature failed to identify any studies pertaining to the influence of online access and the use of academic libraries by high school students. However, studies relative to online catalog users and the use of academic libraries were found. Research associated with the online catalog tended to confirm the idea that younger students preferred the online catalog to the card catalog because of its time-saving features and increased access to library materials from a single location. Literature concerning the use of academic libraries by high school students revealed a determination on the part of a certain number of high school students (usually college-bound) to access academic libraries despite the existence of formidable barriers and a lack of prior academic library instruction.[1]

Study Background

Site Description

The location selected for this study was University High Laboratory School at the University of Illinois at Urbana-Champaign. Students are admitted, regardless of race, color, gender, or creed, on the basis of their ability to meet the academic standards of the school. In a review of previous classes, enrollment in college ranged from 95 percent to 98 percent with 85 percent graduating.[2] An analysis of the study population (members of the classes 1983 through 1986) revealed that all but two participants applied to college during their senior year.

University High School Library Description

The school library, which consists of approximately 13,000 volumes and 1,000 audiovisual items, is a departmental library of the University of Illinois Libraries. As members, students receive a patron identification card that enables them to check out materials from any departmental library, as well as at 27 off-campus libraries, via the online catalog of the University of Illinois Library.[3] Beginning in August 1984, University High School Library was equipped with a public-access computer terminal with which students could search for, and request, materials. Prior to that time, students who wished to use LCS (the University of Illinois Library Computer System) needed to access it on their own initiative at the main, undergraduate, or another departmental library, all located approximately a half mile away.

The collection of the UHS Library may be described as "balanced" within the majority of subject areas. Materials are purchased in several foreign languages, including German, French, Latin, and Russian. As a result of extensive senior debate activities, the level of acquisition in some subject areas is equivalent to many undergraduate collections, particularly in the social sciences.[4]

Research Assignment Description

During their senior year at University High School, each student is required to complete a long-term research project, which involves the preparation of a detailed debate-brief pertaining to a socially relevant topic. For this project, each student is recommended to (1) consult and use all types of libraries, (2) cite approximately 15 to 20 bibliographic sources in a 15- to 20-page written paper, and (3) use a diversity of current materials, such as periodicals, books, government documents and reports, and newspapers. Any source that students cite in their bibliographies must be footnoted in the text of their debate-brief.[5]

University of Illinois Online
Catalog Background and Development

The development of the online catalog began at the University of Illinois in 1978 with the implementation of the Library Computer System.[6] At the time of its installation, LCS was considered to be the initial component of the "online catalog," and was somewhat limited in "content of record and access."[7] LCS, by design, contains a number of short bibliographic records that include "call number, main entry heading, title proper, edition statement, place of publication, date, volume and part information, and status information (holdings, locations charges, etc.)."[8] The holdings of each library "can be searched from any of more than six hundred terminals in the state by codes and search keys."[9] Permissible searches consist of (1) author, (2) author/title, (3) title, and (4) call number. Once found, entries can be used to charge, discharge, renew, reserve, and recall materials. All of these commands (including charging items from remote locations) may be performed directly by library users if they have access to a public computer terminal and a valid identification number.

However, LCS was not viewed as a complete replacement of the card catalog, despite the improvement it represented in searching manual files. A supplementary system, which included (1) the display of the full bibliographic record, (2) access by subject, (3) linkage to LCS, and (4) statewide union catalog capabilities, was needed.[10] In August 1984, such a system was linked to LCS. Entitled Full Bibliographic Record (FBR), it contained information about subject, series, author, and title for most books cataloged since 1975, and most serials cataloged since 1977. FBR presently includes the access points provided on catalog cards, as well as access by additional points of information. For example, it enables users to search the bibliographic file by author (personal and corporate), subject (personal, uniform title, and geographic), and series (personal, title and corporate). To link the two components, a user-friendly interface was designed that "uses natural language to provide a menu-driven system that presents the user with the choice of the most commonly used access commands. These are (1) author, (2) author/title, (3) title, (4) call number, and (5) subject."[11] The interface program is available on IBM Personal Computers. Its improvements over LCS are that (1) the user-friendly interface routes all the relevant inquires to the LCS component without requesting any assistance from the user, (2) users are not required to know command structures as they are for LCS, (3) the user may search by subject, and (4) more detailed circulation and charging information is supplied.

In August 1984, the University High School Library received a public terminal that permitted access to the University of Illinois online catalog (LCS and FBR combined). Its installation established, therefore, an even, two-year division between those students who did and those who did not have access to an on-site OPAC. These two-year pre-online catalog and post-online catalog environments provided the researcher with an opportunity to study the impact which the availability of this technology had upon the use of academic libraries by high school students.

Methodology

The project required the use of two methods to test each hypothesis. The first involved the use of citation analysis. The bibliographic citations were classified into five categories: (1) books and monographs, (2) periodicals, (3) newspapers, (4) school library vertical file materials, and (5) government documents, reports, and pamphlets. Each citation was searched using the online catalogs at the University of Illinois Library, the Champaign and Urbana public libraries, and the card catalog at the University Laboratory School to determine the library facilities used for each citation.

The second method relied upon the use of a survey. A 27-item questionnaire was designed to obtain information concerning means of locating information and the use of finding tools in various libraries. "Finding tool" inquiries requested information regarding student use—or nonuse—of the card and online catalogs, and library preferences from which to check out materials. "Locating information" questions gathered data pertaining to students' actual use of various library facilities and types of materials used from each library. From the classes of 1983 and 1986, 114 usable questionnaires were received, resulting in a response rate of 74.5 percent.

Data Analysis

The student questionnaires were employed in two procedures. First, they were analyzed in the aggregate to permit appropriate comparisons to be made concerning various questions for the classes of 1983 through 1986. Second, the questionnaire responses were examined individually, thus serving as a cross-check to the citation analysis of each student's debate-brief bibliography. The 153 debate-brief bibliographies were computed into aggregate totals for the classes of 1983 through 1986. This procedure permitted a comparison of academic library use between pre-online catalog student users (classes of 1983 and 1984) and post-online catalog student users (classes of 1985 and 1986). The aggregate totals were used as a basis for further statistical treatment to ensure equivalent comparisons.

Once aggregate totals from the debate-brief bibliographies were averaged and proportionately reduced to the equivalent of 1983 total citation means, they were subjected to analysis of variance. Each test statistic was examined to determine support for an alternative hypothesis.

Findings Related to Hypothesis 1

A statistically significant difference was found between pre-online catalog and post-online catalog student users concerning the total number of bibliographic items they cited from academic libraries. On the average, post-online catalog students cited more materials from academic libraries than did pre-online catalog students. Questionnaire data—while not statistically significant—supported acceptance of this hypothesis. Post-online catalog students reported slightly greater use of the University of Illinois Library with respect to the books, periodicals, and newspapers. From 1983 through 1986, the majority of students obtained most of the materials for their debate-briefs from the University of Illinois Library. Academic libraries accounted for a slightly larger percentage of citations in 1985 and 1986 than in 1983 and 1984. The slight tendency of students from the classes of 1985 and 1986 to rely upon an academic library to provide them with the greatest amount of their materials lends support to the hypothesis that access to an academic online catalog in the school library results in greater use of academic libraries.

The findings associated with the increased use of academic libraries by post-online catalog students were anticipated. It was expected that students who had access to an academic online catalog in a school library would use academic libraries to a greater degree than students who had no access to an academic library online catalog. This expectation was based on several results reported in the nationwide online catalog user survey conducted by the Council on Library Resources (CLR).[12]

The CLR survey of on-line catalog users noted several trends that were applicable to the present study population, and that suggested the relational results of this hypothesis. Survey data indicated that youngsters accept an online public access terminal more readily than any other age group. Because the current study population was comprised totally of youngsters, expectations were that they would have fewer reservations about using an online catalog when compared to other age groups, and that they would be less hesitant about using one in a school library than in an academic library.

A second finding of the CLR survey noted that users of online catalogs tend to consult other types of catalogs less frequently. Although both groups in the present study had access to an academic online catalog at other University of Illinois departmental libraries, expectations were that the presence of one in the school library would reduce consultation of a card catalog by post-online catalog students. With the availability of an academic online catalog in the school library, student opportunities for consultation of it, and their concomitant use of academic library materials, was expected to increase.

A related set of CLR findings characterized online catalog users. These characteristics also applied to members of the current study population. In the CLR survey, academic use of the online catalog was found to be course-related and involve users from all subject areas. Users tended to consult the online catalog for subject-related information. Students in the present study were thought to be likely candidates for use of an academic online catalog because of the similar characteristics they exhibited. Each student had a class assignment that required obtaining information from a variety of academic disciplines. Students were assumed to have approached either an online catalog or a card catalog in an effort to find bibliographic materials pertaining to their respective debate subjects. Since post-online catalog students had access to an academic online catalog with subject searching capabilities in the school library, they were expected to cite more academic library materials than their pre-online catalog counterparts.

Findings Related to Hypothesis 2

The evidence suggesting that access to an academic online catalog in the school library is directly related to the diversity of cited library materials was confirmed only partially. The diversity of library materials was measured by the quantity of references cited within four bibliographic areas: (1) academic books, (2) academic periodicals, (3) academic government documents, reports, and pamphlets, and (4) academic newspapers. To determine whether access to an academic online catalog in a school library is directly related to the diversity of cited library materials, the mean number of citations for these bibliographic areas were separately compared. The findings indicate that pre-online catalog and post-online catalog students differed only in their use of academic periodicals. Questionnaire data—while not statistically significant—tended to support an increased use of periodicals and newspapers by post-online catalog students. The increased citing of newspapers, however, was not noted in the debate-brief citation analysis. The increased use of academic periodicals by post-online catalog students was expected. Post-online catalog students not only had access to a school library online catalog, but also had the use of one equipped with FBR and a user-friendly interface. Prior to August 1984, students who wished to search for periodicals were required to perform known-item searching. This involved the somewhat more complicated procedure of typing in letter-combination commands for titles of periodicals with which students were already familiar. With the addition of FBR and the user-friendly interface to the online catalog, two features were included that provided students with further assistance in their search for academic periodicals. The first concerned an improvement in known-item searching via the title-search option. Post-online catalog students, when requesting a title search, were asked to reply if the title for which they were searching was a periodical. If they replied affirmatively, the computer searched for periodicals corresponding to the title search key the student entered into the computer. The second feature involved the availability of the subject search option. Use of the subject search option presents users with a list of related subject headings. If students decided to search under the subject "Volcanoes," for example, they would receive, among other headings, one which reads "Volcanoes—Periodicals." By searching under this heading, they would be provided with a list of periodicals related to the general subject of "Volcanoes."

Several explanations may account for the absence of significant differences between pre-online catalog and post-online catalog student use of academic library books, and government documents and reports: (1) a teacher recommendation that students cite current materials in their debate-briefs, (2) the nature of the different debate topics, and (3) the complexity of government documents and reports.

The recommendation by teachers that students cite recent bibliographic materials in their debate-briefs may have influenced post-online catalog students to cite more materials from academic library periodicals than pre-online catalog students. This opportunity to cite academic library periodicals was not as readily available to students during 1983 and 1984. The citing of academic library periodicals would have satisfied the teacher recommendation concerning the contemporaneous nature of materials in their debate-briefs.

A second variable concerns the nature of the debate subjects. There were particular topics in each class for which most of the available information was in a certain format. For example, a review of the debate topics for the classes of 1985 and 1986 revealed a number of subjects for which bibliographic material may not have been as obtainable as periodical or government document and report materials. Topics such as the "Quarantining of AIDS Victims," "Abolishment of Farm Subsidies," "Revision of the Federal Income Tax System," and "Continuation of Affirmative Action Policies" were topics for which monographic materials may not have been accessible. Although the classes of 1983 and 1984 were also assigned similar types of topics, academic library periodicals were not as attainable for their purposes because the online catalog lacked subject searching capabilities during those years.

The last variable pertains to the level of education required to comprehend government documents and reports. Despite expectations that use of an academic online catalog in a school library would result in increased use of government documents and reports by post-online catalog students, the level of reading and analytical skill required to comprehend some of these may have been too high for college-bound high school seniors. The increased availability of these materials through an online catalog with subject searching capability may have been offset by the level of analytical skill required to correctly interpret materials.

Significance of Study

The results of this study confirm the positive impact that access to an online catalog in a school library has on the use of academic libraries by college-bound high school seniors. Analysis of the data revealed that students who had access to an academic online catalog at University High School Library cited more materials from the University of Illinois Library than students who did not have access to an online catalog. This result was also attributed to two other factors: (1) the availability in 1985 and 1986 of a more advanced form of online catalog, which permitted subject searching and contained full bibliographic records for each item searched, and (2) the continuous availability of instruction in the use of the online catalog in the school library.

The study results also have practical implications for the field of library and information science. The findings affect two library areas: (1) networking, and (2) bibliographic instruction. The availability of a computerized link between the school library and the University of Illinois Library was found to have affected the use of academic libraries by college-bound high school seniors. Students who had access to an academic online catalog in the school library cited more sources from academic libraries than did students who lacked such access. This increased use of academic libraries by college-bound high school students should encourage school librarians to consider the potential that computerized access to a network has for increasing student use of a variety of bibliographic materials.

Libraries should also consider membership in a multitype library network. The fact that all of the students in the study used academic libraries would suggest the need for access to a university or college library. The availability of a multitype network providing access to an academic library and to other types of libraries would offer students the full range of library facilities.

The type of online catalog available significantly influences patron use. During 1983 and 1984, students could access only a less advanced online catalog that was limited to known-item searching. However, during 1985 and 1986, students could access a more sophisticated catalog that permitted subject searching and provided complete location and status information. This factor contributed to the increased use of academic libraries by post-online catalog students. School and academic librarians should investigate carefully the type of computerized access they would have within any particular network.

The features of a particular online catalog also may affect the kinds of materials students use. For example, post-online catalog students may have increased their use of academic periodicals because of the availability of an online catalog in the school library that had improved known-item title and subject searching capabilities. Use of these options enabled students to obtain access to specialized periodicals from which they derived additional information.

The results of this study also suggest the need for a major change in the approach to bibliographic instruction in school libraries. In this project, academic libraries provided over 90 percent of the students with the greatest amount of materials they cited in their debate-briefs. School and public libraries were used only minimally. Although there was a clear pattern of multiple library use, students demonstrated a preference for the use of academic libraries. These findings suggest that school librarians should no longer confine their bibliographic instruction to the finding tools and materials available in their own library; they *must* instruct students in the use of other types of libraries. Such instruction will necessitate the development of institutional relationships by school librarians. School librarians who are not affiliated with a library network may wish to establish some cooperative arrangements with librarians at the nearest academic and public libraries. Once institutional accessibility is obtained, effective bibliographic instruction in the use of these types of libraries can begin.

The major finding of this study showed that students who had access to a computerized academic catalog in the school library cited more materials from academic libraries than students who did not have similar access. The influence of this technology had a positive effect upon student use of bibliographic materials. Online catalogs are becoming a prevalent form of access to bibliographic materials in both academic and public libraries. Their successful use is dependent upon standardized search strategies that are not indigenous to school library bibliographic instruction units.

School librarians must adopt a more catholic approach to bibliographic instruction if their students are to experience success in the use of other types of libraries. For example, *Library of Congress Subject Headings* are used in academic and public libraries, rather than the *Sears List of Subject Headings*, to perform subject searches in an online catalog. Many academic and public libraries use the Library of Congress classification scheme, while the majority of school libraries use the Dewey decimal classification system. Academic and public librarians employ different library terminology in their online catalog instruction compared to the nomenclature that school librarians normally use in reference to the card catalog. School librarians should familiarize their students with these subject and classification differences, and include online catalog terminology in their bibliographic instruction units.

The increased use of academic libraries as a result of access to an academic online catalog in the school library implies also that school librarians may wish to incorporate some actual practice with an online catalog into the bibliographic instruction unit. Periodic visits to academic and public libraries with online catalogs would provide students with some experience and training in the use of an online catalog.

It is important for school librarians to be aware that access to an academic online catalog may change student use of certain kinds of bibliographic materials. Previous research has noted that most students cite materials from books and monographs in their research assignments.[13] In this study, the use of periodicals increased because students had access to an academic online catalog in the school library. School librarians may wish to design bibliographic instruction units that would introduce students to periodical indexes other than *The Readers' Guide to Periodical Literature*, and to periodical titles that would be more relevant to their assignments.

The overall results of this study indicate that bibliographic instruction (especially for college-bound high school students) should change. School and academic librarians must recognize that such students are determined users of other types of libraries. When these libraries are made available to them through the use of online networks, their use of them will increase. School librarians and academic librarians who wish to prepare students to achieve academic excellence should identify the skills and proficiencies which students need in order to cope with the changes and influences caused by recent library technologies.

Notes

[1]Kathleen W. Craver, "Use of Academic Libraries by High School Students: Implications for Research," *RD* 27 (Fall 1987): 53-64.

[2]JoAnne Van Nord. "Background of Student Body," in *North Central Association Evaluation, University High School Library Instructional Materials Center*, compiled by JoAnne Van Nord. (Urbana-Champaign, Ill.: University High School Library, 1972), 10-13.

[3]*University High School Library Procedures and Policies* (Urbana-Champaign, Ill.: University High School Library, 1982), 1-2. Photocopy.

[4]"University High School Library Collection Development Statement" (Urbana-Champaign, Ill.: University Library, University of Illinois, 1984, Typescript), 1-3.

[5]*Preliminary Research Assignment* (Urbana-Champaign, Ill.: University High School English Department, n.d.), 1-7. Photocopy.

[6]*University of Illinois Library at Urbana-Champaign* (Urbana-Champaign, Ill.: University of Illinois Library Office of Development and Public Affairs and the Computer Office of Public Affairs, 1983), 5.

[7]Michael Gorman, "The Online Catalogue at the University of Illinois at Urbana-Champaign: A History and Overview," *Information Technology and Libraries* 4 (Dec. 1985): 306.

[8]Ibid., 307.

[9]Ibid.

[10]Ibid.

[11]Ibid, 310.

[12]Joseph R. Matthews, Gary S. Lawrence, and Douglas K. Ferguson, *Using Online Catalogs: A Nationwide Survey* (New York: Neal Schuman, 1983).

[13]Jacqueline Cooper Mancall, "Resources Used by High School Students in Preparing Independent Study Projects: A Bibliometric Approach" (Ph.D. diss., Drexel University, 1978), 73.

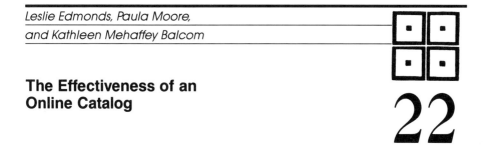

Leslie Edmonds, Paula Moore,
and Kathleen Mehaffey Balcom

The Effectiveness of an
Online Catalog

22

A 1982 nationwide survey of library users commissioned by the Council on Library Resources[1] concluded that there is widespread public acceptance of the online catalog. The research also conjectured that the key issue for librarians is not whether to adopt an online catalog, but how to proceed. The survey included public library users, but reached only a small number of users under the age of 14. A literature search indicates that no systematic study of online catalog use by children has ever been reported. To date, automation research has made only brief reference to this user group, and then the focus has been primarily on acceptance of technology, not the effectiveness of it. Librarians must evaluate the skill levels required by software design to be assured that children's access to materials is not hindered by the introduction of an online catalog.

If public libraries are going to convert to the use of online catalogs for public access, it is important to look carefully at the use of such catalogs by children. The need for evaluation of online catalogs goes beyond acceptance or comfort in the use of the computer. It may be assumed that younger library patrons are more accepting of computer technology because they learn to use computers in school. The more important question is whether children actually can use existing online programs to find needed materials. Of particular concern are developmental skills required by the interactive software. Can children understand information presented on the screens with a program now available? Are they generally capable of understanding search methods used in a program? Does the online catalog offer any advantages or disadvantages as compared to the traditional card catalog? Answers to these questions will help program designers and librarians define the parameters of effective use of

Source: Reprinted from *School Library Journal* (October 1990), 28-32. Copyright © by Reed Publishing, USA.

online catalogs by children and plan modifications in the online catalog, in bibliographic instruction, and reference/reader's advisory services.

This study evaluates children's use of an online catalog to gain bibliographic access to materials at the Downers Grove Public Library (DGPL). To provide a basis of comparison, the study also evaluates children's ability to use the DGPL card catalog. Although most libraries close their card catalogs when introducing an online catalog, the DGPL chose to maintain its card catalogs pending resolution of some specific problems connected with the online database. DGPL touch screen terminals were used to access CLSI's Online Public Access Catalog (OPAC terminal). A specific set of tests was developed to determine if children have the necessary developmental skills to effectively locate and interpret bibliographic information as presented by both forms of the catalog.

Overview

With the cooperation of Downers Grove Elementary School District 58, a sample of children (see figure 1) in the fourth grade (9- to 10-year-olds), sixth grade (11- to 12-year-olds), and eighth grade (13- to 14-year-olds) was tested to

Student Participants by Grade and Gender				
Gender	Grade			Total
	Fourth	Sixth	Eighth	(N = 207)
Male	38 46.91%	35 54.69%	26 41.94%	99 47.83%
Female	43 53.09%	29 45.31%	36 58.06%	108 52.17%
Total	81	64	62	207

Fig. 1. Student participants by grade and gender.

see if their skill development would allow them to follow the online catalog protocols and interpret information presented on the screens in order to identify materials in the library's collection. In addition to observing student use of the library's online and card catalog, general skill levels were measured by a written test. Texts pertaining to the design of instructional programs to teach media skills suggest that fourth-to eighth-graders should have mastered alphabetizing skills as well as basic use of the card catalog. Therefore, it is reasonable to focus on basic alphabetizing skills and knowledge of simple filing rules as prerequisites to effective catalog use and as developmentally appropriate for the children in this study.

Three tests were developed to measure the children's skills and their understanding of and preferences in the use of the card catalog versus the touch screen online catalog. During a visit to the DGPL, children took part in the following activities:

1. Skills Test/Skills included:
    a. The alphabetizing of individual words, names and phrases.
    b. The application of simple filing rules to locate titles, authors, and subjects; for example, knowing when to ignore articles and how to interpret spaces and punctuation.

2. Preference Survey: A survey was taken of the children's preferences between the card catalog and the online catalog.

3. Observation/Interview: Students, selected at random, demonstrated actual skills in manipulating the card or online catalog. The research observers noted:
    a. Ability to find call numbers for items owned by the DGPL.
    b. Efficiency in finding bibliographic information in a known item search.

The research focused on collecting data to answer the following questions:

1. Do older elementary school children use a touch screen online catalog as effectively as a card catalog?

2. What are the impediments to effective catalog (online and card) use by children?

3. Which kind of catalog do children prefer to use? What aspects of the catalog (both online and card) do children identify as helpful or easy to use? What aspects of the catalog (online and card) do children identify as difficult to use or understand?

4. Are there changes in software design, bibliographic instruction, or other public library practices that would make the online catalog easier for children to use?

5. Is independent (unassisted) bibliographic access improved or diminished for students if the library converts from the card catalog to the online catalog?

Children were considered effective or successful in using the catalog if 80 percent or more of the searches resulted in the identification of the call number. They were considered moderately successful if between 60 percent and 79 percent of the searches resulted in identification of the correct call number; they were considered unsuccessful with a rate below 60 percent. Data were also collected to describe the techniques children employ when using a library catalog. The data on the techniques were used to get a sense of the efficiency of the children's searches. When they search a catalog in normal, nonexperimental settings, their searches may be ultimately successful even if errors or misstarts are made. However, their frustration or difficulty with searching may cause them to give up the search and choose other ways of accessing materials at the library.

Methodology

In testing, a great deal of care was taken in selecting the items students would search for during the study observations. A pool of 15 search items was compiled consisting of five authors, five titles, and five subject headings. Items were chosen that would be understandable to the students and that represented "clean" searches in both the card catalog and the OPAC. Titles of children's books were selected that contained easily understood words. The authors' names were distinct yet uncomplicated, i.e., neither "Smith" nor "Mikolaycak" was considered. The subject headings used were all either two or three word phrases that appeared a relatively few number of times in either catalog. Each chosen item was judged to be straightforward and to require only basic knowledge of filing rules to locate. Because the DGPL is part of a cluster of libraries using the same OPAC data- base, each item was checked to ensure that the OPAC screens shown during the search contained no typographical errors. Five OPAC searches required a minimum of eight touches of the terminal screen for successful completion. Another five required nine touches, and the last five required at least ten or eleven. The 15 search items were also checked against the card catalog to ensure that there were no irregularities or errors in filing or in the card format.

The DGPL's children's services coordinator set up a schedule for the class visits during October and November of 1986. Classes of fourth-, sixth-, and eighth-grade students were invited to the public library to participate in the research project. While the nature of the research activities was explained to the teachers of the participating students, the teachers did not direct their students to prepare for their library visit. A signed parent consent form was obtained for each student prior to the library visit.

Staff from the DGPL and students from the University of Illinois' Graduate School of Library and Information Science were trained to administer the skills test and to record observational data consistently. Both the administration of the skills test and the observations were conducted with a high degree of consistency and without difficulty.

Classes visited the library one at a time. Upon arrival, the students received a brief explanation of the activities planned for their visit. The class was randomly divided into two groups. The first group was given the preference survey and the paper-and-pencil skills test. While a half hour was allotted for completion of the skills test and survey, students were neither timed nor rushed. Students were able to finish this written work in the time provided.

The second group was segregated in a room adjacent to the children's services area. Students in this group were randomly selected to conduct searches at either the card catalog or the online catalog. Before beginning a search, students who were chosen to do an OPAC search were shown a sample entry in the online catalog format. The students who were to be observed at the card catalog were shown a sample card entry for the identical title. The observers asked students to identify the author, title, and call number for the sample entry.

Next, students were given a card with a title, author, or subject heading printed on it and were instructed to find either the specific title, any book by the listed author, or any book on the specific subject. Each student selected for observation was given the opportunity to do a title, an author, and a subject search, but all three searches had to be conducted with the same catalog. The order of the search cards alternated between author, title, and subject searches.

Students could decline to do more than one search. In the case of the online searches, the observer excused students after the first or second search if they were unable to experiment with the OPAC, or when the number of touches to the OPAC screen indicated that improvement or success was not likely. For searches on either catalog, students were asked to find the call number when the search item was located. If the student said the call number aloud or pointed to it, the search was considered a success.

Halfway through the class visit, the activities of the two groups were switched. In this way, all students visiting the library completed the skills test and survey, while the majority of students were observed using either the card catalog or the online catalog.

Analysis of Results

Data collected for this study was designed to answer five research questions. Results were also analyzed for performance variations between grades as well as between males and females. Findings related to each question will be discussed in this section.

1. *Do older elementary school children use a touch-screen online catalog as effectively as a card catalog?* Based on the data collected, children do not use the online catalog as effectively as a card catalog. About 65 percent were successful in the card catalog searches, whereas about 10 percent were successful in the online searches. While children made errors in each step of both types of searches, those using the card catalog made fewer errors than those using the online catalog.

2. *What are the impediments to effective catalog (online and card) use by children?* There seem to be several impediments to use of library catalogs by children. First, some of the students studied lacked many of the basic skills necessary to use catalogs or either type easily. These students were generally unsuccessful at alphabetizing full words and were similarly unable to demonstrate mastery of common filing conventions. They also exhibited some problems in correctly identifying titles, authors, and call numbers.

A second impediment involved the use of both the card catalog and the online catalog. Because there is a series of steps involved in using either catalog, children were presented with a sequence of problems to solve. The sequential nature of successful searching appeared to be difficult for younger children (ages 8 to 12) to master due to their age and, thus, stage of development. Sequential searching was also problematic for older students. There were simply too many opportunities for error in the process of using a catalog, between file selection, choosing the correct catalog drawer, or in narrowing down the online alphabetical lists and then locating the search item.

A third hindrance to effective catalog use was the students' inability to conceptualize what letters or words fall *between* entries. This was demonstrated in the scores on question 7 of the skills test which replicated card catalog drawers: "Pretend these are labels on the card catalog. Write down the drawer number where you would look for each author or title." In trying to identify the correct drawer in which various authors and titles were filed, less than half the students scored within the skilled range and fully one-quarter proved unskilled. Their difficulty in visualizing made the task of searching for entries online particularly hard, since searching depended so heavily on the concept of selecting the item that came directly before the search item in each of the OPAC alphabetical lists.

A fourth difficulty was that students could not follow the online protocols to conclude their searches and identify the DGPL call numbers. Of the 35.09 percent who reached the general entry for their search item online, only 10.3 percent were actually able to name the call number.

3. *Which kind of catalog do children prefer to use? What aspects of the catalog (both online and card) do children identify as helpful or easy to use? What aspects of the catalog (online and card) do children identify as difficult to use or understand?* The students preferred to use the card catalog (68 percent) over the online catalog (16 percent). Another 16 percent had no preference (see figure 2).

Preference by Type of Catalog by Grade				
Catalog Format	Grade			Total
	Fourth	Sixth	Eighth	(N=207)
OPAC Terminal	9 11.11%	17 26.56%	7 11.29%	33 15.94%
Card Catalog	60 74.07%	38 59.38%	42 67.74%	140 67.63%
No Preference	12 14.81%	9 14.06%	13 20.97%	34 16.43%
Total	81	64	62	207

Fig. 2. Preference by type of catalog by grade.

Familiarity seemed to be the only common reason that children gave for their preference. The students were not very articulate in explaining their choices ("It's easy." or "Because I like it.") It is likely that children preferred the card catalog because they had used one in their school library. The online catalog may not have been preferred simply because students were unfamiliar with it. If students had had equal experience with both catalogs, the preferences might have been more balanced.

4. *Are there changes in software design, bibliographic instruction, or other public library practices that would make the online catalog easier for children to use?* Several things could be done to improve children's use of both types of catalogs. First, no matter which catalog is to be used, children should have more effective and directed instruction. The public library will need to cooperate with the schools to devise ways to reinforce instruction for children in basic alphabetizing skills and filing rules. Particularly if the card catalog is to be used, this instruction would seem to be the best way to improve student performance, since

changes in the design of the card catalog are impractical. The public library staff needs to make a commitment to tutor students in the use of the card catalog as part of their reference or readers' advisory service. The library might choose to provide a written instruction sheet for students to help them use the catalog. Such instructions could break down the series of problem-solving steps to ensure success at each level.

For use of the online catalog, instruction is also necessary, but schools may have trouble implementing bibliographic instruction if they don't use the same online system. A public library might assist in preparing an instructional unit on the online system for use in the schools. The benefit of class visits must be examined carefully because of the expense and lower likelihood of success. Individual instruction to young patrons and simple, written instructions for the use of the online catalog could also be undertaken by the public library.

While changing the design of the online catalog can be difficult, it is both technically possible and feasible. Online catalogs are an emerging technology and as such, the design of the software will continue to evolve. For children, a better design could eliminate some of the problem-solving steps. There needs, for example, to be fewer screens per search and fewer items on each screen (a smaller percentage of the screen used). The bibliographic entry should be shortened and made easier to read. The DGPL online screens were too cryptic for students to interpret, even when the entry elements were clearly identified. Children would be aided by the used of natural, concise language and clearly written messages. User errors should be tagged so that children know when an error has been made, and so that the mistakes can be easily corrected without returning to the first screen. The great promise of the online catalog is that it can be redesigned, whereas the card catalog cannot.

5. *Is independent (unassisted) bibliographic access improved or diminished for students if the library moves from the card catalog to the online catalog?* If the library does not provide personal assistance to students using the online catalog, bibliographic access by students is greatly reduced by the introduction of an online catalog. However, it must be stressed that fourth grade students did not appear to have mastery of the card catalog either. For younger students, the choice of catalog would not really affect their access since they require assistance in using either catalog.

Conclusions

The results of this research study raise several important issues which need to be explored, both as explanation of the data and as a basis for decision making in the public library setting.

The pattern of performance on both the skills test and in the observation of subjects followed the anticipated developmental model (see figure 3). That is, the younger children did less well on almost every measure. Overall, the fourth graders differed dramatically in their performance, while the sixth and eighth graders were more similar. This would also be expected since the fourth graders would be conforming to Piaget's concrete operations stage and the sixth and eighth graders would be moving into the formal operations stage of development.

Total Skills Test Score by Grade				
Degree of Skill	**Grade**			**Total**
	Fourth	Sixth	Eighth	(N = 207)
Skilled (95-115)	5 6.17%	6 9.38%	13 20.97%	24 11.59%
Moderately Skilled (75-95)	35 43.21%	47 73.44%	48 77.42%	130 62.80%
Unskilled	41 50.62%	11 17.19%	1 1.61%	53 25.60%
Total	81	64	62	207

Fig. 3. Total skills test score by grade.

One would expect that students at the concrete stage of reasoning would rely on trial-and-error problem solving, e.g., using such techniques as card-by-card comparisons or looking inside each drawer to see what part of the alphabet is inside. Fourth graders used these techniques to a greater extent. At the concrete operations stage, children need to depend on manipulation of physical items. While they can understand comparisons between items and changes in items (conservation and reversibility), it is difficult for the child at the concrete stage to use rules, to generalize, or to apply logic to problem solving. It is surprising, therefore, that the fourth graders need to actually look at each card or check individual drawers as a way of using the card catalog. Nor is it unexpected that the OPAC is almost unintelligible to the fourth graders since it is doubtful that the younger children have any way of understanding the size of the database. The format of the screens does not help children "see" what decisions need to be made. Although the OPAC allows patrons to page item-by-item, it is difficult to tell how many items fall between the item presented and the item desired. Since the patron can see how many drawers the card catalog has and how many inches of cards are in each drawer, the card catalog provides this information at a glance. Thus, the patrons can adapt their searches with this information.

The fourth graders' mastery of either library catalog could be improved with instruction and practice and they will naturally need to use a less-efficient approach that allows them to manipulate cards or helps them to see online entries as separate physical items.

The transition to formalized thinking begins at age 11 or 12—the final developmental stage that continues through adulthood. Formal thinking is characterized by the ability to use logic, apply rules, and use conditional (if/then) thinking. These skills are needed for catalog use. Students no longer are dependent on what they see or sense for what they know. The formal operations thinker can "visualize" the alphabet and select where to start looking for an entry without having to see physical cards or compare actual entries. The sixth and eighth graders would both be at the beginning of the formal stage and thus have some mastery of how to apply rules and use conditional logic. It would be expected that the older students would be capable of "figuring out" how to use the catalog given the rules for catalog use. Since older students only had knowledge of the rudimentary rules of catalog use, they may not have had enough knowledge to be successful. Also, students at the beginning of this stage are still learning applications for logic, so they are not always able to apply the correct rules or interpret rules correctly.

Another level of concern is the experience, training, and sophistication of the users of library catalogs. Patrons must be able to remember and apply the correct rule or rules, perform several steps (by applying several rules) in sequence and utilize rules accurately and precisely. A basic concept or rule that needs to be mastered is that of order. Essentially, the catalog users have to understand the concept of alphabetization and be able to locate words and phrases that fall between two points in an alphabetic sequence. To do this, users have to be able to identify what items come before or after a fixed point in the alphabet. The catalog in either format presents an extraordinarily complex set of rules of order to master. While we might think of the task as "knowing the alphabet," it is apparent that the task is closer to acquiring a working knowledge of *AACR2*.

Catalog users, thus, have two challenges. They must know the rules and also understand the logic or the organizational structure on which the rules are based. If users understand the structure but don't know the rules, they may be able to figure out how to do a search but it would not be particularly efficient. If the users know the rules (or many of the rules) but not the structure, any exceptions to known rules will present insoluble problems and it will be difficult to keep all the rules straight.

The children in this study did not have knowledge of many rules, nor did they seem to be able to easily understand the concepts. Naive users of any age will need to increase knowledge, practice sequencing, and concentrate on accurate task performance. The students did not demonstrate understanding of the concepts involved in alphabetizing. Moreover, they did not know many rules and were unable to accurately perform the several steps included in catalog use without making errors. The older students were better able to correct errors and were more knowledgeable than the younger students, though few students really demonstrated sophistication in using the catalog.

Use of the catalog is dependent on developmental level, experience, and training. Because catalog use can be complex, it is important to recognize that children who are not yet developmentally capable of mastering the necessary logic for the catalog may require simpler library catalogs. Another alternative may be providing children with assistance in the use of the existing "adult" catalogs. Thus, our findings suggest that in order to improve children's use of library catalogs, the catalog needs to be simplified (the total number of rules reduced). In addition, better training and guidance must be furnished to these young library patrons.

A Follow-Up

Although CLSI is no longer marketing the particular software package used at Downers Grove, the research presented in this study can be replicated with public access online catalogs currently in use. Librarians who are not yet using an online catalog will find it of value. Also, since research determining student success in using card catalogs is sparse, the methodology used in the Baber research will offer librarians an opportunity to assess student effectiveness in traditional card catalog as well.

As a result of the Baber research project, a balance was struck in the library's children's service department in providing staff assistance at both the catalogs. When working with students in grades six through eight, the staff introduces them to the OPAC rather than the card catalog for author and title searches. The inherent problems within the library's database would render subject searches incomplete and inefficient, however, by utilizing the OPAC and describing the search strategy in an informal, narrative style, students can receive the training and practice necessary for successful OPAC searches. A model for an effective OPAC demonstration still needs to be developed, tested, revised, and implemented.

Instruction presents a unique set of difficulties in the broader perspective of the school's catalog and a public library's online catalog. It is unlikely that the school library will have an online system that is compatible with a public library's catalog system. Moreover, the school media program of bibliographic instruction does not easily lead to effective use of the public library's catalog; teaching a separate set of skills, either through class visits or through limited opportunities for student practice may prove ineffective. In addition, the expense of supplying online terminals to local schools is prohibitive (this may be the case in other school districts). Therefore, it is essential that school and public librarians work together to bridge the gap in technologies and existing instructional programs so that children can become effective catalog users.

Notes

[1]Joseph Matthews, Gary Lawrence, Douglas Ferguson, eds. *Using Online Catalogs: A Nationwide Survey.* (New York: Neal-Schuman Publishers, 1983).

Roberta Welsh Lewis

Elementary School Children Express Their Need for Catalog Information

23

Teachers and librarians must be responsive to the needs of children. To cultivate independent thinkers, educators must encourage independence and provide open access to information. Freedom in the search for information is enhanced by an organizational system that children can understand and use.

Anglo-American Cataloging Rules, 2d edition (*AACR2*), is a logical though intricate system of cataloging to which children should be introduced at a level that can help them meet their informational needs. Since *AACR2* is the predominant system of cataloging today, it should be adopted and explained in incremental lessons to the elementary school student. Within the *AACR2* framework, cataloging can be modified to meet the specific needs of the beginning reader in the search for books.

An informal survey of children's use of catalog data was conducted by soliciting the help of 98 fourth graders in York Elementary School, with 700 students in grades K-4. York is a coastal community in southern Maine, about 65 miles north of Boston.

The help of the students, especially those in classes taught by Robert Griffith and Sue Smith, is acknowledged. Their free expression of needs and ideas helped formulate the core questions of the survey.

Source: Reprinted with permission of the American Library Association, from *JOYS*, Vol. 2, No. 2, "Elementary School Children Express Their Need for Catalog Information," by Roberta W. Lewis, pp. 151-156, © ALA 1989.

General Observations
of Learning Development

Zeek Good-Child, in half-day kindergarten, visits the library every week to browse with his class. Each visit is characterized by calls and scurries as groups of children, like ripples on the beach, advance and recede from stacks to tables. Finally they settle at tables, perching, squirming, and rocking, with an arm or leg preoccupied in perpetual motion. Independent eyes fix on pictures, words, and color captured in books.

Zeek makes a selection and lines up at the computer to have his book stamped and checked out. He says his first name clearly, but his face becomes blank when asked his last name. On a second try, the momentum of the beginning may carry him into at least the first syllable of his last name. Then his name and bar code can be found to complete the checkout.

A few months later, Zeek asks for the sports books. He enters a physically and conceptually new and, to him, uncharted world of books that were grouped by topics in the nonfiction shelves. Now, he and friends cluster in cross-legged bunches, sloshing in the narrow-channel confines of the stacks. Soon Zeek is searching out books on sharks, tanks, and fire engines.

Zeek begins to gravitate with friends to familiar areas. He often obtains a popular book by catching it on the opposite side of the books return chute as a classmate slides it through the opening.

Friendly librarians willingly help him on his search for new topics. After requesting a book about stars, a librarian may lead him to the Dewey decimal "500" section and consecutively pull out several books so that Zeek can see the covers and inside pages. A new book with colorful pictures may interest him or he may just as readily pick up a book on ants that a classmate has just set down.

Zeek's erratic selection method forces consideration of the criteria by which children choose books at the kindergarten and first-grade level.

In second grade, Zeek's reading and writing skills are good enough that he starts to put them to practical use. He recognizes titles by reading the words. The connection between symbolic letter patterns and mental images is beginning to develop in his mind. Zeek's teacher picks an author to study each month, and she fills the classroom with that author's books and illustrations. Zeek wrote to one author who replied with a letter. Soon Zeek can find each author's books on the shelves, and he has yet another way of understanding book organization.

In third grade, when Zeek wants to write about fish, he remembers that he can look under Fish in the card catalog, but he still needs help reading the card and finding the book.

By fourth grade, Zeek is familiar enough with the library space and organization to find what he wants for himself. His reading skills are quite adequate and he enjoys getting into "chapter" books (books with multiple chapters). Conceptually, he can follow difficult sequencing, and in class, he is expected to understand linear relationships, grouping, and some primary and subordinate ordering in math and social studies. It is in the beginning of fourth grade, at nine years of age, that he is formally introduced to library organization by way of a four-session library skills class. As an introduction to Dewey classification, he and the children at his table are asked to sort kitchen utensils into groups. They then sort books by topic and begin to understand the skeleton of order on the library shelves. Zeek learns more detail about the card catalog. With drawers from the card catalog at each table, students practice searching by title, author, and subject.

In three months, Zeek knows he can use the catalog to find books about a subject, and he uses the entries when he needs resources for required reports. Frequently, however, for relaxed reading, he appropriates a book from a friend just before it is returned through the slot.

Learning Theory and Libraries

By observing children's approach to books in the library, from the kindergarten child's wild immersion and random experimentation to the fourth grader's more deliberate focus and search, I made two generalizations.

1. Children have definite criteria by which they select books. From a child's first visit to the library he or she chooses what is attractive. From a quick examination of cover and inside pages, the child accepts or rejects a book. The older child, who can read fluently, must consider more closely the written content.

2. Very young children approach books at random. By the time they are in about fourth grade, many have developed sufficient competency in reading and abstract thinking to make use of a tool as complex as the catalog.

If children can make effective use of the catalog by fourth grade, a question arises: how can the catalog be made more responsive to their needs? If an entry can represent a book, what should be in that entry to give the child more of the critical information needed to decide if that book is the one wanted?

I went to two fourth-grade classrooms to solicit the children's suggestions. I asked for criteria by which they select books for both relaxed reading and report information. Their responses furnished the elements which comprise the first part of the survey, given to all fourth graders (see figure 1 on p. 194).

Student Suggestions

Suggestions from students could be classified under three types.

1. Some suggestions were for information already present on the catalog entry, such as the age of book and number of pages. This may indicate a lack of familiarity with card detail. The number of pages is given in *AACR2*'s area 5 (physical description), but print and detail may be too fine for the children to notice. The age of the book can be figured from the publication date, but this logic most certainly requires more extensive knowledge, familiarity, and sequential thinking than a nine-year-old can implement readily. Their request for age would be difficult to provide in a more direct form, as it would require continual updating of the card. But, children could be shown how to calculate or estimate age, something we do not normally do.

Check what is important to you.

1._____ What it is about
2._____ Type of characters
3._____ Funny or sad
4._____ Setting: Where story takes place
5._____ Illustrator: Who drew the pictures
6._____ Color pictures
7._____ Photographs
8._____ Cartoon pictures
9._____ Chapter book
10._____ Amount of pictures
11._____ Only pictures—no words
12._____ Size of print
13._____ Awards

Do you use the Card Catalog?

1._____ on your own
2._____ with help
3._____ never
4._____ to find where a book is (Easy, PB, Fiction, 543.2, etc.)
5._____ to find another book by an author you like
6._____ to find a book about a certain subject

WOULD YOU LIKE TO GET INFORMATION ABOUT YOUR BOOK FROM THE COMPUTER INSTEAD OF THE CARD CATALOG? _____Yes _____No

Fig. 1. How Do You Pick a Book?

2. Children often asked questions relating to theme, setting, and character. They were unaware that fiction could be searched by subject. One child asked about setting and theme so she could search fiction for report material on a specific country or animal. The questions about character, humor, and theme might better be searched through subject access, but certainly some indication of theme is conveyed through the summary note on the catalog card. The adoption of the annotated card for juvenile material in 1965 adds a descriptive summary, helpful to the child in determining the theme of the book. The summary is not always geared to the young child's vocabulary; it should be focused more specifically on language ability and interests.

3. Many suggestions focused on descriptive elements and included questions on print size, illustration detail, and the presence of chapters. *AACR2*'s area 5 indicates the presence of illustrations and may specify color, the number of illustrations, or the fact that a book is all illustrations. Certainly these elements, important to most children, could be included in area 5 with further information on cartoons, photographs, and type size.

Some children asked that books receiving special awards such as Caldecott and Newbery be identified. The request for noting awards would require an update on cards, but this could be done as book awards are quite limited in number and are very special.

Many children requested an entry on reading level and popularity. Grade level or age level, if stated in the book, may be entered in notes on the card. If defined too narrowly, however, age level designation may hinder rather than assist the child in obtaining useful resources by predefining a reading level and discouraging the child from exploring a wider range of materials. This type of categorization is also not sensitive to individual variations in skills that develop at widely varying rates among individuals.

The questions on the catalog were added in order to determine its level of use and to estimate the amount of flexibility with which individuals make use of its resources. (For responses to catalog use questions see figure 2.)

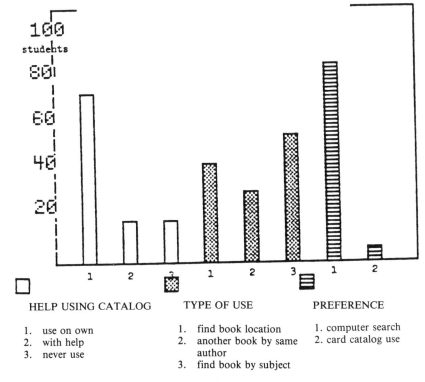

Fig. 2. Use of card catalog by fourth grade students.

Answers to the last question about the child's preference for computer catalogs were often embellished with stars, exclamation points, and other symbols of enthusiasm in support of searching by means of a computer. The responses reflected familiarity with computers, which are highly visible in this school. Each first-grade classroom has its own computer, and upper-grade classrooms share computers. The school is committed to having them in every classroom within three years. Teachers promote their use and all students get computer time.

The nature of the computer lends itself to flexible management of cataloging. Information can be easily updated. Elements such as awards can be added. The computer graphics potential opens up the option of visual codes and picture symbols to indicate the nature of a book. Programmers of cataloging software can be encouraged to be sensitive to the interests and concerns of children.

Summary

To identify children's information retrieval needs, adults should observe and talk with them directly. Meaningful catalog descriptions must satisfy needs by providing useful information. Although the structure of *AACR2* allows for sensitivity to children's needs, the difficulty comes in changing an accepted system and personalizing it. School librarians, while recognizing needs, have great difficulty instituting change because of the time and cost involved. Simply entering cards in the catalog is a major time problem; updating them is impossible.

The computer lends itself to change with ease and speed. It is well received by children and can incorporate pictorial codes for early readers.

Using a computerized catalog, it is possible to develop extensive understanding and adaptability in the use of the cataloging system. There is great value in determining needs perceived by children and thus involving them in their own learning process.

References

Barker, Diane. "Color It Easy." *School Media Quarterly* 7:121-23 (Spring 1974).

Berman, Sanford, ed. *Cataloging Special Materials: Critiques and Innovation.* Phoenix, Ariz.: Oryx, 1986.

DeHart, Florence, and Marylouise D. Meder. "Piaget, Picture Storybooks, and Subject Access." *Technicalities* 5:3-5, 16 (March 1985).

Fasick, Adele M. "Moving into the Future without Losing the Past: Children's Services in the Information Age." *Top of the News* 40:405-7 (Summer 1984).

Intner, Sheila S. "A Giant Step Backward for Technical Services." *Library Journal* 110:43-46 (April 15, 1985).

Pejtersen, Annelise Mark, and Jutta Austin. "Fiction Retrieval: Experimental Design and Evaluation of a Search System Based on Users' Value Criteria (Part 1)." *Journal of Documentation* 39:230-35 (December 1983).

Sussman, Valerie. "Computerizing an Elementary School Library: A First Experience." *Catholic Library World* 58:126-27 (November-December 1986).

Treva, Turner. "Cataloging Children's Materials at the Library of Congress." *The Quarterly Journal of the Library of Congress* 30:152-57 (April 1973).

Truett, Carol. "AACR Who? The Case for Using the New Anglo-American Cataloging Rules in the School Library Media Center." *School Library Media Quarterly* 12:38-43 (Fall 1983).

Wilner, Isabel. "Primary Catalog — Ideas for Young Media Center Users." *School Media Quarterly* 2:369-71 (Summer 1974).

Recommended Reading

Aluri, Rao, D. Alasdair Kemp, and John J. Boll. *Subject Analysis in Online Catalogs*. Englewood, Colo.: Libraries Unlimited, 1991.

Beiser, Karl, and Nancy Melin Nelson. "CD-ROM Public Access Catalogs: An Assessment." *Library Technology Reports* (American Library Association), 25, no. 3, (May-June 1989).

Boss, Richard, and Susan B. Harris. "The Online Patron Access Catalog: The Keystone in Library Automation." *Library Technology Report* (American Library Association), 25, no. 5 (September-October 1989).

Byrne, Deborah J. *MARC Manual: Understanding and Using MARC Records*. Englewood, Colo.: Libraries Unlimited, 1990.

Chan, Lois M., Phyllis A. Richmond, and Elaine Svenonius. *Theory of Subject Analysis: A Sourcebook*. Littleton, Colo.: Libraries Unlimited, 1985.

Cochrane, Pauline A. *Improving LCSH for Use in Online Catalogs*. Littleton, Colo.: Libraries Unlimited, 1986.

Cochrane, Pauline A., ed. *Redesign of Catalogs and Indexes for Improved Online Subject Access: Selected Papers of Pauline A. Cochrane*. Phoenix, Ariz.: Oryx Press, 1985.

Corbin, John. *Directory of Automated Library Systems*. 2d ed. New York: Neal-Schuman Publishers, 1989.

Costa, Betty, and Marie Costa. *A Micro Handbook for Small Libraries and Media Centers*. 3d ed. Englewood, Colo.: Libraries Unlimited, 1991.

Crawford, Walt. *MARC for Library Use: Understanding the US MARC Formats*. 2d ed. White Plains, N.Y.: Knowledge Industry Publications, 1989.

———. *Patron Access Issues for Online Catalogs*. Boston: G. K. Hall, 1987.

DeHart, Florence E., and Marylouise D. Meder. "Cataloging Children's Materials: A Stage of Transition." In *Cataloging Special Materials: Critiques and Innovations*, edited by Sanford Berman, 71-97. Phoenix, Ariz.: Oryx Press, 1986.

Gorman, Michael, ed. *Technical Services Today and Tomorrow.* Englewood, Colo.: Libraries Unlimited, 1991.

Hohn, Harvey. *Technical Services in the Small Library.* Chicago, Ill.: Library Administration and Management Association, American Library Association, 1987.

Hooten, Patricia. *Perspectives on Automation.* Chicago: American Library Association, 1990.

Intner, Sheila. *Access to Media: A Guide to Integrating and Computerizing Catalogs.* New York: Neal-Schuman Publishers, 1984.

Intner, Sheila, and Jean Weihs. *Standard Cataloging for School and Public Libraries.* Englewood, Colo.: Libraries Unlimited, 1991.

Matthews, Joseph R. *Directory of Automated Library Systems.* New York: Neal-Schuman Publishers, 1985.

Matthews, Joseph R., ed. *The Impact of Online Catalogs.* New York: Neal-Schuman Publishers, 1986.

_____. *Public Access to Online Catalogs.* 2d ed. New York: Neal-Schuman Publishers, 1985.

Matthews, Joseph R., Gary S. Lawrence, and Douglas K. Ferguson. *Using Online Catalogs: A Nationwide Survey.* New York: Neal-Schuman Publishers, 1983.

Matthews, Joseph R., Joan Frye Williams, and Allan Wilson. "Microcomputer-based Library Systems: An Assessment, Part I." *Library Technology Reports* (American Library Association), 26, no. 2 (March-April 1990).

_____. "Microcomputer-based Library Systems: An Assessment, Part II." Library Technology Reports (American Library Association) 26, no. 3 (May-June 1990).

Miller, Rosalind E., and Jane E. Terwilliger. *Commonsense Cataloging.* 4th ed. New York: H. W. Wilson, 1990.

Murphy, Catherine, ed. *Online Catalogs in School Library Media Centers: A Planning Guide.* Chicago: American Library Association, 1990.

Saffady, William. *Introduction to Automation for Librarians.* 2d ed. Chicago: American Library Association, 1989.

Understanding MARC (Machine Readable Cataloging). Follett Software Company, 809 Front Street, McHenry, IL 60050-5589. (Available by request from the company.)

Walton, Robert, and Nancy Taylor. *Directory of Microcomputer Software for Libraries*. Phoenix, Ariz.: Oryx Press, 1986.

Zuiderveld, Sharon, ed. *Cataloging Correctly for Kids: An Introduction to the Tools*. 2d ed. Chicago: American Library Association, 1991.

Index